# U•X•L ENCYCLOPEDIA OF
# water science

# U·X·L ENCYCLOPEDIA OF
# water science

## Volume 3
## Issues

### K. Lee Lerner and Brenda Wilmoth Lerner, Editors

Lawrence W. Baker, Project Editor

U·X·L
*An imprint of Thomson Gale, a part of The Thomson Corporation*

## U•X•L Encyclopedia of Water Science

K. Lee Lerner and Brenda Wilmoth Lerner, Editors

**Project Editor**
Lawrence W. Baker

**Editorial**
Charles B. Montney

**Permissions**
Denise Buckley, Shalice Shah-Caldwell, Ann Taylor

**Imaging and Multimedia**
Lezlie Light, Kelly A. Quin, Dan Newell

**Product Design**
Jennifer Wahi

**Composition**
Evi Seoud

**Manufacturing**
Rita Wimberley

©2005 by U•X•L. U•X•L is an imprint of Thomson Gale, a division of Thomson Learning, Inc.

U•X•L® is a registered trademark used herein under license. Thomson Learning™ is a trademark used herein under license.

*For more information, contact:*
Thomson Gale
27500 Drake Rd.
Farmington Hills, MI 48331-3535
Or you can visit our Internet site at http://www.gale.com.

**ALL RIGHTS RESERVED**
No part of this work covered by the copyright hereon may be reproduced or used in any form or by any means—graphic, electronic, or mechanical, including photocopying, recording, taping, Web distribution, or information storage retrieval systems—without the written permission of the publisher.

For permission to use material from this product, submit your request via Web at http://www.gale-edit.com/permissions, or you may download our Permissions Request form and submit your request by fax or mail to:

*Permissions Department*
Thomson Gale
27500 Drake Rd.
Farmington Hills, MI 48331-3535
Permissions Hotline:
248-699-8006 or 800-877-4253, ext. 8006
Fax: 248-699-8074 or 800-762-4058

Cover photographs reproduced courtesy of Photodisc by Getty Images (volume 1, sailboats), courtesy of Digital Vision Ltd. (volume 2, pump), and by permission of Corbis, photograph by Lester Lefkowitz (volume 3, Hoover Dam).

While every effort has been made to ensure the reliability of the information presented in this publication, Thomson Gale does not guarantee the accuracy of data contained herein. Thomson Gale accepts no payment for listing; and inclusion in the publication of any organization, agency, institution, publication, service, or individual does not imply endorsement by the editors or publisher. Errors brought to the attention of the publisher and verified to the satisfaction of the publisher will be corrected in future editions.

---

**LIBRARY OF CONGRESS CATALOGING-IN-PUBLICATION DATA**

UXL encyclopedia of water science / K. Lee Lerner and Brenda Wilmoth Lerner, editors ; Lawrence W. Baker, project editor.
  p. cm.
  Includes bibliographical references and index.
  ISBN 0-7876-7617-9 (set : hardcover : alk. paper) — ISBN 0-7876-7673-X (v. 1 : hardcover : alk. paper) — ISBN 0-7876-7674-8 (v. 2 : hardcover : alk. paper) — ISBN 0-7876-7675-6 (v. 3 : hardcover : alk. paper)
  1. Water—Encyclopedias, Juvenile. 2. Hydrology—Encyclopedias, Juvenile. I. Lerner, K. Lee. II. Lerner, Brenda Wilmoth. III. Baker, Lawrence W.

GB662.3.U95 2005
553.7—dc22
                                                          2004021651

---

This title is also available as an e-book.
ISBN 0-7876-9398-7 (set)
Contact your Thomson Gale sales representative for ordering information.

Printed in the United States of America
10 9 8 7 6 5 4 3 2 1

# Contents

Volume 1: Science

**Reader's Guide** . . . . . . . . . . . . . . . . . . . . . . . . . . . . . . . xiii
**Words to Know** . . . . . . . . . . . . . . . . . . . . . . . . . . . . . . . xvii
**Research and Activity Ideas** . . . . . . . . . . . . . . . . . . . . . xlv

Chapter 1: Basics of Water Science . . . . . . . . . . . . . . . . . . . 1
   Biochemistry (Water and Life) . . . . . . . . . . . . . . . . . . . 1
      Water on Mars (box) . . . . . . . . . . . . . . . . . . . . . . . . 3
      Camels (box) . . . . . . . . . . . . . . . . . . . . . . . . . . . . . 6
   Chemistry of Water . . . . . . . . . . . . . . . . . . . . . . . . . . 8
      Why Is the Ocean Salty? (box) . . . . . . . . . . . . . . . . . 10
   Hydrologic Cycle . . . . . . . . . . . . . . . . . . . . . . . . . . . 12
   Physics of Water . . . . . . . . . . . . . . . . . . . . . . . . . . . . 17
      Buoyancy: Archimedes and the King's Crown (box) . . . 19
Chapter 2: Oceans and Saltwater . . . . . . . . . . . . . . . . . . . 23
   Biology of the Oceans . . . . . . . . . . . . . . . . . . . . . . . 23
      Food Webs (box) . . . . . . . . . . . . . . . . . . . . . . . . . . 25
      Hydrothermal Vents (box) . . . . . . . . . . . . . . . . . . . 26
   Coastlines . . . . . . . . . . . . . . . . . . . . . . . . . . . . . . . . . 29
      Coastal Ecosystems (box) . . . . . . . . . . . . . . . . . . . . 31
      Artificial Reefs (box) . . . . . . . . . . . . . . . . . . . . . . . 32
   Currents and Circulation Patterns in the Oceans . . . . . . 34
      The Coriolis Effect (box) . . . . . . . . . . . . . . . . . . . . 36
   El Niño and La Niña . . . . . . . . . . . . . . . . . . . . . . . . . 39
   Fish (Saltwater) . . . . . . . . . . . . . . . . . . . . . . . . . . . . . 43
      Sharks! (box) . . . . . . . . . . . . . . . . . . . . . . . . . . . . 45
   Geology of the Ocean Floor . . . . . . . . . . . . . . . . . . . . 48
      Plate Tectonics (box) . . . . . . . . . . . . . . . . . . . . . . . 50
      Tsunamis (box) . . . . . . . . . . . . . . . . . . . . . . . . . . . 53

v

Islands . . . . . . . . . . . . . . . . . . . . . . . . . . . . . . . . . . . . . . . . 54
   Hawaiian-Emperor Seamount Chain (box) . . . . . . . . . . 57
Kelp and Seaweed . . . . . . . . . . . . . . . . . . . . . . . . . . . . . . 61
   Giant Kelp (Macrocystis) (box) . . . . . . . . . . . . . . . . . . . 64
Layers of the Ocean . . . . . . . . . . . . . . . . . . . . . . . . . . . . 66
   Upwelling (box) . . . . . . . . . . . . . . . . . . . . . . . . . . . . . . 67
Marine Invertebrates . . . . . . . . . . . . . . . . . . . . . . . . . . . 69
Marine Mammals . . . . . . . . . . . . . . . . . . . . . . . . . . . . . . 74
   Marine Mammals in the Military (box) . . . . . . . . . . . . . 75
   Keiko the Whale (box) . . . . . . . . . . . . . . . . . . . . . . . . . 77
Plankton . . . . . . . . . . . . . . . . . . . . . . . . . . . . . . . . . . . . 79
   Red Tides (box) . . . . . . . . . . . . . . . . . . . . . . . . . . . . . . 83
Tides . . . . . . . . . . . . . . . . . . . . . . . . . . . . . . . . . . . . . . 86
   Tides in the Bay of Fundy (box) . . . . . . . . . . . . . . . . . . 89
Waves . . . . . . . . . . . . . . . . . . . . . . . . . . . . . . . . . . . . . 90
   Surfing the Perfect Wave (box) . . . . . . . . . . . . . . . . . . . 91

Chapter 3: Fresh Water . . . . . . . . . . . . . . . . . . . . . . . . . . . 95
Deltas . . . . . . . . . . . . . . . . . . . . . . . . . . . . . . . . . . . . . . 95
   Life in the Ganges Delta (box) . . . . . . . . . . . . . . . . . . 97
Freshwater Life . . . . . . . . . . . . . . . . . . . . . . . . . . . . . . 100
   Diadromous Fish (box) . . . . . . . . . . . . . . . . . . . . . . . 103
   Stream Shredders (box) . . . . . . . . . . . . . . . . . . . . . . . 107
Groundwater Formation . . . . . . . . . . . . . . . . . . . . . . . 108
   Karst and the Edwards Aquifer (box) . . . . . . . . . . . . . 110
Lakes . . . . . . . . . . . . . . . . . . . . . . . . . . . . . . . . . . . . . 113
   Dying Lakes: Great Salt Lake and Aral Sea (box) . . . . 117
   The Great Lakes (box) . . . . . . . . . . . . . . . . . . . . . . . . 121
Ponds . . . . . . . . . . . . . . . . . . . . . . . . . . . . . . . . . . . . . 123
   Famous and Infamous Ponds (box) . . . . . . . . . . . . . . 125
Rivers . . . . . . . . . . . . . . . . . . . . . . . . . . . . . . . . . . . . . 125
   The Amazon River (box) . . . . . . . . . . . . . . . . . . . . . . 130
Stream Systems . . . . . . . . . . . . . . . . . . . . . . . . . . . . . . 131
   Control of Nature on the Mississippi River (box) . . . 133
Stream Water Flow . . . . . . . . . . . . . . . . . . . . . . . . . . . 136
   Victoria Falls (box) . . . . . . . . . . . . . . . . . . . . . . . . . . 138
   Flash Floods (box) . . . . . . . . . . . . . . . . . . . . . . . . . . 139

Chapter 4: Estuaries and Wetlands . . . . . . . . . . . . . . . . . 141
Estuaries . . . . . . . . . . . . . . . . . . . . . . . . . . . . . . . . . . . 141
   Chesapeake Bay (box) . . . . . . . . . . . . . . . . . . . . . . . 145
Wetlands . . . . . . . . . . . . . . . . . . . . . . . . . . . . . . . . . . 147

Chapter 5: Ice . . . . . . . . . . . . . . . . . . . . . . . . . . . . . . . . . 155
Arctic and Subarctic Regions . . . . . . . . . . . . . . . . . . . 155
   Permafrost (box) . . . . . . . . . . . . . . . . . . . . . . . . . . . 157
Glaciers . . . . . . . . . . . . . . . . . . . . . . . . . . . . . . . . . . . 158
   Avalanche Forecasting (box) . . . . . . . . . . . . . . . . . . . 161

Ice, Sea Level, and Global Climate . . . . . . . . . . . . . . . . . . 163
    Collapse of the Larsen B Ice Shelf (box) . . . . . . . . . . 165
Polar Ice Caps . . . . . . . . . . . . . . . . . . . . . . . . . . . . . . . . 168
    *Endurance:* The Shackleton Expedition (box) . . . . . . . 170
Chapter 6: Water, Weather, and Climates . . . . . . . . . . . . 173
    Climate. . . . . . . . . . . . . . . . . . . . . . . . . . . . . . . . . . . . 173
        Santa Ana Winds (box) . . . . . . . . . . . . . . . . . . . . . 176
    Clouds . . . . . . . . . . . . . . . . . . . . . . . . . . . . . . . . . . . . 177
        Ice in the Air, Pilots Beware! (box) . . . . . . . . . . . . . 180
    Monsoon . . . . . . . . . . . . . . . . . . . . . . . . . . . . . . . . . . 183
    Storms . . . . . . . . . . . . . . . . . . . . . . . . . . . . . . . . . . . . 186
        Waterspouts (box) . . . . . . . . . . . . . . . . . . . . . . . . 188
        Hurricane Andrew (box) . . . . . . . . . . . . . . . . . . . 191
    Weather . . . . . . . . . . . . . . . . . . . . . . . . . . . . . . . . . . 193
        Weather Forecasting (box) . . . . . . . . . . . . . . . . . . 195

**Where to Learn More** . . . . . . . . . . . . . . . . . . . . . . . . . . li
**Index** . . . . . . . . . . . . . . . . . . . . . . . . . . . . . . . . . . . . . lvii

Volume 2: Economics and Uses

**Reader's Guide** . . . . . . . . . . . . . . . . . . . . . . . . . . . . . . xiii
**Words to Know** . . . . . . . . . . . . . . . . . . . . . . . . . . . . . xvii
**Research and Activity Ideas** . . . . . . . . . . . . . . . . . . . . xlv

Chapter 7: Science and Technology. . . . . . . . . . . . . . . . . 199
    Aqueducts . . . . . . . . . . . . . . . . . . . . . . . . . . . . . . . . . 199
        Roman Aqueducts (box) . . . . . . . . . . . . . . . . . . . . 201
    Dams and Reservoirs . . . . . . . . . . . . . . . . . . . . . . . . . 203
        Three Gorges Dam: Triumph or Travesty? (box) . . . . 207
        Aswan High Dam (box). . . . . . . . . . . . . . . . . . . . . 208
    Desalination . . . . . . . . . . . . . . . . . . . . . . . . . . . . . . . 210
    Hydropower . . . . . . . . . . . . . . . . . . . . . . . . . . . . . . . 212
        Iceland (box) . . . . . . . . . . . . . . . . . . . . . . . . . . . . 215
        Tennessee Valley Authority (box) . . . . . . . . . . . . . . 216
        Hoover Dam (box). . . . . . . . . . . . . . . . . . . . . . . . . 217
    Ports and Harbors . . . . . . . . . . . . . . . . . . . . . . . . . . . 219
        The Port of Hong Kong (box) . . . . . . . . . . . . . . . . . 221
    Tide Energy . . . . . . . . . . . . . . . . . . . . . . . . . . . . . . . 223
    Wastewater Management. . . . . . . . . . . . . . . . . . . . . . 225
    Wave Energy . . . . . . . . . . . . . . . . . . . . . . . . . . . . . . 230
Chapter 8: Science and Research . . . . . . . . . . . . . . . . . . 233
    Aquariums . . . . . . . . . . . . . . . . . . . . . . . . . . . . . . . . 233
        Aquariums in the Home (box) . . . . . . . . . . . . . . . . 235
    Ecology. . . . . . . . . . . . . . . . . . . . . . . . . . . . . . . . . . . 237
    Hydrology and Hydrogeology . . . . . . . . . . . . . . . . . . 242

Limnology . . . . . . . . . . . . . . . . . . . . . . . . . . . . . . . 246
   Lake Baikal (box). . . . . . . . . . . . . . . . . . . . . . . . . 249
Marine Archeology. . . . . . . . . . . . . . . . . . . . . . . . . 251
   Alexandria Submerged (box). . . . . . . . . . . . . . . . . 252
Marine Biology. . . . . . . . . . . . . . . . . . . . . . . . . . . . 255
Marine Geology and Geophysics. . . . . . . . . . . . . . . . 259
   Deep Ocean Drilling (box) . . . . . . . . . . . . . . . . . . 262
   Submersibles, ROVs, and AUVs (box) . . . . . . . . . . 263
Oceanography . . . . . . . . . . . . . . . . . . . . . . . . . . . . 264
   Float Research: Athletic Shoe and Rubber
   Duck Spills (box). . . . . . . . . . . . . . . . . . . . . . . . . 268
Remote Sensing . . . . . . . . . . . . . . . . . . . . . . . . . . 270
   Impact of Sound on Marine Animals (box) . . . . . . . 273

**Chapter 9: Economic Uses of Water** . . . . . . . . . . . . . . . 275
Agricultural Water Use . . . . . . . . . . . . . . . . . . . . . 275
   Agriculture in the San Joaquin Valley (box) . . . . . . . 276
Aquaculture . . . . . . . . . . . . . . . . . . . . . . . . . . . . . 278
   Catfish Farming (box). . . . . . . . . . . . . . . . . . . . . 280
   Salmon Farming (box) . . . . . . . . . . . . . . . . . . . . 281
Commercial and Industrial Uses of Water. . . . . . . . . . 283
   Commercial Fishing (box) . . . . . . . . . . . . . . . . . . 285
Economic Uses of Groundwater . . . . . . . . . . . . . . . 287
   Dowsing (box). . . . . . . . . . . . . . . . . . . . . . . . . . 289
Minerals and Mining . . . . . . . . . . . . . . . . . . . . . . 292
   Manganese Nodules (box). . . . . . . . . . . . . . . . . . 293
   Placer Deposits and the California Gold Rush (box) . 296
Municipal Water Use. . . . . . . . . . . . . . . . . . . . . . 297
   New York City Municipal Water (box) . . . . . . . . . . 299
Petroleum Exploration and Recovery . . . . . . . . . . . . 300
   Oil and Gas in the North Sea (box) . . . . . . . . . . . 302
Residential Water Use . . . . . . . . . . . . . . . . . . . . . 306
Salt. . . . . . . . . . . . . . . . . . . . . . . . . . . . . . . . . . . 308
Shipping on Freshwater Waterways . . . . . . . . . . . . . 310
   Freshwater Shipping in the American Frontier (box). 312
   Shipping on the Great Lakes (box) . . . . . . . . . . . . 314
Shipping on the Oceans. . . . . . . . . . . . . . . . . . . . 315
Surface and Groundwater Use. . . . . . . . . . . . . . . . 319
   Colorado River (box). . . . . . . . . . . . . . . . . . . . . 320
Tourism on the Oceans . . . . . . . . . . . . . . . . . . . . 321
   The *Titanic* (box). . . . . . . . . . . . . . . . . . . . . . . . 323
Transportation on the Oceans . . . . . . . . . . . . . . . . 325
Whaling . . . . . . . . . . . . . . . . . . . . . . . . . . . . . . . 329

**Chapter 10: Recreational Uses of Water** . . . . . . . . . . . . 333
Dangerous Waters . . . . . . . . . . . . . . . . . . . . . . . 333
   Hypothermia (box) . . . . . . . . . . . . . . . . . . . . . . 335

Lost at Sea (box) . . . . . . . . . . . . . . . . . . . . . . . . . . . 338
Mines (box) . . . . . . . . . . . . . . . . . . . . . . . . . . . . . . . 339
Recreation in and on Freshwaters . . . . . . . . . . . . . . . . . . 341
Swimming (box) . . . . . . . . . . . . . . . . . . . . . . . . . . . 342
Water Skiing and Wakeboarding (box) . . . . . . . . . . . 343
Whitewater Rafting (box) . . . . . . . . . . . . . . . . . . . . . 345
Recreation in and on the Oceans . . . . . . . . . . . . . . . . . . 347
Swimming the English Channel (box) . . . . . . . . . . . . 348
Chapter 11: History and Culture . . . . . . . . . . . . . . . . . . . . . 351
Arid Climates . . . . . . . . . . . . . . . . . . . . . . . . . . . . . . . . . . 351
Las Vegas Water Use (box) . . . . . . . . . . . . . . . . . . . . . 353
Exploration of the Oceans . . . . . . . . . . . . . . . . . . . . . . . 354
Cousteau and *Calypso* (box) . . . . . . . . . . . . . . . . . . . 357
Beebe Expeditions (box) . . . . . . . . . . . . . . . . . . . . . . 358
Water and Cultures in the Ancient World . . . . . . . . . . . 361
Ancient Egypt and the Nile River (box) . . . . . . . . . . 363
Ancient Polynesians (box) . . . . . . . . . . . . . . . . . . . . . 364
Southwestern Native Americans (box) . . . . . . . . . . . 366
Water and Cultures in the Modern World . . . . . . . . . . . 369
Life Below Sea Level in the Netherlands (box) . . . . . . 370
Joining Waters: The Impact of Canals (box) . . . . . . . . 373

**Where to Learn More** . . . . . . . . . . . . . . . . . . . . . . . . . . . . . . . li
**Index** . . . . . . . . . . . . . . . . . . . . . . . . . . . . . . . . . . . . . . . . . . lvii

Volume 3: Issues

**Reader's Guide** . . . . . . . . . . . . . . . . . . . . . . . . . . . . . . . . . . xiii
**Words to Know** . . . . . . . . . . . . . . . . . . . . . . . . . . . . . . . . . xvii
**Research and Activity Ideas** . . . . . . . . . . . . . . . . . . . . . . . xlv

Chapter 12: Environmental Issues . . . . . . . . . . . . . . . . . . . . . 377
Acid Rain . . . . . . . . . . . . . . . . . . . . . . . . . . . . . . . . . . . . . 377
Art and Acid Rain (box) . . . . . . . . . . . . . . . . . . . . . . . 378
Black Forest (box) . . . . . . . . . . . . . . . . . . . . . . . . . . . . 382
Beach Erosion . . . . . . . . . . . . . . . . . . . . . . . . . . . . . . . . . 383
Carolina Outer Banks (box) . . . . . . . . . . . . . . . . . . . . 385
Coastal Development Laws and Acts (box) . . . . . . . . 386
Bioaccumulation of Heavy Metals . . . . . . . . . . . . . . . . . 387
Eating Tuna (box) . . . . . . . . . . . . . . . . . . . . . . . . . . . . 389
Desertification . . . . . . . . . . . . . . . . . . . . . . . . . . . . . . . . . 390
1930s U.S. Dustbowl (box) . . . . . . . . . . . . . . . . . . . . . 391
Eutrophication . . . . . . . . . . . . . . . . . . . . . . . . . . . . . . . . 394
Gulf of Mexico (box) . . . . . . . . . . . . . . . . . . . . . . . . . . 396
Floods and Flood Control . . . . . . . . . . . . . . . . . . . . . . . 397
Venice in Peril (box) . . . . . . . . . . . . . . . . . . . . . . . . . . 401

- Global Climate Change ........................... 404
  - Arctic Melting (box) ......................... 406
  - Kyoto Treaty (box) .......................... 408
- Groundwater ................................... 411
- Habitat Loss and Species Extinction ............... 414
  - Kesterson National Wildlife Refuge and
    Selenium (box) .............................. 417
- Industrial and Commercial Waste ................. 418
  - Love Canal (box) ............................ 420
- Landfills ...................................... 422
- Non-point Sources of Pollution ................... 425
  - Agricultural Runoff (box) ..................... 429
- Oil Spills ..................................... 430
  - *Prestige* Oil Spill Near Spain (box) ........... 431
  - *Exxon Valdez* (box) ......................... 433
- Overuse ...................................... 435
  - Overfishing ................................. 436
- Sediment Contamination ........................ 438
  - PCB Effects on Bird Populations (box) ......... 440
- Species Introduction ........................... 442
  - Zebra Mussels in the Great Lakes (box) ....... 444
- Water Conservation ............................ 445
  - The Hetch-Hetchy Debate: What Use Is
    the Use of Wilderness? ...................... 451
- Water Politics: Issues of Use and Abuse ........... 454
  - Ogallala Water Mining ....................... 457
- Water Pollution ................................ 458
  - Sewage (box) ............................... 460
  - Ocean Dumping (box) ........................ 462
- Watersheds ................................... 463

## Chapter 13: Legal and Political Issues ............ 471
- Endangered Species Laws ....................... 471
  - Marine Mammal Protection Act of 1972 (box) ... 473
  - Endangered Species Act of 1973 (box) ......... 474
  - CITES (box) ................................ 475
- Exclusive Economic Zones ....................... 476
- Fishing, Commercial Regulation (Fresh and Salt Water) 479
- International Non-profit Organizations ............ 483
  - Nature Conservancy (box) .................... 486
- International Water Laws and Enforcement ........ 488
  - U.S. Coast Guard (box) ...................... 491
- Strategies for Sustainable Water Development ..... 493
  - UN Role in Sub-Saharan Africa (box) .......... 496
- Surface and Groundwater Rights .................. 498
- U.S. Agencies and Water Issues .................. 502
  - U.S. Geological Survey (box) ................. 503

    Environmental Protection Agency (EPA) (box) . . . . . 505
    U.S. Department of the Interior (box). . . . . . . . . . . . 506
    Water Quality and Contamination Cleanup . . . . . . . . . . 506
    CERCLIS Superfund (box) . . . . . . . . . . . . . . . . . . . 508

**Where to Learn More** . . . . . . . . . . . . . . . . . . . . . . . . . . . li
**Index** . . . . . . . . . . . . . . . . . . . . . . . . . . . . . . . . . . . . . . . lvii

# Reader's Guide

Water is important and special because it takes part in almost all of the processes that form and shape the Earth. Water is also essential to life. Without water, life—in all its many forms—would not be possible. The study of water science helps toward understanding how and why water plays such an important role.

Water also unites and divides us. Water is the subject of numerous treaties, laws, and agreements between nations, states, and communities. However, because water is an increasingly important and scarce resource, there are often complex legal and political issues surrounding the use of water. Many wars and court cases have arisen over who owns a body of water, who has a right to use it, or how water should be divided and used among those who claim it. To assure an adequate supply of water to meet broad needs of humans around the world, the development of scientifically sound strategies for sustainable water development are critical.

In many cases, disputes over water are related to preserving the quality of waters that nourish and protect both human and natural communities. To better understand these issues, one also needs to know the essentials of water science.

## Scope and format

*U•X•L Encyclopedia of Water Science* takes an international perspective in exploring water science and water issues. The encyclopedia features more than one hundred entries in three volumes, with each volume broken into separate chapters:

Volume 1 (Science): Basics of water science; Oceans and saltwater; Fresh water; Estuaries and wetlands; Ice; Water, weather, and climates

Volume 2 (Economics and Uses): Science and technology; Science and research; Economic uses of water; Recreational uses of water; History and culture

Volume 3 (Issues): Environmental issues; Legal and political issues

Within each chapter, entries are arranged alphabetically. Among the topics covered in Volume 1 are the Hydrologic cycle; Kelp and seaweed; Lakes; Wetlands; Glaciers; and Clouds. Volume 2 covers Dams and reservoirs; Marine biology; Petroleum exploration and recovery; Tourism on the oceans; Dangerous waters; and Exploration of the oceans. And Volume 3 includes topics such as Acid rain; Groundwater issues; Oil spills; Sediment contamination; Endangered species laws; and Exclusive economic zones.

Each entry provides definitions for scientific terms and sources for further research. In addition, a general glossary, a research and activities section, and a cumulative index to the set are included in each volume. Numerous sidebars highlight significant facts and describe water-related activities. More than 150 black-and-white photos—as well as a different set of color photo inserts in each volume—help illustrate *U•X•L Encyclopedia of Water Science*.

**Acknowledgments**

In compiling this edition, the editors have been fortunate in being able to rely upon the expertise and contributions of the following scholars who served as academic advisors, contributing advisors, and writers for *U•X•L Encyclopedia of Water Science*:

Juli Berwald, Ph.D., Geologist (ocean sciences), Chicago, Illinois

Marcy Davis, M.S., Science writer, Austin, Texas

Laurie Duncan, Ph.D., Marine geologist, Austin, Texas

Brian D. Hoyle, Ph.D., Microbiologist, Halifax, Nova Scotia, Canada

Joseph P. Hyder, University of Tennessee College of Law, Knoxville, Tennessee

Adrienne Wilmoth Lerner, University of Tennessee College of Law, Knoxville, Tennessee

Todd Minehardt, Ph.D., Science writer, Austin, Texas

Yavor Shopov, Ph.D., President, Commission on Physical Chemistry and Hydrogeology of Karst, Institute of Statistics, UNESCO, Sofia, Bulgaria

The editors extend special thanks to Carol Nagel and Meggin Condino at Thomson Gale for their invaluable advice and faith in our efforts. Finally, and most importantly, the editors would like to thank U•X•L senior editor Larry Baker. His dedication, skill, and creativity were essential to the production of this book.

Additional thanks go to copyeditor Mya Nelson, proofreader Erin Braun, indexer Sandi Schroeder of Schroeder Indexing Services, and typesetter Datapage Technologies International, Inc., for their fine work.

## Dedication

The editors lovingly dedicate this book to the brave men and women of the U.S. Navy and the U.S. Coast Guard.

"The sea, washing the equator and the poles, offers its perilous aid, and the power and empire that follow it.... 'Beware of me,' it says, 'but if you can hold me, I am the key to all the lands.'" —Ralph Waldo Emerson (1803–1882), *The Conduct of Life*, "Wealth"

## Comments and suggestions

We welcome your comments on *U•X•L Encyclopedia of Water Science*. Please write: Editors, *U•X•L Encyclopedia of Water Science*, U•X•L, 27500 Drake Rd., Farmington Hills, MI 48331; call toll-free: 1-800-877-4253; fax: 248-699-8097; or send e-mail via http://www.gale.com.

*K. Lee Lerner and Brenda Wilmoth Lerner, editors*

# Words to Know

## A

**Abiotic:** Nonliving part of the environment.

**Abyssal plain:** Vast, flat areas of the deep-ocean floor.

**Abyssopelagic zone:** The deep ocean that extends from 13,000 feet (4,000 meters) below the surface to the seafloor.

**Acid deposition:** The collective term for dry deposition and wet deposition of acids as a result of air pollution.

**Acid rain:** The result of acidic chemicals reacting in the atmosphere with water and returning to Earth as contaminated rain, fog, or snow.

**Aeration:** Adding oxygen, nitrogen, and other gasses necessary for respiration into water.

**Agar:** A mixture of sugars found in some types of seaweed that can form a solid surface used in laboratories to grow bacteria.

**Air mass:** Large body of air with only small variations of temperature, pressure, and moisture.

**Air pressure:** Force exerted by the weight of a column of air above a particular location.

**Algae:** Fresh and salt water plants that can convert the Sun's energy into food; they range in size from microscopic cells to forms that are bigger than a person.

**Algal bloom:** The rapid and huge increase in numbers of algae that can occur in the presence of a food source such as phosphorus.

**Alpine glacier:** Mass of moving ice that is confined by mountain valleys.

**Ambergris:** A highly prized fat found in the intestines of some whales.

**Anadromous:** Fish that are born in fresh water and then move to marine water as adults.

**Annelid:** A segmented worm such as an earthworm or a polychaete worm.

**Antarctic ice cap:** Ice covering the continent of Antarctic and Southern Ocean region around the South Pole.

**Anticyclone:** An atmospheric system associated with dry, clear weather with winds that spiral out away from a center of high atmospheric pressure.

**Aquarist:** Person who keeps an aquarium.

**Aquatic:** Relating to water.

**Aqueduct:** A channel or conduit, usually resembling a bridge, that carries water on land or over a valley, from a higher point to a lower one.

**Aquiclude:** Permeable (leaky) layers of rock or soil that confine and pressurize groundwater within aquifers.

**Aquifer:** An underground rock formation that contains water.

**Archaeological context:** The natural surroundings, physical location, and cultural origin of archaeological artifacts or sites.

**Archimedes principle of buoyancy:** An object submerged in a fluid is pushed upward by a buoyant force equal to the weight of the fluid it displaces.

**Arctic:** Region of the Earth between the North Pole and the Arctic circle.

**Arctic Circle:** Invisible circle around the North Pole above latitude at 66°33' North.

**Arctic ice cap:** Ice covering the Arctic Ocean and land areas north of the Arctic Circle in the North Pole.

**Arid:** Lack of rainfall. An arid climate has an annual rainfall of only 10 inches or less per year.

**Artesian flow:** Water that rises to the land surface from confined aquifers without pumping.

**Arthropod:** A member of a group of invertebrates that has jointed appendages and an external skeleton.

**Artifact:** Any object made or modified by humans.

**Atmosphere:** A unit to measure pressure; one atmosphere is 14.7 pounds per square inch, which is the standard atmospheric pressure measured at sea level.

**Atmospheric (barometric) pressure:** Pressure caused by the weight of the atmosphere over a surface or object.

**Atoll:** Ring-shaped coral island that surrounds a shallow lagoon.

**Atom:** The smallest unit that has all the chemical and physical characteristics of an element.

**Autecology:** Ecological study of individual organisms or individual species.

**Autonomous underwater vehicle (AUV):** Remote-controlled motorized crafts that are designed to study and withstand the pressure of the deep ocean.

**Autotroph:** Organism that uses inorganic substances to produce energy.

# B

**Bacterioplankton:** Plankton composed of bacteria, often serving as the basis of the aquatic food chain.

**Baleen:** Bristly plates that hang from the upper jaws of baleen whales; acts like a sieve for the microscopic animals during feeding.

**Ballast water:** Water that is pumped into the hull of a ship to keep the ship balanced correctly in the water when it is empty.

**Barge:** Large, usually flat boat used for shipping.

**Barometer:** An instrument used to measure atmospheric pressure.

**Barrage:** Artificial obstruction such as a dam constructed in a water channel to increase water depth or divert flow.

**Barrier Island:** Long, narrow coastal island built up parallel to the mainland.

**Basalt:** Black iron- and magnesium-rich volcanic rock common in ocean basins.

**Base level:** The water level at the outlet of a stream, usually sea level; streams cannot erode below this level.

**Bathymetry:** The three-dimensional shape of the seafloor.

**Bathypelagic zone:** The layer of the ocean below the mesopelagic zone and above the abyssopelagic zone; generally it extends between 3,250 feet (1,000 meters) and 13,000 feet (4,000 meters) below the surface of the ocean.

**Bathyscaphe:** A submersible vehicle that is capable of going to the deepest parts of the ocean and withstanding extreme pressure.

**Beach:** Region of sand or rock that slopes down to the water of a lake or ocean.

**Benthic:** Animals, plants, and microorganisms that live on the floor of the ocean.

**Bioaccumulation:** Tendency for substances to increase in concentration in living organisms as they take in contaminated air, water, or food.

**Biodiversity:** The variety of living organisms and the ecosystems in which they occur.

**Bioluminescence:** Light that is generated by chemical reactions in bacteria, animals, and plants.

**Bioremediation:** The use of living organisms such as bacteria to remove pollutants from natural resources, such as water.

**Biosphere:** All the biological communities (ecosystems) that exist in the world.

**Biotic:** Living part of the environment.

**Black smoker:** Underwater seep of volcanic magma that deposits minerals.

**Boreal forests:** Treed areas of the northern temperate regions of North America, Europe, and Asia that are dominated by evergreen trees like firs, pines, and spruces.

**Brackish:** Water with a salinity (salt content) between that of freshwater and ocean water.

**Braided stream:** Streams with many channels that split apart and rejoin.

**Brine:** Water that contains a high concentration of salt.

**Bulk carrier:** A ship that carries large quantities of raw material, such as steel, timber, or grain, in large cargo holds.

**Buoyancy:** Ability of an object to float in a liquid.

**Buoyant force:** Upward force exerted by a liquid on an object; an object will float if the buoyant force of the liquid is greater than the downward force of gravity.

## C

**Caldera lake:** Lake filling a large circular depression left by a volcanic eruption or collapse.

**Canal:** Man-made or artificially improved waterway used for travel, shipping, irrigation, or hydropower.

**Canoe:** Boat pointed at both ends and typically with an open top, or deck.

**Carbonate:** Rock or loose sediment composed of the mineral calcite or calcium carbonate.

**Cargo:** Goods that are being transported.

**Cargo hold:** A section of a ship that is divided from other sections for the transport of a single type of cargo.

**Cartilage:** Tough but flexible material, found between bones in humans and in the skeletons of sharks and rays.

**Cetacean:** A member of the group of marine mammals that includes whales, dolphins, and porpoises.

**Channel:** The water-filled path of the stream, river, or man-made waterway.

**Chemical oceanology:** Study of the molecules and atoms that are dissolved in the ocean.

**Chemistry:** The science of the composition, structure, and properties of matter.

**Chemosynthesis:** The use of chemicals, rather than sunlight, for the production of food.

**Cistern:** A man-made reservoir for storing water.

**Clearcut:** The total removal of trees and much of the vegetation from a section of forest.

**Climate:** Long-term meteorological conditions or average weather.

**Climate effect:** Temperature and moisture patterns that characterize a large region over tens, hundreds, or even thousands of years.

**Climate zone:** Areas of the world with a characteristic climate. Climate zones are described as arid, Mediterranean, mountain, polar, temperate, and tropical.

**Cnidarian:** A member of a group of invertebrates that includes corals, jellyfish, and sea anemones; these organisms have stinging cells to capture prey.

**Coastal zone:** The shallow part of the ocean extending from the high-tide mark on land to the edge of the continental shelf.

**Coastline:** The land that lies next to the sea.

**Commercially extinct:** When an animal becomes too rare to be worth hunting.

**Community:** All of the organisms that live in a certain locations.

**Compound:** Substance in which two or more elements are joined together.

**Computer model:** Description of a system, theory, or phenomenon entered into a computer that includes its known properties and conditions and can be used to predict future conditions and events within the system.

**Condensation:** The transformation (phase change) of a gas to a liquid.

**Conservation:** Protection, management, or restoration of natural resources such as soil, forests, wetlands, minerals, and water.

**Container ship:** A ship that transports cargo in sealed containers that may be unloaded directly onto trains or trucks.

**Contaminant:** Polluting substance that has harmful effects on biological life and other natural systems.

**Contamination:** Polluted or containing unwanted substances.

**Continental glacier:** Very large, dome-shaped mass of glacial ice that completely covers the terrain beneath it; also called ice sheet.

**Continental shelf:** The edge of a continent that gently slopes in relatively shallow water before dropping off steeply to the great depths of the open ocean.

**Convection:** Circulation of a gas or liquid driven by heat transfer and gravity.

**Convention on International Trade in Endangered Species of Wild Fauna and Flora (CITES):** A 1973 treaty that restricts international commerce between participating nations for plant and animal species that are believed to be harmed by trade.

**Coral:** A rocklike deposit formed of the calcium carbonate skeletons of a group of small sea animals.

**Coral reef:** Tropical marine feature created by numerous colonies of tiny coral animals; coral reefs contain a great diversity of marine animals.

**Coriolis effect:** The effect of the Earth's rotation on the atmosphere and oceans that causes deflection to the right in the northern hemisphere, and deflection to the left in the southern hemisphere.

**Crest:** The highest point of a wave. Also, the highest level of floodwaters during a flood.

**Cretaceous period:** A division of geologic time from 65 to 144 million years ago; along with the Jurassic and Triassic, this period comprised the Mesozoic Era known as "the age of the dinosaurs."

**Crevasse:** A large crack or fissure in the surface of a glacier.

**Cruise ship:** A large ship, once used as the primary means of transporting people across an ocean, that now serves as a vacation destination, while visiting various ports of interest.

**Crustacean:** A member of a group of arthropods that includes brine shrimp, barnacles, copepods, shrimp, lobsters, crabs, and euphausids.

**Curation:** Cleaning, preserving, and storing artifacts recovered from archaeological sites for further study.

**Current:** The circulation of ocean waters that produces a steady flow of water in a prevailing direction.

**Cyclic changes:** Changes that repeat themselves over time.

**Cyclone:** Rotating atmospheric system of winds that flow into a low-pressure center. Cyclones rotate counterclockwise in the northern hemisphere and clockwise in the southern hemisphere.

# D

**Dam:** A physical barrier constructed across a river or waterway to control the flow or raise the level of water.

**Decibel:** Unit that measures the loudness or intensity of sound.

**Deep-sea fishing:** Form of fishing that requires boating several miles out to sea in order to catch fish that live far from shore, such as marlin, tarpon, and barracuda.

**Deforestation:** Large-scale removal of trees from a woodland.

**Delta:** The sedimentary deposit that forms at the mouth of a river. Delta means "triangle" in Greek, and river deltas are usually triangular.

**Density:** The amount of mass-per-unit volume of a substance. In water, density is primarily determined by the combination of salinity and temperature.

**Dentricles:** V-shaped structures that make up the rough skin of a shark.

**Deposition:** Process by which dirt, silt, and sand is moved from its original place by wind or water and deposited elsewhere.

**Depositional coastline:** A coastline formed from the sediment of carbonates, plants, and animals that have hard mineral shells made of calcium carbonate.

**Desalination:** Process of removing salt from sea water or water contaminated with salt.

**Desert:** An area of land that receives less than 10 inches (25.4 centimeters) of precipitation per year.

**Desertification:** Gradual changes that take place over a region or area of land that ultimately result in the formation of a desert.

**Detergent:** A chemical used as a cleaning agent because it encourages the formation of an oil-in-water emulsion.

**Diatoms:** Single-celled phytoplankton that produce a thin shell made of silica (glass).

**Dinoflagellates:** Single-celled phytoplankton that move by propelling whip-like appendages called flagella.

**Dipolar molecule:** A molecule that has a positive charge at one end and an equal, but opposite, negative charge at the other end.

**Discharge zone:** Land area where groundwater flows out of aquifers on to land surface.

**Dispersant:** A chemical agent that reduces the surface tension of liquid hydrocarbons, encouraging the formation of an oil-in-water emulsion. This reduces the volume of residual oil on shorelines or the water surface after a spill.

**Dissolution:** When water breaks rocks into dissolved chemicals; a form of erosion.

**Distillation:** The purification of water by heating.

**Distributary:** Channel of water that runs through deltas.

**Diversion:** Changing the direction of a water body such as a stream or river by building canals, dams, or channels.

**Divide:** High point or ridge that separates drainage basins, and in which water flows down in all directions.

**Diving suit:** Sealed suit that receives a constant supply of air, usually surface air supplied by hoses; used for early ocean dives.

**Doldrums:** A zone of dead air and still water, usually at the equator where the trade winds and equatorial currents converge.

**Downwelling:** Ocean zones where surface water sinks into the deep ocean.

**Dowsing:** Pseudoscientific practice of using alleged spiritual powers and a "divining rod" to locate underground water.

**Drag:** A force that resists movement.

**Drainage basin:** Land area from which surface runoff drains into a stream or lake.

**Dredge:** Device for scooping or digging rock and sediment from the seafloor.

**Dredging:** A process where a ship drags a hook or grate along the bottom of a waterway in order to remove the accumulated silt and mud.

**Drought:** A temporary but extended period of abnormally low rainfall.

**Dry deposition:** Acidic gases and solid particles containing acids that settle out of the air and land on surfaces.

**Dynamic equilibrium:** State of balance attained by maintaining equal rates of input and withdrawal from a system.

# E

**Echinoderm:** A member of the group of invertebrates that includes feather stars, sea stars, brittle stars, sea urchins, and sea cucumbers.

**Echolocation:** The ability of dolphins, bats, and some other animals to detect objects and prey by emitting sound waves that bounce off objects and return to the animal's ears or other sensory organ.

**Echosounder:** A tool that bounces sound waves off the ocean floor to record water depths or create maps of the ocean floor.

**Ecology:** Study of the relationships among organisms and between organisms and their environment.

**Ecosystem:** Community of plants and animals that interact with each other and with their physical environment.

**Ecotourism:** Tourism that focuses on nature and the environment without harming it.

**Ectotherm:** An animal that has a body temperature similar to that of its environment.

**Effluent:** Wastewater that has been treated to remove most impurities.

**Electrical current:** Flow of electricity.

**Electromagnetic spectrum:** The range of electrical waves of varying wavelengths that make up light. The visible range is only a small portion of the full spectrum.

**Electron:** A particle with a negative charge that orbits the nucleus of an atom.

**Element:** A substance that cannot be divided by ordinary chemical means.

**Embayment:** Indentation in the shoreline that forms a bay.

**Endangered:** A species that is in danger of becoming extinct within the foreseeable future throughout all or a significant portion of its natural habitat.

**Endangered Species Act:** Law passed in 1973 that identifies species that face possible extinction and implements measures to prevent extinction; species may be listed as either endangered or threatened under the act.

**Endotherm:** An animal that can maintain a relatively constant body temperature regardless of its environment.

**Endothermic:** Chemical reaction or phase change that absorbs energy.

**Environmental impact study:** A survey conducted to determine if a landfill project could have negative effects on the environment.

**Environmental Protection Agency:** Federal agency responsible for enforcing laws designed to protect the environment, including air quality, water quality, wetlands, hazardous wastes, and other environmental matters.

**Epilimnion:** The surface of a lake that extends as deep as light penetrates.

**Epipelagic zone:** The surface of the ocean where light penetrates; also called the photic zone.

**Equatorial current:** A sustained pattern of water flowing westward near the equator.

**Erosion:** Wearing away of soil, rock, sand, or other material by the action of wind and water.

**Erosional coastline:** A coastline formed by rising tectonic plates that gradually wears away.

**Escherichia coli:** Type of bacteria that is found in the intestines of warm-blooded animals including humans; some types can cause illness if ingested.

**Estuary:** Wide part of a river where it nears the sea; where fresh and salt water mix.

**Eutrophic:** Waters with a good supply of nutrients.

**Eutrophication:** Proliferation of plant life, especially algae, that results when excess nutrients are added to lake or pond water, which reduces the oxygen content and often causes the death of animals.

**Evaporation:** The change of liquid water to water vapor.

**Exclusive economic zone:** A 200-mile (322-kilometer) area extending from a nation's coastline that permits that nation to extract resources such as oil, gas, and fish and to pass laws to protect those resources.

**Exothermic:** Chemical reaction or phase change that produces heat.

**Export:** Raw materials or goods that are shipped, traded, or sold to other nations.

**Extinction:** The total disappearance of a species; the irreversible loss of a living species.

**Eye:** Small circular area of relative calm at the center of a cyclone.

# F

**Ferry:** Ship that transports cars and people across bodies of water on a regular schedule.

**Filtration:** The process by which pollutants are removed from water.

**Fishing regulations:** Restrictions placed on where, when, and how fish may be caught.

**Fixed wave power device:** Wave power electrical generator that is attached to the seafloor and/or shore.

**Fjord:** A long, narrow, deep glacial valley flooded by the sea.

**Flash flood:** Flood that rises and dissipates rapidly with little or no advance warning, usually as the result of intense rainfall over a relatively small area.

**Floating wave power device:** Wave power electrical generator that is floating in shallow water.

**Floodplain:** Flat land adjacent to rivers that are subject to flooding during periods of heavy rainfall.

**Food chain:** Relationship of organisms in an ecosystem in which each member species feeds on other species.

**Food web:** The predator and prey relationships between animals and plants.

**Free diving:** Underwater swimming without the use of a breathing apparatus; also known as skin diving or breath-hold diving.

**Frond:** A long, feathery leaf, or the blade of a kelp plant or sea plant.

**Front:** The boundary between two air masses of different temperature and humidity.

## G

**Generator:** Machine that converts mechanical energy to electrical energy.

**Geothermal:** Heat from Earth; energy obtained from the hot areas under the surface of the Earth.

**Glacial erratic:** Boulders carried by glaciers and deposited away from their original location.

**Glacial flour:** Sediments that have been crushed and ground into a fine texture beneath a glacier.

**Glacial outwash:** Sand and gravel deposited by water melting from a glacier.

**Glacial till:** Sediments, or the rock, gravel, and sand carried and deposited by a glacier.

**Glacier:** Large mass of moving ice.

**Global warming:** Increase in the average temperature of the Earth's surface.

**Gorge:** A deep, narrow ravine, often with a river or stream running through it.

**Graben:** Rifts or holes formed when tectonic plates pull away from each other; when filled with water they can form large lakes.

**Graded profile:** A stream or river with a constant slope (incline).

**Graded stream:** A stream that has achieved a constant slope (profile) by reaching a balance of erosion and deposition.

Gravity: The natural force of attraction between any two objects that depends upon the mass of the objects and the distance between the objects. Planets, like Earth, draw objects toward their surfaces. Attraction is directly proportional to the product of the masses of the bodies and inversely proportional to the square of the distance between the bodies.

Gray water: Water that has been used for bathing, in the kitchen, or other purposes that do not generate highly-contaminated wastewater.

Greenhouse effect: The process where light from the Sun is reflected off Earth's surfaces and then trapped by clouds to warm Earth's atmosphere and surface.

Greenhouse gases: Gases in Earth atmosphere's that include water vapor and carbon dioxide, methane, nitrous oxides, ozone, halogens (bromine, chlorine, and fluorine), halocarbons, and other trace gases (gases found in very relatively small amounts).

Greenhouse layer: Layer of gases in the atmosphere that lets pass incoming solar rays and traps escaping heat.

Gross tons: A marine term equal to 100 cubic feet (about 10 cubic meters) used to describe the size of a boat, ship, or barge.

Groundwater: Freshwater that resides in rock and soil layers beneath Earth's land surface.

Groyne: A wall-like structure that sticks out into the water from the beach, which is intended to trap material.

Guyot: A flat-topped submarine mountain.

Gyres: Large circular patterns created by surface water currents in the oceans.

# H

Habitat: The environment in which a species naturally or normally lives and grows.

Hadal zone: The layer of the ocean in deep trenches and submarine canyons at depths that can extend down to 35,750 feet (11,000 meters).

Halite: A mineral composed of sodium chloride, commonly known as rock salt.

Halocline: Layer of water where the salinity changes rapidly with depth.

Headland: Point that extends into the ocean; usually a high rocky point surrounded by sea cliffs.

**Heavy metal:** Element such as lead or mercury that tends to be toxic to plant and animal life, even when present in a low concentration.

**Heterotroph:** Organism that consumes another organism to obtain energy.

**Himalaya Mountains:** Tall mountain range in central Asia that includes nine of the world's ten highest peaks, including the tallest one, Mt. Everest.

**Holdfast:** The part of a seaweed that allows the plant to attach to a rock.

**Holoplankton:** Plankton that spend their entire life cycle floating and drifting among the currents.

**Homeostasis:** Tendency for a system to resist change.

**Hovercraft:** Ship that floats over the surface of the water on a cushion of air.

**Humidity:** Water vapor (moisture) in the air.

**Hurricane:** An organized storm (tropical cyclone) with sustained winds of 74 miles per hour (119 kilometers per hour) or greater in the Atlantic Ocean, Gulf of Mexico, Caribbean Sea, or eastern Pacific Ocean.

**Hydrocarbon:** Chemical substance made up of carbon and hydrogen; propane, gasoline, kerosene, diesel fuel, and lubricating oil are common hydrocarbons.

**Hydrofoil:** Ship that has wing-like foils under the hull of the ship that provide lift that raises the hull of the ship out of the water.

**Hydrogeologist:** Scientist who studies the properties and distribution of freshwater, especially as it relates to the soil and rock structure of the Earth.

**Hydrologic potential:** Potential energy in water stored in reservoirs above the elevation of a river downstream.

**Hydrologist:** Scientist who studies the properties and distribution of Earth's freshwater.

**Hydrophilic:** Easily dissolvable in water.

**Hydrophobic:** Not easily dissolvable in water.

**Hydrosphere:** The whole body of water that exists on or around Earth, including water in the atmosphere, lakes, oceans, rivers, and groundwater.

**Hydrothermal deposit:** Mineral-containing geologic unit that was formed by hot waters percolating through source rocks.

**Hydrothermal vents:** Volcanic-powered, hot spring openings in the ocean floor that spew out a fluid that is rich in chemicals and minerals.

**Hypolimnion:** The deep part of a lake where no light penetrates.

**Hypopycnal flow:** River water that floats on top of sea water as it flows out to the ocean; it is caused by the fact that river water is less dense than salty sea water.

**Hypothermia:** Condition in which the body becomes too cold to function properly.

**Hypoxia:** Condition in which the concentration of oxygen in body tissues is too low for the body to function normally.

## I

**Ice budget:** The total amount of frozen water on Earth.

**Ice cap:** Ice at the poles; large dome-shaped glaciers that are smaller than ice sheets.

**Ice front:** The ice at the lowest end of a glacier.

**Ice sheet:** Very large, dome-shaped mass of glacial ice that covers a large continental area; also called continental glacier.

**Ice shelf:** A floating platform of ice where an ice sheet flows out over water.

**Ice stream:** Portion of a glacier or ice sheet that flows faster than the surrounding ice.

**Iceberg:** Large chunk of ice that breaks off from glaciers and floats in the oceans.

**Ichthyology:** The scientific study of fish.

**Import:** Raw materials or goods that are produced in a foreign country and brought into another.

**In situ:** In place.

**Industrial Revolution:** Period of rapid industrial growth, usually dated from 1750 to 1900, that resulted in a shift from economies based on agriculture and small businesses to economies based on industry and large corporations.

**Influent streams and ponds:** Bodies of surface water in recharge zones that contribute groundwater.

**Interdistributary:** Land or water that is between distributaries in deltas.

**Internal combustion engine:** An engine that takes the energy in fuel and combusts (burns) it inside the engine to produce motion.

**International Maritime Organization (IMO):** International agency of the United Nations that is concerned with shipping regulation and safety.

**International organization:** A group that includes two or more countries and that operates in more than one country.

**Intertidal:** The zone of the seashore between the high tide point and the low tide point.

**Inuit:** The native human inhabitants of the Arctic coastal regions of Eastern Asia (Siberia), North America and Greenland; also known as Eskimo, although this term has fallen out of favor.

**Invertebrate:** An animal without a backbone.

**Ion:** An electrically charged atom or group of atoms.

**Irrigation:** Diverting freshwater from lakes and rivers for use in agriculture to provide water for crops.

## J

**Jet stream:** High-speed winds that race around the planet at about five miles above the Earth.

**Jetty:** Structure built out into the sea, a lake, or a river to protect the harbor or shore against waves or tides.

## K

**Karst:** Landscape with caverns, sinkholes, underground streams, and springs created by erosion of limestone rock layers by groundwater.

**Kayak:** Boat that is pointed at both ends and has a closed deck except for a small hole where the paddler sits.

**Kettle:** Round depression left in glacial sediment after melting of a buried block of ice; it forms lakes and ponds when filled with water.

**Kettle pond:** Small round pond that forms when a melting glacier leaves chunks of ice buried in its deposits.

## L

**Lagoon:** A shallow body of water that is separated from the sea by a reef or narrow island.

**Lake overturn:** Mixing of lake waters from temperatures causing changes in the water layers' density.

**Land bridge:** Strip of dry land that connects islands or continents when it is exposed by lowered sea level during glacial periods.

**Latitude:** Imaginary lines that tell how far north or south a place is from the equator.

**Lava:** Hot, liquid rock that reaches the Earth's surface through a volcano or opening in Earth's crust.

**Leachate:** An acidic wastewater that contains contaminants from decomposed materials in a landfill.

**Lentic:** Relating to waters that are moving, like in rivers and streams.

**Levee:** A natural or man-made wall along the banks of a stream channel that helps confine floodwaters within the channel.

**Limnology:** Study of the ecology of continental surface waters including lakes, rivers, wetlands, and estuaries.

**Liner:** A sheet of plastic or other material that is put on top of clay on the inside of a landfill to prevent material from leaking out of the landfill.

**Lithosphere:** Rocky outer shell of Earth that is broken into large, rigid pieces called plates.

**Littoral zone:** Shallow, sunlit zone along lake shores where rooted plants grow.

**Lock:** One in a series of gates that allows boats or ships to pass through multiple water levels.

**Longshore current:** Near-shore current that runs parallel to a coastline.

**Lotic:** Relating to waters that are stationary, like in ponds and lakes.

# M

**Macroplankton:** Plankton large enough to be seen by the naked eye, including larval forms of jellyfish and some species of crustaceans.

**Magnetometer:** Used in marine archaeology to locate shipwrecks by finding metal objects used in the ship's construction such as nails, brackets, decorative ironwork, or artillery.

**Malacostraca:** A class of marine invertebrates that includes shrimp, lobsters, crabs, and euphausids.

**Mammal:** A vertebrate that nurses its young with milk, breathes air, has hair at some point in its life, and is warm-blooded.

**Mariculture:** Farming of marine animals and aquatic plants in a controlled marine environment.

**Marine biology:** Study of life in the ocean.

**Marine geology:** Study of the formation and structure of underwater land and rock formation.

**Marine Mammal Protection Act:** Law that seeks to increase the population of marine mammal species by prohibiting the hunting, capture, or killing of marine mammals.

**Marsh:** Wetland dominated by grasses, reeds, and sedges.

**Meandering stream:** A stream with a channel that follows a twisting path of curves and bends.

**Mesopelagic zone:** The layer of the ocean below the epipelagic zone and above the bathypelagic zone; generally it extends from about 500 feet (150 meters) to about 3,250 feet (1,000 meters).

**Metabolic rate:** The rate at which the biochemical processes occur in an organism.

**Metal:** Substance that is a conductor of electricity and heat.

**Meteorology:** The science of atmospheric conditions and phenomena.

**Mid-ocean ridge:** A continuous chain of low, symmetrical volcanoes that extends through all the ocean basins.

**Milankovitch cycles:** Predictable changes in Earth's average temperature that are caused by changes in Earth's position relative to the Sun.

**Mines:** Explosive devices that usually explode when an object makes contact with them; sea mines usually float on or just below the surface.

**Molecule:** A group of atoms arranged to interact in a particular way; the smallest part of a substance that has the qualities of that substance.

**Mollusk:** A member of a group of invertebrates that includes the snails, clams, oysters, scallops, mussels, squid, and octopuses.

**Monsoon:** A wind from the southwest that brings heavy rainfall to India and other parts of southern Asia during the summer.

**Moraine:** A ridge formed by the unsorted gravel, sand, and rock pushed by a glacier and deposited at the outer edge, or front, of the glacier.

**Mousse:** A water-in-oil emulsion that is formed by turbulence of the surface water after a petroleum spill to the aquatic environment.

**Municipality:** A village, town, or city with its own local government that provides services for its residents.

# N

**National Weather Service:** Government agency that predicts the weather and warns the public of dangerous weather situations and their consequences, including severe weather and flood warnings.

**Native species:** A species naturally occurring in an environment.

**Natural gas:** Naturally occurring hydrocarbon gas.

**Natural resources:** Economically valuable materials that humans extract from the Earth; water is one of humans' most essential natural resource.

**Navigable:** Describes a body of water wide and deep enough for boats or ships to travel.

**Navigation:** The ability to determine the correct position of a ship in the ocean and the direction to sail in order to reach the desired destination.

**Navigation channel:** Passage in a waterway that is naturally deep or dredged to permit the passage of ships, or a defined, well-marked passage that leads from the docks to open waters; also called ship channel.

**Navigation rights:** The right of the ships from one nation to pass through certain waters, particularly the territorial waters of another nation.

**Neap tide:** Lowest tides of the month that occur at the second and fourth quarters of the Moon.

**Neutron:** A particle found in the nucleus of an atom that has no electric charge.

**Non-point source pollution:** Water pollution that comes from several unidentified sources, such as contaminated rain, runoff, or groundwater.

**Nor'easter:** A gale or storm blowing from the northeast, particularly common in New England and eastern Canada.

**Nutrient:** Chemical such as phosphate and nitrate needed by organisms in order to grow.

## O

**Ocean currents:** The circulation of ocean waters that produce a steady flow of water in a prevailing direction.

**Oligotrophic:** Describing a body of water in which nutrients are in low supply.

**Open-pit mine:** Large craters dug into the earth to extract ore that is near the surface.

**Ore:** Naturally occurring source of minerals.

**Organic:** Of or relating to or derived from living organisms.

**Overfishing:** Catching a species of fish faster than it can naturally reproduce resulting in a decline in the overall population of that species.

**Ozone layer:** Region in the outer atmosphere that absorbs the Sun's harmful ultraviolet radiation.

## P

**Pangea:** A super-continent that existed about two hundred million years ago when all of Earth's continental land masses were joined.

**Parts per million (ppm):** The number of particles in a solution per million particles of the solution.

**Pathogen:** Organisms (such as bacteria, protozoa, and viruses) that can cause disease.

**Peat:** Compressed organic material found in bogs.

**Permafrost:** Frozen layer of soil beneath the top layer of soil that has remained frozen for two or more years.

**Permeability:** The ability of fluid to move through a material.

**Pesticides:** Substances used to kill or harm unwanted plants, insects, or rodents.

**Petroleum:** A naturally occurring liquid mixture of hydrocarbons that is mined and refined for energy and the manufacturing of chemicals, especially plastics. Also known as crude oil.

**Phase change:** Transformation of a substance between one phase of matter (solid, liquid, or gas) to another.

**Phosphorus:** An element used as a food source by a variety of plants and microorganisms.

**Photosynthesis:** The process where plants use sunlight, water, and carbon dioxide to produce their food.

**Physical oceanography:** Study of the physical properties of the ocean including temperature, salinity and density, the ability to transmit light and sound, and the flow of currents and tides.

**Phytoplankton:** Plankton composed of plants and plant-like bacteria, such as algae.

**Pinniped:** A member of the group of marine mammals that include seals, sea lions, fur seals, and walruses.

**Placer deposit:** Water-deposited mineral source, such as gold nuggets in streams.

**Plankton:** Small, often microscopic, organisms that float in the ocean.

**Plate tectonics:** The theory that Earth's lithospheric plates move over time. It explains geological patterns of earthquakes, mountain chains, volcanoes, and rock types.

**Platform:** Large buildings, attached to the sea floor or floating, that house workers and machinery needed to drill for oil or gas.

**Playa:** Flat areas at the bottom of desert basins that occasionally fill with water.

**Pleistocene Epoch:** Division of geologic time from 10,000 to 2 million years ago; also known as the Ice Age.

**Point-source pollution:** Water pollution that enters the water body from a particular site.

**Point-source wastewater:** Wastewater that enters natural waters from defined locations.

**Polar:** A molecule that has a positively charged part and a negatively charged part.

**Polychaeta:** The largest class of segmented worms that live in the ocean.

**Population:** Group of organisms all belonging to the same species that live in a specific location.

**Porosity:** Amount of empty space within a rock or soil body.

**Port:** City or town on a harbor where ships dock and cargo is loaded or unloaded.

**Potable:** Water that is safe to drink.

**Precipitation:** Transfer of water as rain, snow, sleet, or hail from the atmosphere to the surface of Earth. In chemistry or geochemistry: The process in which ions dissolved in a solution bond to reform a solid.

**Proton:** A positively charged particle that is located in the nucleus of an atom.

**Purification:** Process by which pollutants, mud, salt, and other substances are removed from the wastewater.

# R

**Rainshadow:** An area that has decreased precipitation because a barrier mountain range causes prevailing winds to lose their moisture before reaching it.

**Recharge zone:** Area where water enters groundwater reservoirs by infiltrating through soils, stream beds, and ponds.

**Reclamation:** Draining submerged or wetter land to form dry, usable land.

**Reef:** An underwater ridge of rock or coral near the surface of the ocean.

**Remote sensing:** The use of devices to collect and interpret data; in marine archaeology, remote sensing is used to locate, map, and study underwater sites.

**Remotely operated vehicle (ROV):** Motorized crafts designed to withstand the increased pressure of the deep ocean.

**Reservoir:** Natural or man-made lake or body of water, often constructed to control a body of water.

**Reservoir rocks:** Rocks where petroleum collects.

**Residence time:** Time an average water molecule spends in one of the reservoirs of the hydrologic cycle.

**Respiration:** Process in which an organism uses oxygen for its life processes.

**Ring of fire:** A zone of large volcanoes and earthquakes that surrounds the Pacific Ocean.

**Riparian zone:** Narrow strip of vegetation that is found bounding the edge of a natural water body such as a stream or river.

**River system:** A river and its network of headwater streams and tributaries. All the streams that contribute water to the main river.

**Runoff:** Excess water when the amount of precipitation (water falling to Earth's surface) is greater than the ability of the land to soak up the water.

## S

**Sailing:** Moving across the water in a boat powered by wind energy harnessed by sails.

**Saline lake:** Saltwater lake that contains high concentrations of dissolved salts.

**Salinity:** A measure of the salt concentration of seawater.

**Sanctuary:** A habitat where killing animals or plants is prohibited.

**Sanitation:** Maintaining clean, hygienic conditions that help prevent disease through the use of clean water and wastewater disposal.

**Saprotroph:** Organism that decomposes another organism into inorganic substances and in the process obtains energy for itself.

**Scuba diving:** "Scuba" is the acronym for self-contained underwater breathing apparatus, referring to the air tanks and mouthpieces used by divers.

**Sea ice:** Frozen seawater floating on the ocean surface.

**Seafloor spreading:** The process by which a new oceanic seafloor is created by small volcanic eruptions at mid-ocean ridges.

**Seamount:** An underwater mountain.

**Sedge:** Grass-like plants.

**Sediment:** Particles of gravel, sand, and silt.

**Seismic waves:** Vibrations emitted by earthquakes and large explosions that travel as waves through the Earth.

**Semipermeable:** Descriptive of a material that allows the passage of some molecules and prevents the passage of others.

**Sensor:** Device that can detect the waves that have bounced back from the object they contacted.

**Sewer system:** Network of channels or pipes that carry wastewater to a treatment facility for purification.

**Shoreline:** A strip of land within a coastal zone that is submerged by high tide; also called shore zone.

**Sidescan sonar:** Type of sonar that emits sound energy over a wide path, tens or hundreds of miles (kilometers) across, allowing scientists to map large areas of the ocean.

**Silt:** Sedimentary particles smaller than sand particles, but larger than clay particles.

**Sinkhole:** A crater that forms when the roof of a cavern collapses; usually found in limestone rock.

**Sludge:** A semisolid residue, containing microorganisms and their products, from any water treatment process.

**Snorkel:** A hollow tube attached to a mouthpiece that can jut out above the surface of the ocean to allow a diver to breath.

**Snorkeling:** Form of diving in which the diver swims at or near the surface of the water using a snorkel to breathe surface air.

**Snow line:** The lowest elevation where snow stays on the ground or glacier surface without melting.

**Solar salt production:** A process that yields sea salt by allowing the sun to evaporate saltwater.

**Solution:** A liquid that contains dissolved substances.

**Solution mining:** Producing table salt by pumping water underground where it dissolves halite, then returning the solution to the surface where the salt is recovered through evaporation.

**Solvent:** A substance, most often a liquid, into which other compounds can dissolve.

**Sonar:** Derived from "SOund NAvigation and Ranging," sonar uses sound waves to locate underwater objects.

**Source rocks:** Mud layers rich with plant and animal material that become rocks where temperature and pressure transform the plant and animal material into petroleum.

**Species:** Group of organisms that have a unique set of characteristics, such as body shape and behavior, and are capable of reproducing with each other and producing offspring.

**Sponge:** One of the least complex multicellular animals; a member of the phylum Porifera.

**Spring tide:** Highest tides of the month that occur at the new and full Moon.

**Stratified:** Layered.

**Stream:** Moving surface fresh water driven towards sea level by gravity.

**Stromata:** Holes on the surface of leaves that can let water vapor pass out of the plant into the air.

**Subarctic:** Region just below the Arctic Circle, to the edge of the northern forests in North America, Europe, and Asia.

**Subduction:** Process by which oceanic seafloor is recycled into Earth's interior at deep ocean trenches.

**Submersible:** A craft designed to carry a pilot and scientists for underwater study of the deep ocean.

**Superfund:** A program managed by the Environmental Protection Agency that identifies, investigates, and cleans up the worst hazardous waste sites in the United States.

**Surface mixed layer:** The surface of the ocean where wind acts as a mixer, dissolving gases such as oxygen into the water.

**Surface water:** Water that is located on the surface, naturally in the form of streams, rivers, lakes, and other waterways, or in reservoirs, swimming pools, and other containers that have been built.

**Sustainability:** The use of a natural resource in a manner where it can be maintained and renewed for future generations.

**Swamp:** Wetland dominated by trees.

**Swash:** The forward and backward motion of water where waves break upon the shore.

**Synecology:** Ecological study of groups of organisms and how they work together.

## T

**Tanker:** A ship that transports liquid cargo, usually oil or chemicals.

**Tectonic plate:** Moving plates of Earth's crust.

**Temperate zone:** Region characterized by moderate temperatures, rainfall, and weather and overall climate that is neither hot nor cold, wet nor dry.

**Tentacles:** Long appendages on sea organisms that contain suckers or stinging cells and are used to grasp food and move around.

**Terra cotta:** Ceramic materials made from baked clay used in Ancient Rome for aqueduct pipes, dishes, and some tools.

**Territorial water:** Ocean waters governed by a nation; most territorial waters extend for 12 miles (19.3 kilometers) from a nation's coastline.

**Thermal spring:** Natural spring of water at a temperature of 70°F (21°C) or above; commonly called a hot spring.

**Thermocline:** The part of the ocean below the epipelagic zone where the temperature changes very quickly with depth.

**Threatened:** Descriptive of a species that is likely to become endangered in the foreseeable future.

**Tidal fence:** Device installed in an area with highly-changing tides that makes electricity by harnessing tidal energy.

**Tidal flat:** A broad, flat area of coastline alternately covered and exposed by the tides.

**Tidal wave:** The swell or crest of surface ocean water created by the tides. Also refers to an unusual water rise along a coastline as created by a storm or undersea earthquake.

**Tide:** Periodic rise and fall of sea level along coastlines caused by gravitational and rotational forces between the Sun, Moon, and Earth.

**Tornado:** A violently rotating column of air that is in contact with the ground.

**Trade winds:** Strong winds that blow from east to west in the subtropics on either side of the equator; named for their part in propelling European sailing ships to the East and West Indies to conduct trade.

**Transpiration:** The process where water is absorbed by a plant through its roots and passes into the air from the leaves as water vapor.

**Treaty:** An international agreement between two or more nations in written form and governed by international law.

**Tributary:** Smaller streams that flow into a larger stream or river.

**Tropical storm:** A low pressure storm system formed in tropical latitudes with sustained winds between 39 and 74 miles per hour (63 and 119 kilometers per hour).

**Tropics:** Warm, humid region lying north and south of the equator.

**Trough:** The lowest point in a wave; occurs between the crests.

**Tsunami:** Very large ocean wave created by an undersea earthquake or volcanic eruption.

**Tundra:** Treeless plains of the arctic and subarctic between the northern forests and the coastline of the Arctic Ocean.

**Turbine:** Device that converts the flow of a fluid (air, steam, water, or hot gases) into mechanical motion for generating electricity.

**Twister:** Common name for a tornado.

**Typhoon:** Tropical cyclone in the western Pacific or Indian oceans.

## U

**United Nations:** An association of countries founded in 1945 that is devoted to the promotion of peace, security, and cooperation between nations.

**United Nations Law of the Sea:** International law that governs the rights and responsibilities of nations and their approach to the oceans.

**Upwelling:** An area where cold, often nutrient-rich water rises from the deep ocean to the surface.

**U.S. Department of the Interior:** Department in the U.S. government that is responsible for the conservation of natural resources and the administration of government-owned land.

**U.S. Geological Survey:** Division of the U.S. Department of the Interior that is responsible for the scientific analysis of natural resources, the environment, and natural disasters.

## V

**Vertebrate:** An animal that has a bony spine that contains a nerve (spinal) chord.

## W

**Wall cloud:** An area of clouds that extends beneath a severe thunderstorm and sometimes produces a tornado.

**Wastewater:** Water left over after it has been used, such as any water that empties into a drain or sewer.

**Water allotment:** An individual portion of water granted by a water right.

**Water chemistry:** The balance of nutrients, chemicals, and minerals in water.

**Water footprint:** The amount of water used by an individual, business, community, or nation.

**Water right:** Grants a right to use water but not ownership of the waterway.

**Water table:** The zone above which the spaces in the soil and rocks are not completely filled with water and below which the soil and rock spaces are completely filled with water.

**Water treatment:** A series of steps that makes water potable and removes chemicals and microoganisms that could be harmful to the natural environment.

**Watershed:** The land area that drains water into a river or other body of water.

**Waterspout:** A column of rotating air, similar to a tornado, over a body of water.

**Wave base:** Water depth at which water is undisturbed by a passing wave. Wave base is at a depth equal to half the horizontal distance between two neighboring wave crests (one-half wavelength).

**Wave refraction:** Wave fronts bending when they approach a coastline at an angle.

**Wavelength:** Distance of one full wave; can be measured from crest to crest or trough to trough.

**Weir:** A low dam built across a stream or any flowing body of water, usually with rocks, to raise its level or divert its flow.

**Wet deposition:** Precipitation that has become acidic as a result of air pollution.

**Wetlands:** Areas of land where water covers the surface for at least part of the year and controls the development of soil.

# Z

**Zone of infiltration:** Shallow soil and rock layers with pore space that are at least partially filled with air; water table is the bottom of this zone.

**Zone of saturation:** Soil and rock layers with pore spaces that are completely filled with fluid; water table is the top of this zone.

**Zooplankton:** Small, often microscopic, animals that float in the ocean.

# Research and Activity Ideas

The following research and activity ideas are intended to offer suggestions for complementing science and social studies curricula, to trigger additional ideas for enhancing learning, and to provide cross-disciplinary projects for library and classroom use.

- **Experimentation:** The following resources contain simple experiments that illustrate the physical properties of water:

Project WET (Water Education for Teachers), an international nonprofit water education program and publisher located at Montana State University. http://www.projectwet.org/index.html.

*Janice VanCleave's Oceans for Every Kid: Easy Activities That Make Learning Science Fun,* by Janice Van Cleave, Wiley, 1996.

*Exploring the Oceans: Science Activities for Kids,* by Shawn Berlute-Shea and Anthony B. Fredericks, Fulcrum, 1998.

*Oceans Alive: Water, Wind, and Waves,* by Doug Sylvester, Rainbow Horizons, 2001.

*Why Is the Ocean Salty?* by Herbert Swenson, U.S. Government Printing Office, Superintendent of Documents. Prepared by the U.S. Geological Survey to provide information about the earth sciences, natural resources, and the environment.

- **Adopt a creature:** Take a class vote to choose a freshwater or marine creature to adopt whose species is stressed or endangered. Research the life of the creature, prepare a class display, and learn about the latest efforts to conserve the species and its habitat. Suggestions for creatures to adopt include the:

Manatee: Information about adopting a manatee can be found at the Save the Manatee Club Web site, http://www.savethemanatee.org/default.html.

Humpback whale: Information about adopting a humpback whale can be found at the Whale Center of New England Web site, http://www.whalecenter.org/adopt.htm.

Sea turtle: Information about adopting a sea turtle that has been fitted with a transmitter for tracking can be found at the Seaturtle.org Web site, http://www.seaturtle.org/tracking/adopt/.

Whooping crane: Information about adopting a whooping crane can be found at the Friends of the Patuxent Wildlife Center Web site, http://www.friendspwrc.org/.

Salmon: Information about participating in the Adopt-a-salmon program can be found on the U.S. Department of Fish and Wildlife Web site, http://www.fws.gov/r5cneafp/guide.htm.

• **Newspaper search:** Locate and review newspapers for the following disasters using the dates given. Assess if reporters grasped the cause and extent of the event. Choose interesting accounts to read to the class. The events are: hurricane in Galveston, Texas, on September 8, 1900; drought in the southern plains of the United States, 1930–39 (also called the Dust Bowl); tsunami in the Gulf of Alaska on March 28, 1964; Arno River floods in Florence, Italy, on November 4–5, 1966; and *Amoco Cadiz* oil spill off the coast of Brittany, France, on March 16, 1978. Old issues of local newspapers are likely available at your public library, a nearby college or university library, or from the local newspaper office itself.

• **At the movies:** Watch one of the following popular movies, each of which contains content about Earth's water sources or its ecosystems. *20,000 Leagues Under the Sea* (1954), *Jaws* (1977), *Into the Deep* (1991), *A River Runs Through It* (1992), *Free Willy* (1993), *The Living Sea* (1995), and *Finding Nemo* (2003). Applying your knowledge of water science, how was the issue portrayed in the movie? Whether the movie was a drama, comedy, or documentary, was the science portrayed accurately? Were there misconceptions about water science issues that it relayed to the audience?

- **Debate #1:** Divide the class into two groups, one in favor of the United States ratifying the United Nations Law of the Sea and the other against. Students should defend their positions about the environmental, economic, and political benefits or hardships that adopting the law would bring the United States, and whether U.S. ratification would change the state of the world's oceans.

- **Debate #2:** Divide the class into two groups, one in favor of large dam projects on major rivers and the other against. Students should research China's Three Gorges project, the Sardar Sarovar Project in India, and the Hoover and Glen Canyon dams. Debate the issue, with students defending their positions on hydroelectric power, water supply, flood control, and recreation enabled by dams, along with the environmental impacts, displaced persons, and detriments of flooding an area for a reservoir that occur when large dams are constructed.

- **Interviews:** Make a list of persons who have visited or lived near beaches, lakes, rivers, or wetlands for a long period of time. Parents or grandparents would be good candidates. Interview them about the changes in the area that they have noticed over time, such as changes in the water quality or quantity, new or reduced populations of water creatures, habitat change, and encroaching development. Develop questions ahead of time. Tape record the interview if possible or take careful notes. Transcribe the recording or notes into a clear written retelling of the interview. This process is known as taking and recording an oral history. Share the oral history with the class.

- **Aquarium:** Plan a class trip to a local aquarium. Notice the environment required for particular species such as water salinity, depth, temperature, presence of other unique features (coral reef, rocks, caves, plants) and available food sources. Design a model aquarium of several compatible species, labeling the particular features needed by each species. If a home aquarium sounds like an interesting hobby, the following Web sites provide helpful information for getting started: "Aquariums as a Hobby" from SeaWorld's *Animals: Explore, Discover, Connect* Web site at: http://www.seaworld.org/infobooks/Aquarium/Aquarium.html and "Starting a New Aquarium" from the *World of Fish* Web site at: http://meltingpot.fortunecity.com/oltorf/729/id18.htm.

- **Conserve water:** Make a checklist of ways to conserve water in the home. Include: using low-flush toilets (or placing a closed container of water in non-low-flush toilet tanks), checking faucets for leaks, using aerators on faucets, collecting rainwater for watering gardens, watering landscapes during early morning hours, landscaping with native plants that demand less water, installing low-flow shower heads, and using other water-saving measures found while researching the topic of water conservation. Inspect your home according to the checklist to learn ways that your family can help conserve water and discuss this with family members. Make checklists to distribute to other students at your school.

- **Stay informed:** Three current challenges facing the world's oceans are often featured in the news media. Watch and listen for reports about diminishing coral reefs in the Caribbean Sea and in the Pacific Ocean, about warming ocean temperatures, and for reports about noise pollution interfering with marine mammal communication. Get the details of one of these current issues with research. Web sites of oceanographic institutes and universities are good places to begin collecting information.

- **"Water Science for Schools"** The U.S. Geological Survey maintains the Web site "Water Science for Schools," which provides teachers and students with information and activities for learning about water science and water resources. The Web site is located at: http://ga.water.usgs.gov/edu/ and includes excellent information about the water cycle, Earth's water resources, and how humans use water. The site includes pictures, data, maps, and an interactive center.

- **Map project:** Research the watershed areas of local rivers, lakes, and streams. Using colored chalk or highlighters, color-code and shade the watershed areas on a large street map. Post the map in the community to raise awareness of the watershed, along with measures people can take to protect it from contamination.

# U•X•L ENCYCLOPEDIA OF
## water science

# Chapter 12
# Environmental Issues

## Acid Rain

Acid rain is a general term describing the pollution that occurs when acids fall out of the atmosphere (mass of air surrounding Earth). The principal pollutants that produce acids in the atmosphere are sulfur dioxide ($SO_2$) and nitrogen oxides, like nitrogen oxide (NO) and nitrogen dioxide ($NO_2$). These compounds combine with water in the atmosphere to form sulfuric acid ($H_2SO_4$), and nitric acid ($HNO_3$). Acid rain has significantly affected the waters that flow into lakes and rivers, as well as the lakes and rivers themselves. In turn, the plants and animals that depend on lakes, rivers and oceans are harmed by acid rain.

When describing acid rain, scientists use the more precise term acid deposition. Scientists distinguish between two types of acid deposition: dry and wet. Dry deposition includes acidic gases and solid particles containing sulfuric and nitric acid that settle out of the air and land on the ground or other surfaces. Dry deposition usually occurs very close to the point where the pollutants are released. Wet deposition occurs when precipitation, such as rain, sleet, fog, and snow, becomes acidic and falls to the ground. Wet deposition can occur hundreds of miles (kilometers) from the place where the air pollution originates.

### Acid rain and the pH scale

The scale that is used to measure the acidity of a substance is called the pH scale. The pH scale runs from 0 to 14. If a material has a pH of 7 it is neutral, meaning that it is neither acidic nor alkaline (basic). Substances with pH values less than 7 are acidic and substances with pH values greater than 7 are alka-

> ### Art and Acid Rain
>
> Acid deposition is extremely corrosive, especially to soft stones. Many famous buildings throughout the world show signs of acid damage. For example, the Parthenon in Athens, the Coliseum in Rome, and the Taj Mahal in India have all been damaged by acid deposition. Monuments in Poland and stained glass windows in Sweden have also suffered from corrosion. Several famous cathedrals in England including St. Paul's, York Minster and Westminster Abbey have shown the effects of acid deposition. Most of this damage is the result of dry deposition.
>
> All of the acid damage on famous structures results in very high restoration costs. In 1984 the Statue of Liberty in New York harbor had to be dismantled at substantial cost because of damage to its metal frame and copper covering by acid deposition. A study in England showed that if sulfur emissions were reduced by 30%, the savings in repair to these famous buildings could be as high as $20 billion.

line. Distilled water is neutral, with a pH of 7. Lemon juice and vinegar are both acidic; they have pH values of 2.3 and 3.3, respectively. Baking soda, with a pH of 8.2, and milk of magnesia, with a pH of 10.5, are both alkaline. Combining an alkaline substance with an acidic substance results in a substance with a pH value that is closer to 7 than either of the original substances. This is called neutralization.

A substance that has a pH of 3 is ten times more acidic than a substance that has a pH of 4; a substance that has a pH of 3 is one hundred times more acidic than a substance with a pH of 5, and so on. Given their respective pH values of 2.3 and 3.3, lemon juice is a ten times stronger acid than vinegar.

Natural rain water is slightly acidic. Chemical reactions between pure water and carbon dioxide in the atmosphere result in a weak acid. The pH of natural rainwater is between 5 and 6. This acidity is useful because when the rain falls to the ground, it can dissolve minerals in the soil that plants use to grow. Acid rain is anywhere from ten to ten thousand times more acid than natural rain, with a pH between 4.5 and 1.5.

## WORDS TO KNOW

**Acid deposition:** The collective term for dry deposition and wet deposition of acids as a result of air pollution.

**Dry deposition:** Acidic gases and solid particles containing acids that settle out of the air and land on surfaces.

**Wet deposition:** Precipitation that has become acidic as a result of air pollution.

### The major sources of acid deposition

Acid deposition forms from the burning of fossil fuels, which are used in cars, factories, electricity generation, and other industries. Fossil fuels were formed over thousands of years by dead plants and animals. After these plants and animals died they were buried under sediments (particles of sand, silt, and clay). The intense pressure and increases in temperature under these sediments chemically changed the dead plants and animals into the fuels that are used to drive cars and generate electricity today. When fuel is burned it not only releases the energy that is used to power electrical devices, but it also releases chemicals, such as sulfur dioxide and nitrogen oxides that form acid rain.

Car exhaust is a major source of the nitrogen oxides in the air. A second major source of nitrogen oxides in the air come in smelting plants (factories that process metal), electrical facilities, and factories. Factories and power plants are also the major source of

Acid rain and other pollution scar a village monument in Derby, England. © *Chinch Gryniewicz/Corbis.* Reproduced by permission.

sulfur compounds that cause acid rain. The U.S. Environmental Protection Agency (EPA) reports that about two-thirds of all sulfur dioxide and one-quarter of all nitrogen oxides in the atmosphere originate from coal burning electric power plants.

## Acid deposition in lakes and rivers

Under natural conditions, rainwater, which is slightly acidic, runs through the soils near a lake. These soils often contain limestone or calcium, which is alkaline and neutralizes the acid. The water in a healthy lake usually has a pH around 6.5, which allows for the growth of a variety of plants, invertebrates (animals without a backbone), and fish.

When acid rain falls on the ground and runs into lakes, initially it is neutralized by the alkaline substances in the soils. Eventually however, these substances are used up and the water that runs into lakes and rivers is extremely acidic. This causes lakes to become acidic as well. This acidity is highly damaging to the plants and animals that live in lakes. For example, at pH values lower than about 6, crustaceans, mollusks, snails, salmon, rainbow trout, many insects, and plankton cannot survive. At pH values lower than about 5.5, small fish such as whitefish and grayling will die. At pH values lower than about 4.5, all but the hardiest life dies.

In addition, as more acidic water passes through the soils, chemical reactions occur in the soils that cause harmful minerals such as aluminum to be released. These minerals run into the lake where they are taken up by plants and invertebrates. The plants and invertebrates are then eaten by fish, which are consumed by birds that live nearby. Because the birds must eat so many fish in order to survive, the aluminum is concentrated in their bodies. High levels of aluminum cause the birds to lay eggs with very fragile shells. Often the eggs break or become dry inside. Other times, baby birds are born with physical deformities.

The EPA completed a survey of one thousand lakes in the United States in areas where acid deposition is suspected to be a problem. They found that 75% of the lakes surveyed did suffer from acidity. In addition, nearly half the streams sampled showed evidence of acidity. The major places where acid deposition was found to be a problem in the United States were Adirondacks and Catskill Mountains in New York State, the Appalachian mountains along the east coast, the northern Midwest, and mountainous areas of the Western United States. The report also mentioned that air pollution in the United States contributed to acidification of lakes and streams in Canada.

### Acid deposition in oceans

Because of its chemical composition, the nitrogen and sulfur-based acids that cause acid deposition in fresh water lakes and rivers do not have a strong effect on the acidity of the ocean. However, carbon compounds in the atmosphere are responsible for increased acidity. Burning of fossil fuels releases carbon dioxide ($CO_2$) into the atmosphere. Carbon dioxide levels in the atmosphere are currently the highest they have been in 55 million years. When it combines with seawater, this carbon dioxide produces carbonic acid, which makes seawater more acidic. This acidity will have a very negative effect on all marine organisms that make shells out of calcium carbonate, such as corals and mollusks, because it reduces the availability of calcium ions (the building blocks of shells) in seawater.

## Acid deposition in forests

The ways that acid rain harms forests are complicated and interconnected. Acid rain harms both the soils that trees use to grow and the trees themselves. As acid rain falls on the soil in a forest, it washes away nutrients such as calcium and magnesium that are needed by trees to grow. In addition, acid rain releases from the soil toxic (poisonous) minerals such as aluminum that are then absorbed by the plants' roots. This causes severe damage to the trees' roots and weakens the trees. As acid rain falls on the trees themselves, it burns the needles at the top and at the tips of branches, which are then shed. This reduces the ability of the trees to make food from photosynthesis (process of converting the energy of sunlight into food) and to grow. Trees are then more vulnerable to environmental stresses like disease, drought (prolonged periods of dry weather), and insects. A tree that is exposed to acid rain will absorb extra alkaline substances from the soil, making the soil acidic. This means that the acid rain falling on the soil makes the soil even more acidic, compounding the problems of acid rain.

Decline in forests due to acid rain has been a serious problem throughout the Northern Hemisphere. In the 1990s surveys of the Black Forest in Germany showed that half of the trees were dead or dying as a result of acid deposition. Between 1970 and 1998 nearly half the red spruce trees in the northeastern United States died. Many sugar maples in Canada and the United States are also dying. Throughout Scandinavia, forests are dying because of acid rain. Most of the acid rain that affects these countries travels hundreds of miles (kilometers) from its sources in other parts of Europe.

Acid rain damage in a German forest. © *Boussu Regis/Corbis Sygma. Reproduced by permission.*

## Black Forest

Beginning in the 1960s scientists noticed that many of the trees of Central Europe were dying. In particular, in the Black Forest, which is located in Southwestern Germany, a large number of trees showed signs of weakening and dying. The term daldsterben, or tree death, was coined to describe the problem. The first trees to be struck with the affliction were the pines, followed by deciduous trees (trees that lose their leaves each year). By 1990 at least half the trees in the Black Forest were harmed. Many trees dried out and died, while others dropped leaves or became discolored. The problem was eventually attributed to acid deposition in the forest. Although several types of remediation techniques, such as replanting trees, were tried, none have yet been successful. Scientists assume that the damage to the soil has made it so acidic that new trees can no longer grow in these ancient forests under current conditions.

### Corrosion due to acid deposition

Acid deposition damages most surfaces on which it falls. In particular, dry deposition etches the paint on cars, corrodes metals, and deteriorates stone. In particular, buildings made of limestone and marble contain a lot of calcium carbonate. The acid in dry deposition, reacts with the calcium carbonate to form a powder. This powder is easily washed away when it rains. A variety of famous buildings and sculptures, especially in Europe, have been damaged by acid deposition.

### The acid rain program

In 1990 the EPA established the Acid Rain Program as part of the Clean Air Act. The goal of the program is to reduce the emissions of sulfur dioxide and nitrogen oxides. Much of the work in this program involves creating the correct economic incentives for factories and electrical plants to improve the quality of the materials they release into the air. Companies decide how they want to achieve emissions reductions. Some may choose to install special devices on their smokestacks that cleanse the pollutants out of the emissions. Others may use fuel that is less polluting or may use renewable energy sources. Finally, companies can trade for emissions allowances (the amount of pollutants that can be legally released) from companies that have already reduced their emissions below the standard levels.

The Acid Rain Program has been more successful at controlling sulfur pollutants than nitrogen pollutants. Since 1980 sulfur emissions from large factories have fallen by nearly one-half, from 9.4 to 4.7 million tons of sulfur dioxide a year. Much of these improvements in emissions have occurred in the parts of the country where pollution is the biggest problem, such as in Ohio and Indiana. As a result the concentration of sulfuric acid in the Northeast and the Mid-Atlantic states has fallen by about 25% and lakes in these regions are showing signs of recovery. The emissions of nitrogen oxides have remained fairly constant over the last decade. As a result, the deposition of nitric acid into the environment has remained essentially unchanged.

*Juli Berwald, Ph.D.*

## For More Information

### Books
Morgan, Sally. *Acid Rain (Earth Watch)*. London: Franklin Watts, 1999.

Raven, Peter H., Linda R. Berg, and George B. Johnson. *Environment*. 2nd ed. Fort Worth, TX: Saunders College Publishing, 1998.

Sylvester, Doug. *The Environment: Global Warming, Ozone, Acid Rain And Pollution*. San Diego: Rainbow Horizons, 1998.

### Periodicals
"Acid Oceans Spell Doom for Coral." *The Daily Star* (August 31, 2004): 1A. This article can also be found online at http://www.thedailystar.net/2004/08/31/d40831011715.htm (accessed on September 3, 2004).

### Websites
"Acid Rain." *Encyclopedia of the Atmospheric Environment*. http://www.ace.mmu.ac.uk/eae (accessed on September 3, 2004).

"Acid Rain." *U.S. Environmental Protection Agency*. http://www.epa.gov/airmarkets/acidrain (accessed on September 3, 2004).

United States Geological Survey. "Acid Rain: Do You Need to Start Wearing a Rainhat?" *Water Science for Schools*. http://ga.water.usgs.gov/edu/acidrain.html (accessed on September 3, 2004).

# Beach Erosion

Erosion is the removal of soil and sand by the forces of wind and water and it has occurred for as long as land has met water. Erosion is a continual natural process; material is constantly being shifted around to change the shape of a stream, riverbank, or beach. Today, when much available land bordering the ocean (coastlines) is developed for housing, the erosion of beaches is an important concern. Wave action can cause erosion that can remove the support for a house, causing it to tumble into the ocean. Along the 80,000 miles (128,748 kilometers) of coastline in the United States, beach erosion has become a big problem. While erosion is a natural process, humans have caused the rate of erosion to increase. The main factor causing the increased erosion damage is development.

Waves continually change a beach's shape by moving sand, small rocks, and debris. *M. Woodbridge Williams, National Park Service. Reproduced by permission.*

### WORDS TO KNOW

**Coastline:** The land that lies next to the sea.

**Erosion:** Wearing away of the land that occurs by natural forces such as wind and waves.

**Groyne:** A wall-like structure that sticks out into the water from the beach, which is intended to trap material.

### How beach erosion occurs

A beach is the rocky or, most often, sandy zone where the land meets the lake or ocean. This wind also moves the water towards the land, pushing the water to form waves. As the depth of the water decreases towards the beach, the waves change shape. Eventually, the top of the wave crashes over and down onto the beach. Then the water is pulled back out as the next wave makes its way towards the coastline.

This constant movement of water in and out across the sand or rocks is similar to the action of sandpaper on wood. Each wave can wash away or as least slightly move a tiny portion of the beach. Over a very long period of time, all these tiny events add up to the rearrangement of the beach. Sometimes, beach erosion occurs at a faster rate, as storms bring larger waves that crash more forcefully onto the beach. Storm waves carry more energy than calm waves, and can quickly wear away beach material.

For all the sand lost from a beach, the action of the waves also brings an equal amount of sand ashore. Thus, although the shape of a beach will change, the beach itself will remain.

### Problems caused by erosion

Although erosion is a natural process and does not completely remove a beach, scientists are concerned about beach erosion because human activities have altered the way erosion occurs. Coastlines are attractive places and many people want

## Carolina Outer Banks

Beach erosion makes seaside homes more vulnerable to storm surges. Families must often evacuate when hurricanes threaten. © *Jason Reed/Reuters/Corbis. Reproduced by permission.*

The Outer Banks are series of dunes that stretch for 130 miles (209 kilometers) in the sea off the coast of North Carolina. Among the well-known attractions of the Outer Banks is Kitty Hawk, site of Orville and Wilbur Wright's famous 1903 flight, and a series of distinctive lighthouses.

The Cape Hatteras lighthouse is also an example of the power of erosion. When the lighthouse was built in 1870 it stood about 1,500 feet (457 meters) back from the waves crashing on the beach. By 1999 erosion had brought the waves to within 150 feet (46 meters) of the lighthouse. To preserve the structure, engineers picked up the lighthouse, put it on a movable treadmill similar to the ones used to transport Apollo spacecraft to the launch pad in the 1970s, and moved the lighthouse further inland.

One of the reasons that erosion claimed so much land was a manmade attempt to stop the process. In the 1970s the United States Navy built two groynes just north of the lighthouse. The groynes were put there to protect a building. Unfortunately, they accelerated the erosion downstream to the point where moving the lighthouse was necessary to save it.

---

to live or visit there. Many beaches are now completely lined by buildings, parking lots, and roads. The beachfront areas of Miami Beach, Atlantic City, and Honolulu, are three examples of heavily developed beaches in the United States. The large area of land covered by concrete does not allow rainwater to soak into the ground and gently trickle out over the beach at many different points. Instead, the water empties onto the beach at only a few streams. The streams wear away selected portions of the beach, which can make erosion more severe.

## Development and erosion

The desire for a home right on the ocean has lead many people to literally build their houses on top of sand dunes, which are hills of sand heaped up by the wind. Dunes are not permanent structures; they naturally wear away. To attempt to reduce erosion, people have built structures like seawalls and narrow strips that jut out into the water (a groyne). These structures break the pattern of the waves in a small area. The United States government spends over $150 million each year to build beach-protective structures. Homeowners also spend a great deal of money.

While a small section of a beach may be protected by these structures, other areas of the beach are often more affected by the resulting interrupted wave action. To compensate, sand must often be added to a beach if the beach is to be preserved. In parts of Florida, beach repair of this type averages about $1 million per mile of beach every year.

The use of seawalls, in some areas, especially where they are built by homeowners intermittently along a coast, has proven to be unwise. Rather than allowing the incoming energy of a wave to disappear over the area of a beach, a seawall can actually accelerate the speed of incoming water flowing around or over it. This speeds up the removal of material from the beach. In some areas where seawalls have been in place for many years, the beach has often completely disappeared and the waves lap the base of the wall. Where seawalls are built along a large, continuous area such as in Galveston, Texas, and are constructed high enough that waves do not crash over them, they cause less slow beach erosion. The Galveston seawall also protects against the rapid beach erosion that occurs during hurricanes.

### Reducing beach erosion

Many areas have passed laws to prevent the destruction of sand dunes, which serve as a natural protective barrier against erosion during storms. Where sand dunes are destroyed by humans or erosion, artificial barriers of wire or tree limbs secured in dune-forming areas help to speed their formation. Protected dunes along seashores are rich in plant life, which serves to further strengthen the dunes because of the root networks of the tall grass-like plants. Although dunes provide little protection for narrow beaches, they help decrease erosion in broad beaches, such as those in Florida and Texas.

---

### Coastal Development Laws and Acts

The need to protect coastlines from erosion and overdevelopment has lead the United States to enact various rules and regulations.

In 1972 the federal government created the Coastal Zone Management Act. This voluntary program helped encourage coastal states to make changes that would help protect beaches by sharing the cost of some of this development. In the years since then, the act has been revised to make money available to projects that seek to restore coastal areas to a more natural state and to keep beaches from being bought by private owners.

The state of California has a series of regulations that together make up the California Coastal Act. The rules help control what type of development can occur along the coast and how much of the coast is available to the general public. A similar coastal management program exists in Atlantic coast states including Maine and New Jersey.

A strategy that scientists are evaluating to reduce erosion is to build up the bottom of the ocean farther out from the beach, creating an off-shore ridge with sand and materials such as steel from aircraft and ships, or stone. Incoming waves break over the ridge of piled up material instead of breaking on the beach. Researchers are examining whether this disrupts the natural environment in a negative manner.

The most popular method to keep the sandy beaches that are so desirable to homeowners and recreational beachgoers is to bring sand to the beach. Often sand will be taken from the ocean bottom further away from shore and sent through a pipe to the beach. This temporary measure only delays the effects of erosion, and is often repeated.

*Brian Hoyle, Ph.D.*

## For More Information

### Books

Cambers, Gillian. *Coping with Beach Erosion.* Paris: United Nations Educational, Scientific and Cultural Organization, 1998.

Douglas, Scott L. *Saving America's Beaches: The Causes of and Solutions to Beach Erosion.* Singapore: World Scientific Publishing Company, 2002.

Steele, Philip W. *Changing Coastlines (Earth's Changing Landscape).* North Mankato, MN: Smart Apple Media, 2004.

Wood, Timothy. *Breakthrough: The Story of Chatham's North Beach.* Chatham, MA: Hyora Publishers Publishers, 2002.

### Websites

DeVitt, Terry. "Beach Erosion." *The Why Files.* http://whyfiles.org/091beach/credits.html (accessed on September 7, 2004).

# Bioaccumulation of Heavy Metals

Some of the substances that make up Earth's crust are elements, substances that cannot be naturally broken down into simpler substances. A few of these elements are poisonous even if present in a low concentration. These are known as heavy metals. Examples of heavy metals include mercury, cadmium, arsenic, chromium, thallium, and lead.

A school of bluefin tuna snagged during a mattanza (a mass tuna catch) that periodically occurs off the coast of Sicily, Italy. © *Jeffrey L. Rotman/Corbis. Reproduced by permission.*

## WORDS TO KNOW

**Bioaccumulation:** The buildup of a substance in a living thing to a concentration that is greater than the concentration of the substance in the natural environment.

**Heavy metal:** A group of metal elements that are poisonous even when present in low concentrations.

### The heavy metal-water connection

There is a connection between heavy metals and water. Because heavy metals are part of Earth's crust, they can be worn away by the action of weather. When they are worn off of rock, they can collect in surface or groundwater (fresh water in rock and soil layer beneath Earth's surface). Depending on the chemistry of the water, the metals might stay in the water, or come out of the water and gather on an available surface such as plants. Heavy metals can, therefore, enter peoples' bodies via drinking water and food.

Heavy metals get into fresh and salt water when water or other fluids are added to the water body. Examples include industrial waste, sewage (even treated sewage can contain high levels of heavy metals), run-off (water that flows over surfaces) after a rainfall and from mining operations.

Microorganisms, plants, and animals depend on water for life. Heavy metals can bind to the surface of microorganisms and may even penetrate to the inside of the cell. Inside the microorganism, the heavy metals can be chemically changed as the microorganism uses chemical reactions to digest food. A well-known example is the ability of some bacteria to change mercury to a modified form called methylmercury. Methylmercury can be absorbed much more easily than mercury into the bodies of insects and other small organisms. When these small organisms are eaten by bigger living organisms such as fish, the heavy metals enter the fish. But, instead of staying in the fish for only a short time, the metals can remain in the fish for extended periods. As the fish eats more of the smaller organisms, the amount of heavy metals increases. As bigger organisms eat the smaller organisms (making up the food chain), the heavy metals build-up in concentration in the larger living things. This increase in concentration of substances over time and in bigger living organisms is called bioaccumulation. For example, at the top of the ocean food chain, fish such as tuna can contain significant quantities of mercury.

### The effects of heavy metals

Bioaccumulation of heavy metals is dangerous to human health. Lead, cadmium, cobalt, nickel, and mercury can affect the formation of blood cells. The build-up of heavy metals can cause malfunctions in the liver, kidneys, the circulatory system (responsible for the circulation of blood throughout the body), and the movement of nerve signals. Some heavy metals may also play a role in the development of various cancers.

**Lead** The lead atom (smallest component of an element having the chemical properties of the element) is similar in size and shape to the calcium atom. Lead can substitute in the body for calcium, particularly in bone. In children, where bones are still developing and the child is not taking in the required amount of calcium, the lead can become stored in the bone. If the lead gets out of the bone, as can happen when a child gets a suitable amount of calcium, the free lead can cause damage to nerves and to the brain.

**Mercury** Mercury, especially the form methylmercury, is very dangerous to people. Methylmercury is produced by microorganisms that live in the water. A lengthy exposure to mercury (such as can occur when mercury-containing fish are eaten) can damage the liver and cause brain damage. If a pregnant women takes in too much mercury it can cause birth defects in her child.

### Effect of bioaccumulation on water organisms

Many organisms that live in fresh and salt water are harmed when heavy metals accumulate inside them. Shellfish do not

---

### Eating Tuna

The hazards of eating mercury-contaminated fish came to public attention in 1956, when 121 people around Minamata Bay in Japan were poisoned after eating fish that had been contaminated by mercury spilled from a nearby industry. Forty-six of the 121 people died. The symptoms of lack of coordination, paralysis, difficulty swallowing, convulsions, and brain damage became known as Minamata Disease.

After shrimp, tuna is the most popular seafood in the United States. The presence of mercury in tuna has lead to a great deal of concern about the safety of canned tuna, which is used to make a popular lunchtime sandwich for school-aged children. Calculations have shown that a 45-pound child who eats one 6-ounce can of chunk white tuna a week takes in an amount of mercury that exceeds the dose recommended as safe by the United States Environmental Protection Agency. Nevertheless, as of 2004, no firm rules have yet been put into place about how much tuna people should eat until scientists confirm the amounts and sources of mercury that are harmful to humans.

have any mechanism to prevent bioaccumulation. This actually makes the shellfish a good indicator to scientists that a problem of heavy metal accumulation may exist in a certain area. If shellfish are found with unacceptably high levels of heavy metal, scientists are alerted to the possibility of contamination in organisms throughout the body of water.

The problem of bioaccumulation of heavy metals is proving difficult to solve. Much work still needs to be done by scientists to develop reliable methods of detecting the presence of unacceptable levels of heavy metals, and in protecting waterways from exposure to heavy metal-containing pollution.

*Brian Hoyle, Ph.D.*

**For More Information**

**Books**

Botkin, Daniel B., and Edward A. Keller. *Environmental Science: Earth as a Living Planet.* New York: Wiley, 2002.

Gedicks, Al. *Resource Rebels.* Cambridge, MA: South End Press, 2001.

Smol, John. *Pollution of Lakes and Rivers.* London: Arnold Publishers, 2002.

**Websites**

"Eutrophication (Nutrient Pollution)." *University of Manitoba, Experimental Lakes Area.* http://www.umanitoba.ca/institutes/fisheries/eutro.html (accessed on September 1, 2004)

"Eutrophication." *U.S. Environmental Protection Agency.* http://www.epa.gov/maia/html/eutroph.html (accessed on September 1, 2004)

## Desertification

Desertification is a term used to describe the gradual changes that take place over a region or area of land that ultimately result in the formation of a desert. Although many places in the world are called deserts, scientists usually define a desert as a region or area that receives less than 10 inches (25.4 centimeters) of water from precipitation (rain, slow, sleet, or hail) during a year.

Desertification harms many people. During the late 1960s and early 1970s, desertification brought on by a severe drought

## 1930s U.S. Dustbowl

A cloud of topsoil lifts from drought stricken farms and contributes to the accelerated loss of soil during the 1935 Dust Bowl. *AP/Wide World Photos. Reproduced by permission.*

During the Great Depression of the 1930s, the United States and Europe suffered difficult economic times. Jobs were scare and unemployment was high. Farms failed and many farmers were forced to abandon the land that had once supported their families and communities. In some areas of the United States, people suffered from malnutrition and starvation.

In addition to economic hardships, there was also a severe drought (an extended period of time with little or no rain over an area) over large portions of the Midwest throughout the 1930s. The drought also contributed to farm failures.

The combination of lack of irrigation (the watering of land and crops), and natural drought resulted in the loss of topsoil (a process scientists call deflation of the soil). The topsoil dried it became lighter and easily blown by the wind. As a result, great windstorms of dry dust blew millions of pounds of topsoil from once fertile farms and the large portions of the American Midwest, particularly Oklahoma and Kansas, became known as the Dust Bowl.

In some areas, the amount of dust and topsoil in the air was so great that dust storms decreased the visibility to just a few feet. The dust in the air became so choking that it was life-threatening to babies, small children, the elderly, and the sick. According to the 1934 *Yearbook of Agriculture,* nearly 35 million acres of cultivated land (land normally plowed and watered by farmers) became desertlike and unable to support the growth of crops. More than 200 million additional acres of land also showed signs of becoming desert-like and were in the process of desertification.

An improved economy late in the decade and the return of normal levels of rainfall, reversed the process of desertification over most of the Dustbowl region.

---

(an extended period with little or no rain) in the Sahel region of Africa devastated the local agriculture of six African countries located on the southern border of the Sahara Desert. International relief measures were unable to prevent the death of thousands of people who suffered from the resulting famine (lack of food). Millions of animals that normally relied upon eating the grass that grew in the already dry region also died. The deaths of the animals resulted in further starvation of the people living in the region.

### WORDS TO KNOW

**Desert:** An area of land that receives less than ten inches (25.4 centimeters) of precipitation per year.

**Precipitation:** Transfer of water as rain, slow, sleet or hail from the atmosphere to the land or ocean surface.

Dry areas of North America—particularly in the southwestern and western United States—are also vulnerable to desertification. Some scientists estimate that up to nine out of ten such areas can be described as undergoing some form of desertification.

## How desertification changes the environment

As the process of desertification takes place, the land loses its ability to support agriculture. Areas that were once arid (dry), but that could still support the growth of some crops or the grazing of animals, become barren as the desertification progresses. For example, grasslands may undergo desertification to become deserts.

During desertification, an area undergoes many changes, but it does not lose its ability to support crops or animals all at once. Neither does it completely lose its ability to support life. Even a desert can support the sparse growth of vegetation that live in areas with little moisture. As desertification proceeds, however, the land gradually loses its ability to support plants that require higher levels of water, and only plants that are able to live and thrive on less water survive.

A farmer surveys the parched soil of his drought stricken South Texas farm. *Jim Sugar Photography/Corbis-Bettmann. Reproduced by permission.*

The loss of water also changes the way the land responds to wind and occasional rains. Over time, desertification results in changes to the landscape that result in the formation of areas of high erosion (areas where soil and rock are lost or worn away by water) and the formation of dramatic land features (such as flat-topped mesas or buttes). As desertification continues, the topsoil (uppermost layer of soil) dries and becomes lighter. It is easily blown away by the wind is and the remaining sand or soil may form dunes (hills of sand created by wind). The wind over the region or area then shapes the dunes in very specific ways. For example, scientists can look at the pattern of dunes and tell how the winds blow throughout the year.

The loss of water over time also changes the chemistry of the land. As the land becomes drier, the concentration of salt increases in the water that does remain. If the concentration of salt become too high (a process termed salinization), the remaining water can become too salty for humans to drink or use for watering crops.

## Causes of desertification

In addition to a decline in the amount of rain that falls each year, a number of other factors are important in determining whether a region or area will undergo desertification. Factors such as wind, amount of sunlight, and use of the land also influence how fast desertification takes place.

Desertification can be caused or reversed by natural forces and cycles in the climate such as rainfall and wind patterns. For example, rainshadow deserts may form in area with little precipitation because a barrier such as a mountain range causes moisture-rich winds to lose their moisture before reaching the area.

Improper use or overuse of water resources by humans can also cause desertification. If, for example, humans overuse water to water lawns, not enough water may remain available in local groundwater or aquifers support surrounding areas needing water to grow grasses that support cattle and other grazing animals. In addition, if too many animals are introduced into an area, they can overgraze by eating too much of the available vegetation. The loss of too much natural grass and vegetation can speed up the processes of land erosion, which will speed up the process of and desertification.

Other human activities such as deforestation (the overcutting of trees) and mining may cause desertification. The introduction of new species of plants and animals not native (naturally occurring) to a region or area—especially plants or animals that may require more water than the native species already living in the area—may result in desertification.

## Halting desertification

Under the right conditions, if the use of land is carefully regulated and special practices are started to conserve water, desertification can be greatly slowed or even reversed. In this way, water conservation helps keep lands productive.

In many dry regions, water conservation practices are new to the societies that live there and it remains the custom to simply abandon dry lands in search of areas with more water available to support crops and animals. As the world's population increases, however, this practice cannot continue indefinitely, and water conservation practices have become increasingly important.

Desertification can also be reversed by natural forces and cycles in the climate.

*K. Lee Lerner*

## For More Information

### Books

Burroughs, William, ed. *Climate: Into the 21st. Century.* New York: Cambridge University Press, 2003.

Bush, Mark B. *Ecology of a Changing Planet.* Upper Saddle River, NJ: Prentice Hall, 1997.

### Websites

"From the Dust Bowl to the Sahel." *National Atmospheric and Space Administration: Earth Observatory.* http://earthobservatory.nasa.gov/Study/DustBowl (accessed on September 7, 2004).

"National Weather Service Climate Prediction Center." National Oceanic and Atmospheric Administration. http://www.cpc.ncep.noaa.gov/ (accessed on September 7, 2004).

"Surviving the Dust Bowl: The American Experience." *Public Broadcasting System/WGBH.* http://www.pbs.org/wgbh/amex/dustbowl/ (accessed on September 7, 2004).

"Water." *National Environment Research Council Centre for Ecology and Hydrology.* http://www.ceh.ac.uk/science_topics/water.htm (accessed on September 7, 2004).

"World Climates." *Blue Planet Biomes.* http://www.blueplanetbiomes.org/climate.htm (accessed on September 7, 2004).

# Eutrophication

Eutrophication is a process in which a body of water changes with time as deposits of nutrients and sediments (particles of sand, silt, and clay) from the surrounding area accumulate.

## The process of eutrophication

In eutrophication, the chemical characteristics of the water changes. The biology of the water, in terms of the types of organisms that can live in that water body, also changes. Eutrophication involves an increase in the level of plants' food sources in the water. Younger water bodies that have lower levels of nutrients do not support much life. As the nutrients increase, more life can develop in the water. Indeed, the word eutrophic comes from the Greek word *eu* meaning "well" and *trophic*, meaning "feeding." The term *eutrophic*, therefore, literally means "well nourished." At the other end of the scale is an overgrowth of plants including the microscopic chlorophyll-containing algae, which will rob the lake of oxygen and cause the deaths of animals and other aquatic life.

## Consequences of eutrophication

While eutrophication is a natural process that occurs over thousands of years, it has become associated with what can happen to water when human activities alter the water composition. This form of eutrophication has sometimes been called cultural eutrophication.

The human-made form of eutrophication occurs when food sources for plants and microorganisms find their way into the water. Fertilizer, cleaning detergents, and other human products contains compounds such as phosphorus, nitrogen, and carbon that cause the growth of plants and specifically of algae. Rain washes these compounds off of farm fields, lawns, golf courses, roads, and parks into stream, rivers, ponds, lakes, and ocean waters.

Eutrophication that is artificially accelerated, mainly because of the addition of fertilizer from agricultural run-off and homeowner's lawns and other chemicals from paved surfaces such as parking lots, can destroy the recreational quality of a lake for people. A formerly beautiful lake can become a smelly dead zone.

In the 1970s and 1980s in a benchmark series of studies that has set the standard for the discipline, Canadian scientists studied the effects on the controlled addition of various fertilizers to a series of small lakes. Because the lakes were isolated, the scientists were able to study what affect each fertilizer had on the health of the lake. These studies demonstrated that, among the various compounds that were added to test sections of lakes, phosphorus was the key chemical that drove the eutrophication process. One lake was split in half by a plastic divider. Carbon and nitrogen were added to one half of the lake and carbon, nitrogen, and phosphorus were added to the other half. The half that received phosphorus developed huge numbers of a type of microorganism called blue-green algae. This rapid and huge increase in numbers of algae is called an algal bloom. The resulting algal bloom used much of the available oxygen in the water,

## WORDS TO KNOW

**Algal bloom:** The rapid and huge increase in numbers of algae that can occur in the presence of a food source such as phosphorus.

**Estuary:** An area where a freshwater body meets the sea.

**Phosphorus:** An element used as a food source by a variety of plants and microorganisms.

## Gulf of Mexico

In the Gulf of Mexico eutrophication has occurred on a vast scale. The eutrophic "dead zone," an area where the oxygen content in the water is too low to support many fish and plants that normally live in the Gulf, extends along the coasts of Louisiana and Texas for hundreds of miles (kilometers). The zone grows larger in the summer months as the tropical waters become warmer, and shrinks in the fall as the water temperature cools. The excess nutrients are deposited by the waters that flow into the Gulf of Mexico from the Mississippi River, and large oxygen-depleting algal blooms are the result.

Surveys have shown that the eutrophic area during summer months is about 6,950 square miles (18,000 square kilometers), or about the size of New Jersey. The fishing industry along the Gulf that normally brings in over $26 billion dollars worth of shrimp, crab, and fish each year has felt an impact of the dead zone. Fishing fleets are forced to travel farther out to sea for their catch, around or past the barren area.

A number of government organizations including the U.S. Environmental Protection Agency are working to understand the causes of the Gulf eutrophication and to lessen the damage. This task is challenging as the Mississippi River delivers water from a large portion of the central United States, and the Mississippi River basin contains over half of all U.S. farms. Controlling the nutrients entering the Mississippi will be a multi-state effort between federal, state, and local governments.

causing the death of fish and other creatures that depend on oxygen for survival. This experiment was key in convincing people around the world that the addition of phosphorus compounds to water was a problem. Later, laws were enacted in Canada that banned the use of most phosphorus compounds in laundry detergent (phosphorus was initially added to laundry detergent to add softness to clothes). As well, these studies have helped drive the creation of environmental regulations elsewhere.

Another source of nitrogen and phosphorus is sewage. In many large cities throughout the world, millions of gallons of raw sewage are still pumped into local waters every day. Whether rain-washed or flushed, nitrogen and phosphorus compounds entering a water body can be used as a source of food by microorganisms in the water, in particular algae.

### Effects of eutrophication

The human-made form of eutrophication occurs much faster than natural eutrophication. Instead of a water body changing over thousands of years, a lake undergoing eutrophication as a result of excess runoff (surface water that flows off land) of nitrogen-, phosphorus- and carbon-containing compounds can go from being clean, clear, and home to a variety of life, to a green algae-filled body in only a few years. Reversing the damage from human-made eutrophication in a body of water can be a difficult process. This is especially true in lakes where the replacement of water, as water flows into the lake at one end and flows out at the other, occurs slowly. During the 1960s Lake Erie underwent eutrophication. For over a decade, scientists assumed that the lake might never recover. Fortunately, environmental measures such as reducing the use of detergents that contain phosphorus and careful management of agriculture near the lake has helped restore Lake Erie to health.

Harmful effects of eutrophication are also found in the Chesapeake Bay. The bay, located in Maryland, is a large estuary (area where freshwater meets saltwater). In the 1970s the bay was healthy and home to a wide variety of underwater life. But as massive amounts of nutrients from agricultural and urban activities slowly washed into the bay, the blooms of algae cut off sunlight and reduced the oxygen in the water. As a result, animal life in the bay, such as the famous Maryland crabs, are reducing in numbers. Citizen groups and government agencies are joining forces to restore the water quality of the Chesapeake bay by reducing the amount of sediments and nutrients that are introduced into the bay, and by protecting the nearby forests and wetlands that serve as natural filters for contaminants. Their joint goal is to restore the Chesapeake water quality to a level that will sustain its natural plant and animal inhabitants by the year 2010.

*Brian Hoyle, Ph.D.*

## For More Information

### Books

Dennis, Jerry. *The Living Great Lakes: Searching for the Heart of the Inland Seas.* New York: Thomas Dunne Books, 2003.

National Research Council. *Clean Coastal Waters: Understanding and Reducing the Effects of Nutrient Pollution.* Washington: National Academy Press, 2000.

### Websites

"Eutrophication (Nutrient Pollution)." *University of Manitoba.* http://www.umanitoba.ca/institutes/fisheries/eutro.html (accessed on September 1, 2004).

"Eutrophication." *U.S. Environmental Protection Agency.* http://www.epa.gov/maia/html/eutroph.html (accessed on September 1, 2004).

"Tributary Strategies: Charting the Path to a Healthy Bay." *Chesapeake Bay Program.* http://www.chesapeakebay.net/wqctributarytech.htm (accessed on September 1, 2004).

# Floods and Flood Control

Floods occur when a normally drier land area is temporarily submerged in water overflowing from rivers, dams (barrier to contain the flow of water), runoff, or tides. Runoff is water

## WORDS TO KNOW

**Crest:** The highest water level during a flood; also the highest level of floodwaters during a flood.

**Dam:** A physical barrier constructed across a river or waterway to control the flow or raise the level of water.

**Drainage basin:** Land area from which surface runoff drains into a stream or lake.

**Flash flood:** Flood that rises and dissipates rapidly with little or no advance warning, usually as the result of intense rainfall over a relatively small area.

**Floodplain:** Low-lying area near a water source that is normally dry, but is subject to overflow by a river, lake, or water from a man-made water barrier.

**Levee:** A long, narrow embankment usually built to protect land from flooding.

**National Weather Service:** Government agency that predicts the weather and warns the public of dangerous weather situations and their consequences, including severe weather and flood warnings.

that accumulates and flows after heavy rainstorms or snowmelts. Floods occur in all fifty states and around the world. Floods can be caused by several factors: heavy rainfall over a short period, moderate rainfall over a long period, melting snow, hurricane storm surge (a dome of water that builds up as a hurricane moves over water), ice or debris jams on rivers, and dam failures.

Floods can cause great harm to people and property. Floods are the deadliest form of natural disasters, killing more Americans every year than tornados, lightning, earthquakes, and forest fires combined. Due to the potential harm, government agencies work to prevent and predict floods.

### Describing floods

Scientists describe floods according to three criteria: the maximum height of the water above normal levels during the flood, the time period required for the flood waters to rise and fall, and the size and frequency with which similar floods are likely to occur.

**Height of the floodwater.** In describing the maximum height of a flood, scientists refer to the crest of a river (its maximum height during a flood) or the height of the floodwaters over the floodplain. A floodplain is a low-lying area near a water source that is normally dry, but is subject to overflow by a river, lake, or water from a man-made water barrier. In Florence, Italy in 1966 for example, the Arno River crested at about 20 feet (6 meters) over flood stage (the level at which water leaves its banks and begins to flood), and filled the nearby Santa Croce church, home to countless masterpieces of art, with over 8 feet (2.4 meters) of water and mud. Watermarks indicating the height of the flood are still visible today along the walls of the church.

When describing floods according to the time period required for the water to rise and fall, scientists often refer to flash floods. Flash floods are floods that occur in only a few hours or even minutes, usually due to heavy rainfall or a dam break. Flash floods can also occur when ice or debris to obstruct the flow of river water, causing water to back up upstream. When the ice or debris breaks loose, a wall of water rushes downstream and can cause flash floods.

**Speed of the flood.** Flash floods are dangerous because they are usually accompanied by fast moving water. Fast moving water usually occurs in drainage ditches, canyons, and in rivers and creeks. Flash floods can produce fast-moving walls of water up to 20 feet (6 meters) high. However, it does not take 20 feet of water to cause death or major damage. Two feet of fast moving water can wash away cars, and flash floodwaters only 6 inches (15 centimeters) deep have knocked down people. Weather forecasters are especially alert to notifying the public about conditions that are favorable for the development of flash floods, but people should also be wary of low-lying roads and other areas during heavy rains.

Floods that are slower to develop than flash floods can also be just as deadly and damaging. These floods occur when an area receives moderate rainfall over a period of days or weeks, and streams and rivers accumulate more water than they can handle. As the water has nowhere else to go, it spills over the banks of the river and onto the floodplain. Flooding can even occur where no rain has fallen. Bulging rivers can force floodwaters tens or even hundreds of miles (kilometers) downstream.

**Size and frequency of the flood.** Scientists also categorize floods according to the size of the flood and the likelihood of another similar flood in the same place within a one-year time-

Flood waters overwhelm a water treatment plant near the Raccoon River, Iowa. *AP/Wide World Photos. Reproduced by permission.*

frame. For example the 1966 flood in Florence, Italy was described as a 100-year flood, which means that the chance of a similar flood occurring within the same year in Florence was 1 in 100. A 5-year flood has a 5 in 100, or 20% chance of a similar flood happening in the same place within a year. The classifications of 5-year flood, 10-year flood, 25-year flood, 50-year flood, 100-year flood, or 500-year flood, actually refer more to size of the flood than to predictions when a similar one will happen again in the future. The water volume of the flood increases along the scale as the frequency decreases. A 5-year flood is almost always a mild occurrence, whereas a 500-year flood tends to have very high and violent water flow, and covers a wide area of the floodplain.

## Flood damage

Since the 1970s, an average of 140 Americans have died in floods every year. The deadliest flood in American history occurred in Johnstown, Pennsylvania, a town that was built on the floodplain near the fork of the Little Conemaugh and Stony Creek Rivers. On May 31, 1889 an upstream dam on the Little Conemaugh ruptured. The wall of water that rushed downstream resulted in a flash flood that killed 2,200 people when it reached Johnstown. In 1972 232 people died in Rapid City, South Dakota, during a flash flood. Many of the people that were killed were spectators who were swept away while admiring the floodwaters.

Floods can also cause significant property damage. Flood damage includes damage and destruction of houses, businesses, automobiles, crops, and personal property. Floods are responsible for over $2 billion of damage every year in the United States. The Great Midwest Flood of the Mississippi and Missouri Rivers in 1993 caused between $15 and $20 billion in damages and 50 deaths. This slow-forming flood covered thousands of square miles (kilometers) with water in most Midwestern states. Residents downstream placed sandbags along the banks of the river to create a barrier before the floodwaters reached them, but the river engulfed large parts of farmland and cities all along its floodplain. The floodwaters remained for 144 days.

## Flood watches and warnings

The National Weather Service issues four types of flood warnings: flood watches; flash flood watches; flood warnings; and flash flood warnings. The National Weather Service is a government agency that predicts the weather and warns the

## Venice in Peril

Venice, Italy, is built in a lagoon (a shallow body of water separated from the ocean by a sandbank or by a strip of low land) bordered by the Adriatic Sea and tidal marshland. The city's canals and seaport made Venice a successful seaport and center of trade for centuries. However the same sea that allowed Venice to flourish also threatens its historic architecture. Venice is sinking.

The lagoon around Venice floods as many as 200 days a year. These floods routinely send water into Venice's squares and buildings. The frequency of floods in Venice has increased over the last century. Venice now floods 30 times more often than it did over 100 years ago.

There are several reasons for the sinking of Venice and the resulting floods. Groundwater (fresh water in the rock and soil layers beneath Earth's land surface) in the area around Venice was pumped out at a great rate during the twentieth century. The removal of groundwater lowered the water table (level below the land surface at which spaces in the soil and rock become saturated with water) in Venice, resulting in soil compaction. Soil compaction refers to the same amount of soil being packed into a smaller space. Soil compaction in Venice led the city to sink. This sinking process is also known as subsidence. Since 1950 Venice has sunk nearly 8 inches (20 centimeters). Flooding in Venice may have also increased due to a ship canal that was dug in the 1950s. Many scientists also calculate that rising sea levels that result from climate change may also lead to increased flooding.

Scientists have developed several plans to save Venice from ruin. Construction is underway on a mobile flood barrier where the lagoon meets the Adriatic Sea. Large gates will be attached to the sea floor at these locations. When sea levels are expected to rise and flood Venice, these large gates will rise up and prevent seawater from entering the lagoon. This four-billion-dollar project is expected to be completed in 2011. These mobile flood barriers will protect Venice from rising seawater for the next 100 to 150 years.

Scientists are also studying the possibility of raising Venice by injecting fluids into the soil far below the city. Fluid pumping would replace water that was removed from Venice's water table during the twentieth century. Engineers hope the fluid pumping can raise the city 8 to 12 inches (20 to 30 centimeters).

---

public of dangerous weather situations. Knowing what these watches and warnings mean can save lives.

A flood watch means that weather conditions are favorable for floods to form. A flood watch is usually issued during long periods of moderate rainfall. A flash flood watch means that flooding could occur within six hours or less after the rain ends. Flash flood watches are usually issued during periods of heavy rainfall when waters may rise quickly.

A flood warning means that flooding is occurring. Rivers and creeks are rising. People in low-lying areas should be prepared to evacuate if waters in their area begin to rise. A flash flood warning means that water levels are rising quickly and will threaten life and property within six hours. Upon receiving a flash flood warning, people in low-lying areas or areas near creeks and rivers should move to higher ground immediately.

Forecasters advise people to remain indoors during a flood watch or warning and go out only if necessary to evacuate. Keep a weather radio nearby and have an escape plan. Never walk through running water; find a way around it. Even a small creek or drainage ditch can be deadly during a flood. Also, never drive across a road that has water on it, even if it looks safe to do so. Judging the depth of water over a road is difficult, especially at night. In the United States more flood victims die in their cars than anywhere else.

**Flood control**

Given the awesome and destructive power of flood waters, humans have long sought to tame rivers and streams to prevent future flooding. Rivers that have many streams that feed them are more likely to flood than rivers with few streams. In the United States, the Mississippi River drainage basin accommodates more water than any other drainage basin. A drainage basin is an area of land in which all of the creeks, streams, and rivers drain into a common source. The Mississippi River drainage basin is the third largest drainage basin in the world. Approximately 41% of all water in the lower 48 states drain into the Mississippi River. The Mississippi River drainage basin covers over 1.2 million square miles (3.1 million square kilometers) and all or part of 31 states. This results in the Mississippi River handling a great amount of water. Flood waters anywhere in the drainage basin will eventually all flow into the Mississippi River, potentially causing it to flood as well.

Spanish explorers recorded flooding of the Mississippi River in 1543. The floodwaters remained for 80 days. Flooding in the early twentieth century devastated the lower Mississippi River drainage basin. In 1927 floodwaters covered over 26,000 square miles (67,300 square kilometers). This huge flood led Congress to pass a law called the Flood Waters Control Act of 1928, which sought to control the waters of the lower Mississippi River. The result of this law was the Mississippi River and Tributaries Project. The project sought to allow the Mississippi River to handle a flood 11% larger than the flood of 1927. The project was designed to prevent flooding along about 600 miles (957 kilometers) of the river from Cape Girardeau, Missouri to New Orleans, Louisiana.

The project led to the construction of a series of dams and levees (walls built to hold back and channel flood water) to control the Mississippi River. Deep channels called floodways also provide a path for floodwaters. Dams can be opened to allow water out of the river and into these floodways. Most floodways are located near areas that flood easily (low-lying floodplains).

The Tennessee Valley Authority, a government agency that controls dams and generates electricity, also runs a flood control program. The Tennessee Valley Authority controls 34 dams that prevent flooding along the Tennessee River, Ohio River, and Mississippi River. The dams release water from reservoirs before flood season. A reservoir is the water that is backed up behind a dam. Lowering the reservoirs allows them to hold more water during the flood season. The floodwaters are then slowly released from behind the dams to prevent flooding downstream. The Tennessee Valley Authorities flood control system prevents over $200 million in flood related damage every year.

*Joseph P. Hyder*

## For More Information

### Books
Duden, Jane and Kay Ewald. *Floods! Rising, Raging Waters.* Des Moines, IA: Perfection Learning, 1999.

McCullough, David. *The Johnstown Flood.* New York: Simon & Schuster, 1968.

### Websites
"Flood Control." *Tennessee Valley Authority.* http://www.tva.gov/river/flood.htm (accessed on September 7, 2004).

"Floods." *Federal Emergency Management Agency for Kids.* www.fema.gov/kids (accessed on September 7, 2004).

"Floods." *National Oceanographic and Atmospheric Administration.* http://www.noaa.gov/floods.html (accessed on September 7, 2004).

"The Mississippi River and Tributaries Project." *US Army Corps of Engineers.* http://www.mvn.usace.army.mil/pao/bro/misstrib.htm (accessed on September 7, 2004).

"The Sinking City of Venice—NOVA Online." *PBS.* http://www.pbs.org/wgbh/nova/venice/ (accessed on September 7, 2004).

## WORDS TO KNOW

**Climate:** Long-term meteorological conditions or average weather.

**Cyclic changes:** Changes that repeat themselves over time.

**Evaporation:** The process whereby water changes to a gas or vapor.

**Greenhouse effect:** The process where light from the Sun is reflected off Earth's surfaces and then trapped by clouds to warm Earth's atmosphere and surface.

**Greenhouse gases:** Gases in Earth atmosphere's that include water vapor and carbon dioxide, methane, nitrous oxides, ozone, halogens (bromine, chlorine, and fluorine), halocarbons, and other trace gases (gases found in very relatively small amounts).

**Respiration:** Process in which an organism uses oxygen for its life processes.

**Transpiration:** Evaporation of water from the leaves or stems of plants.

**Water vapor:** Water in the form of gas in the atmosphere.

# Global Climate Change

Global climate change, often simply referred to as "global warming," is a complex and scientifically controversial issue that attributes an increase in the average annual surface temperature of Earth to increased concentrations of carbon dioxide and other gases in the atmosphere (air surrounding Earth). Many scientists disagree on how to best interpret data related to climate change. Scientists also argue about which data (for example, measurements of changes of thickness in arctic ice, measurements of sea temperatures at critical locations, or measurements of certain chemicals in the atmosphere, etc.) should be used to make informed decisions about the extent and rate of global climate change.

Climate describes the long-term conditions or average weather for a region. Throughout Earth's history, there have been dramatic and cyclic changes (changes that repeat themselves in cycles that can last from thousands to millions of years) in climatic weather patterns corresponding to cycles where glaciers of ice advance and retreat over the landscape. These glacial cycles occur on the scale of 100,000 years. However, within these larger glacial cycles are shorter duration warming and cooling trends that last from 20,000 to 40,000 years.

Scientists estimate that approximately 10,000 years have elapsed since the end of the last ice age, and examination of physical and biological evidence establishes that since the end of the last ice age there have been fluctuating periods of global warming and cooling.

## Concerns over global warming

Global warming actually describes only one of several components involved in climate change and specifically refers to a warming of Earth's surface outside of the range of normal fluctuations that have occurred throughout Earth's history.

Measurements made of weather and climate trends during the last decades of the twentieth century raised concern that global temperatures are rising not in response to natural cycles, but rather in response to increasing concentrations of atmospheric gases that are critical to the natural and life-enabling greenhouse effect.

The greenhouse effect describes a process wherein infrared radiation (a form of light) from the Sun is reflected off Earth's surfaces, but then trapped by clouds to warm Earth's atmos-

Fongafale Island, the capital of Tuvalu—one of the smallest countries in the world—is threatened by rising sea levels. © *Matthieu Paley/Corbis. Reproduced by permission.*

phere and surface (the light is reflected through the atmosphere and back towards Earth's surface). Although the greenhouse effect is essential to life on Earth, if changes result in too strong a greenhouse effect, the changes in Earth's climate could be dramatic and occur much faster than do natural cycles.

Observations collected over the last century indicate that the average land surface temperature increased by 0.8–1.0°F (0.45–0.6°C). The effects of temperature increase, however, cannot be easily identified or measured because an overall increase in Earth's temperature may actually cause temperatures at certain locations to decrease because of increased cloud cover associated with increased precipitation (the transfer of water as rain, slow, sleet, or hail from the atmosphere to the surface of Earth).

Measurements and estimates of global precipitation and the sea level changes (the height of Earth's oceans) indicate that precipitation over the world's landmasses has increased by approximately 1% during the twentieth century. Further, as predicted by many global warming models, the increases in pre-

## Arctic Melting

Evidence of melting pack ice located in the Canadian Arctic. © *Eric and David Hosking/Corbis. Reproduced by permission.*

Reliable information concerning changes in Arctic and Antarctic ice is difficult to obtain and scientists do not always draw the same conclusions from the data. As a result, conflicting information and ideas exist about the causes and state of Arctic and Antarctic melting. Some scientists argue that ice melting could be due to short-term fluctuations in climate or ocean currents. Many more scientists, however, agree that global climate warming is contributing to the loss of polar ice.

Observations and measurements that indicate ice is melting in the Arctic Sea, and in the ice surrounding Antarctica, is supported by submarine based measurements. Sonar readings (a measuring device that can send out sound signals and measure how long those signals take to travel to objects, bounce back, and return) show that the distance between the surface of the ocean and the bottom of the ice is decreasing and that ice in some areas is 40% thinner than it was just 40 years ago.

Because ice takes up more room than does liquid water, when Arctic ice melts, it does not directly raise the level of the oceans. In contrast, because much of it is over land, melting Antarctic ice can contribute liquid water to the oceans. Along with other factors, melting ice can result in sea level increases that threaten coastal areas with flooding.

Scientists at the National Aeronautics and Space Administration (NASA) use satellites to measure ice cover, and their results also show Arctic ice cover decreasing. Between 1978 and 2000, half a million square miles (1.3 million square kilometers) of apparently permanent Arctic ice melted away. At that rate of loss, some scientists argue that the permanent ice caps may be in danger of disappearing before the end of the century. As more ice disappears, it increases the temperature of Arctic waters because, while ice reflects the majority of the Sun's rays back into space, darker blue ocean waters are capable of absorbing much more heat-generating light from the Sun.

Although the long-term economic consequences may be dire, over the short term, some companies may try to exploit the melting ice to increase shipping through the Arctic sea. Many potential routes that now require expensive icebreakers offer significantly shorter routes (and thus lower cost routes) between parts of Europe and the Far East when compared to southerly routes through the Panama or Suez canals.

---

cipitation were not uniform. High latitude regions (regions far north or south of the equator) tended to experience greater increases in precipitation, while precipitation declined in tropical areas.

Measurements and estimates of sea level show increases of 6–8 inches (15–20 centimeters) during the twentieth century. Geologists and meteorologists (scientists who study Earth's processes, climate, and weather) estimate that approximately 25% of the sea level rise resulted from the melting of mountain glaciers. The remainder of the rise can be accounted for by an increase in the amount of ocean water in response to higher atmospheric temperatures.

### Changes in the normal greenhouse effect

Because the majority of data clearly show that Earth's temperature has risen over the last century, the key question for scientists is whether increases in global temperature are part of a natural cycle of change or whether human activity is responsible for the changes.

Estimates of greenhouse gases (those gases that contribute to the greenhouse effect) in the atmosphere that existed prior to the nineteenth century (estimates that are made from current measurements of arctic ice) indicate that over the last few million years the concentration of greenhouse gases remained relatively unchanged prior to the European and American industrial revolutions (the time in history, roughly since 1850, when large scale industry and manufacturing that relied on machines powered by gas and oil began).

During the last 150 years, however, increased emissions from internal combustion engines and the use of certain chemicals have increased concentrations of greenhouse gases. Although most greenhouse gases occur naturally, the evolution of an industrial civilization has significantly increased levels of these naturally occurring gases. Many scientists argue that these increases are responsible for an abnormal amount of global warming.

### Greenhouse gases

Important greenhouse gases in the modern Earth atmosphere include water vapor and carbon dioxide, methane, nitrous oxides, ozone, halogens (bromine, chlorine, and fluorine), halocarbons, and other trace gases (gases found in very relatively small amounts).

The sources of the greenhouse gases are both natural and man-made. For example, ozone is a naturally occurring greenhouse gas found in the atmosphere. Ozone is constantly produced and broken down in natural chemical reactions that take place in the atmosphere. In contrast, some chemicals that can

> ## Kyoto Treaty
>
> The Kyoto Protocol is an agreement between governments to reduce the amount of greenhouse gases emitted by developed countries. The protocol is intended to be the first legally binding global agreement to cut greenhouse gas emissions and was part of the United Nations Framework Convention on Climate Change (UNFCCC). The agreement, reached in December 1997 at a United Nations conference in Kyoto, Japan, seeks to reduce the amount of greenhouse gases emitted by developed countries by 5.2% below their 1990 levels by the year 2012.
>
> More than 100 countries fully accepted the agreement. The United States, however, ultimately rejected the Kyoto Protocol because many legislators thought the costs to the American economy would be too high. In addition to economic worries, U.S. lawmakers worried that the protocols ignored emissions from developing countries. Emissions from developing countries are predicted to become a highly significant percentage of global greenhouse gas emissions by 2015. In 2003, President George W. Bush (1946–) said that the United States would not ratify (fully accept and implement into law) the Kyoto Protocol. The U.S. rejection was critical because the protocol only comes into force when 55 leading countries, representing 55% of the greenhouse gas emissions produced by developed countries, ratify the agreement. The United States is a largest emitter of greenhouse gases—with one of the highest levels of emissions per capita (per person)—and accounts for 36.1% of all emissions. Without U.S. cooperation, the protocols—fully accepted by countries and groups of countries represented by the European Union— fall short of the 55% target. As of July 2004, the accepting leading countries accounted for only 44.2% of emissions.
>
> Although environmentalists in America and Europe argue that the treaty is an essential first step toward saving Earth's climate, many scientists now argue that the Kyoto protocols, even if fully implemented, will be ineffective in slowing the increases in greenhouse gases and that much stricter limits will be needed.

alter the ozone's chemical reactions enter the atmosphere primarily as the result of human use of products that contain chlorofluorocarbon gases (CFCs), such as in cans of hairspray or spray paint (CFCs in spray cans are not permitted in the United States). There is scientific evidence that CFCs can lead to an overall reduction in ozone.

Alterations in the concentrations of greenhouse gases result from either the overproduction or underproduction of naturally occurring chemicals such as ozone.

Water vapor (water in the form of gas) and carbon dioxide are natural components of respiration (the process in which an organism uses oxygen for its life processes), transpiration (evaporation of water from the leaves or stems of plants), evaporation (the process whereby water changes to a gas or vapor), and decay processes. Carbon dioxide is also a by-product of combustion (burning). The amount of water vapor released through evaporation increases directly with increases in the surface temperature of Earth. Within normal limits, increased levels of water vapor are usually controlled by increased warming and precipitation. Likewise, concentrations of carbon dioxide (and other gases such as methane) are usually maintained within normal limits by a variety of physical processes and chemical reactions.

Although occurring at lower levels than water vapor or carbon dioxide, methane is also a potent greenhouse gas. Nitrous oxides, enhanced by the use of nitrogen fertilizers, nylon production, and the combustion of organic material—including fossil fuels— have also been identified as contributing to a stronger greenhouse effect.

Measurements made late in the twentieth century showed that since 1800, methane concentrations have doubled and carbon dioxide concentrations are now higher than at any time during the last 160,000 years. In fact, increases in carbon dioxide over the last 200 years—up until 1973—were greater than at any time in Earth's history. Although the rate has slowed since 1973, corresponding to the time when widespread pollution controls were first introduced, the rate remains high relative to other periods in Earth's history.

A school of fish hovers about a coral reef in the Indian Ocean. Even slight global climate change can affect fragile ecosystems such as coral reefs. © Stephen Frink/Corbis. Reproduced by permission.

### The debate over global climate change

The fact that increased levels of greenhouse gases have occurred at the same time as recent increases in global temperature has generally strengthened arguments predicting increased global warming over the next few centuries. In 2001, the United Nations Intergovernmental Panel on Climate Change (IPCC) asserted that human activity was responsible for much of the recent climate change resulting in global warming.

In the alternative, some scientists remain skeptical because the Earth has not actually responded to the same extent as expected. For example, some estimates based upon the rate of change of greenhouse gases predicted a global warming of .8°F to 2.5°F (0.44°C to 1.39°C) over the last century. However, the actual increase—if measured at .9°F (.5°C)—is significantly less. Moreover, this amount of global warming may be within the natural variation of global temperatures. Most scientists agree, however, that an enhanced greenhouse effect will result in some degree of global warming.

Whether recent global warming and changes in sea levels are natural, induced my human activity, or a mixture of natural and human-induced is an important scientific argument. Although the causes are debated, however, there is good agreement that events that normally take place over much longer periods (thousands of years) are now occurring over hundreds of years, even as quickly as decades. Most importantly, the global warming trend is unarguably altering ecosystems, sometimes harmfully to both life and economies.

Global warming results in melting ice at the North and South Poles that increase sea levels of water. Small changes in sea levels can quickly make land unusable for agriculture (salt water, for example, can destroy rice fields.)

*Paul Arthur and K. Lee Lerner*

## For More Information

### Books

Alley, Richard. *The Two-Mile Time Machine.* Princeton, NJ: Princeton University Press, 2002.

Burroughs, William, ed. *Climate: Into the 21st Century.* New York: Cambridge University Press, 2003.

Weart, Spencer R. *The Discovery of Warming.* Cambridge, MA: Harvard University Press, 2003.

### Websites

"Antarctic Ice Shelves and Icebergs in the News." *National Snow and Ice Data Center.* http://nsidc.org/iceshelves/ (accessed on September 7, 2004).

"Global Warming: Frequently Asked Questions." *National Oceanic and Atmospheric Administration.* http://www.ncdc.noaa.gov/oa/climate/globalwarming.html (accessed on September 7, 2004).

"Global Warming." *United States Environmental Protection Agency.* http://yosemite.epa.gov/oar/globalwarming.nsf/content/index.html (accessed on September 7, 2004).

# Groundwater

Many of Earth's groundwater supplies are threatened, mainly by human population growth and contamination. Groundwater is freshwater that resides underground; it collects following the movement of water from the surface down through soil and rock. As the water moves downward, a zone or line is formed underground, above which the spaces in the soil and rock are filled with air and water (called the zone of infiltration) and below which water occupies every available opening (called the zone of saturation). The water table is at the top of the zone of saturation, and groundwater lies beneath the water table.

In a desert, groundwater is a vital source of life to plants, which can produce roots that are dozens of feet (meters) long, to reach down from the dry surface to the water below. Groundwater is also important to humans for drinking water, growing crops (irrigation), and other uses. For example, in the year 2000, about 21% of the 408 billion gallons of water used in the United States each day came from underground sources. Over the course of a year, that adds up to about 32 trillion gallons of groundwater!

## Threats to groundwater

The main reason that groundwater is threatened has to do with the chemistry of water. Many other compounds (substances formed by the joining of two or more elements) can easily dissolve into the liquid form of water. Liquids into which other compounds dissolve in are called solvents, and water is known as the "universal solvent." If there is a toxic (poisonous) chemical near to groundwater, chances are good that it will also be able to dissolve into and contaminate the groundwater. Toxins (poisonous substances) that cannot dissolve in water (such as oils), can still ruin the quality of groundwater if exposed to an underground water source.

**"Out of sight, out of mind."** Because many areas have a plentiful supply of groundwater, this resource can easily be overlooked. In Canada for example, before 1990, water scientists found that although 30% of Canadians relied on groundwater for their drinking water, the government had not formed laws to help protect groundwater quality. Since that time, the number of Canadians depending upon groundwater for drinking water has increased, but Canada still has no groundwater protection policy.

## WORDS TO KNOW

**Aquifer:** Underground rock or sediment layer that yields water of adequate quantity and purity for human use.

**Irrigation:** In agriculture, a process where dry land or crops are supplied with water.

**Pesticides:** Substances used to kill or harm unwanted plants, insects, or rodents.

**Sinkhole:** A crater that forms when the roof of a cavern collapses; usually found in limestone rock.

**Solvent:** A substance, most often a liquid, into which other compounds can dissolve.

**Water table:** Level below which all pore space in rocks and soil are filled with water; also the top of the zone of saturation.

**Zone of infiltration:** Soil and rock layers above which the spaces in the soil and rock are filled with air and water.

**Zone of saturation:** Soil and rock layers with pore spaces that are completely filled with fluid.

**Individual versus community groundwater use.** A well that supplies one house does not usually harm a groundwater source. This is because the amount of water that is taken from the ground is more than balanced out by the amount of water that goes back into the ground as rainfall, melting snow, floodwater or other sources. However, when a community relies on one or a series of wells for its water supply, the total amount of water that is withdrawn from the groundwater source can be large. If an area experiences a drought (prolonged shortage of rainfall), water consumption rises, or wells are placed too close together, then more groundwater can be taken than is replenished. Rather than drawing water from different parts of the geographical area where water from the region collects (the aquifer), wells very near one another can draw water from the same part of the aquifer, depleting it faster than if the wells were further apart.

These imbalances cannot continue indefinitely or the groundwater supply will run out. The city of Las Vegas, Nevada is an example of a community whose demand for water is causing problems to the underground supply of water. So much groundwater has been taken from the ground around Las Vegas due to a growing population's demand for water, that areas of the land have dropped by over five feet (1.5 meters) in the past century.

**Other sources of groundwater depletion.** Some industries use large amounts of groundwater. In the oil industry, for example, groundwater (along with surface water) is forced down into oil wells to help bring the hard-to-pump oil up to the surface. While much of this water is eventually returned to the ground, some is lost, mainly through evaporation, or is so polluted that it cannot be put back into the environment. Mines that are made by digging huge holes in the ground (quarries) also help deplete groundwater. Groundwater will often leak out of the walls of the quarry and pool in the bottom of the hole. The quarry acts as a sponge, drawing water out of the surrounding ground. Even though the water can be pumped out and returned to the surrounding ground, the rate of water loss from the ground is sometimes higher than the rate at which the water returns to the ground.

Nature is another source of groundwater depletion, in the form of a drought. Without rainfall to replenish the groundwater, an underground water source can quickly run dry with continued use.

## Groundwater contamination

Most of the chemicals and microorganisms in water will be removed as it seeps down through layers of soil and rock to reach the water table. Soil and rocks filter the chemicals and microorganisms in water by sticking to the contaminants or because they are too large to pass through the tiny cracks in the rock. This cleaning effect is not, however, always foolproof. There can be breaks in the soil-rock barrier that allow chemicals and microorganisms to rapidly move down to the groundwater, where they collect and contaminate the groundwater.

**Pesticides in groundwater.** Only a few generations ago, the contamination of groundwater by chemicals designed to kill weeds and other pests (pesticides) was not a concern. But as the population of the United States has grown, and with the demand to produce more crops from each acre of land, scientists began to develop chemical pesticides. The use of pesticides has increased the amount of food that can be grown. Indeed, the United States has become the largest producer of food in the world, partially due to the fact that crops are protected from destruction by insects and other pests with the use of pesticides.

A scientist tests a sample of groundwater taken from a landfill in California. © *Jim Sugar/Corbis. Reproduced by permission.*

This increase in production has come with a big disadvantage, the contamination of groundwater (along with surface bodies of water and soil) by the pesticides. Because pesticides can take decades to get from the surface to groundwater, the problem with pesticides in groundwater could become worse in the future. Organizations such as the U.S. Environmental Protection Agency are working to understand pesticide contamination of groundwater and to try to set standards for how much pesticide can be safely applied to the land.

**Other sources of groundwater contamination.** Another example of how groundwater can be contaminated is via a sinkhole; a crater formed on the surface when the rook of a cavern located directly below collapses. The sinkhole creates a kind of water freeway; water can move easily down through the many open spaces in the rock to the groundwater zone. Sinkholes often occur in limestone rock. In states enriched in limestone,

**Groundwater** | **413**

such as Iowa, sinkhole-related contamination of groundwater is a concern. In just the northeast part of Iowa, almost 13,000 sinkholes are known to exist.

Groundwater can also be contaminated when underground storage tanks, such as the tanks located underneath gas stations, develop a leak. As the toxin leaks out of the tank, it can make its way to the groundwater. When the chemicals disperse (spread) in the groundwater, a wide area (many city blocks) around the tank can become contaminated. As this type of groundwater contamination is harder to detect, most communities have systems in place to check underground storage tanks for leaks on a regular basis.

Since water moves downward to the groundwater, any contaminant that is on the surface may also be carried down. Along with pesticides, surface contaminants can also include wells in fields that are designed to help drain excess water, water containing salt that is applied to roads in northern climates to prevent ice from forming, old uncovered wells that contain animal or other waste, and the burial of waste material in landfills.

*Brian Hoyle, Ph.D.*

### For More Information

#### Books
Glennon, Robert. *Water Follies: Groundwater Pumping and the Fate of America's Fresh Waters.* Washington, DC: Island Press, 2004.

#### Websites
Environment Canada. "Groundwater." *The Green Lane.* http://www.ec.gc.ca/water/en/nature/grdwtr/e_gdwtr.htm (accessed on September 1, 2004).

"Get Informed." *The Groundwater Foundation.* http://www.groundwater.org/gi/gi.html (accessed on September 1, 2004).

U.S. Geological Survey. "Pesticides in Ground Water." *Water Science for Schools.* http://ga.water.usgs.gov/edu/pesticidesgw.html (accessed on September 1, 2004).

## Habitat Loss and Species Extinction

Habitat (natural environment) loss is the number one threat to the survival of many animal species (organisms that share a unique set of characteristics), and water is part of any habitat.

Coastal marshes and wetlands in the United States and elsewhere are shrinking every year. Wetlands are areas of land where water covers the surface for at least part of the year and controls the development of soil; marshes are wetlands dominated by grass-like plants. Wetlands in particular support a great variety of bird, fish, and other animal life, and can be used by migrating (periodic traveling) birds as a stop-off point on their long journeys. Without the wetlands, the number of species that can live on the land declines. Habitat loss is primarily caused by human activities, such as logging, development, fishing, and recreation.

Edward Wilson (1929–), a renowned entomologist (scientist who studies insects) has written that the current rate at which life is becoming extinct has not been seen since the time of the dinosaurs 65 million years ago. Wilson estimates that the current rate of extinction (the rate at which every member of a species dies) is 100,000 times faster that what is considered the natural rate and that, in the next 25 years, one of every five species of insect, bird, and animal could die out. Along with the loss of diversity, the possible extinction of even one insect has great importance. Insects, for example, are near the bottom of a natural system of life in which creatures of prey are eaten by predator creatures, called the food web, or the food chain. If the bottom of the food chain is disturbed, it could impact animals along the rest of the chain, including humans.

## Development and overuse

Coastal marshes and wetlands in the United States and elsewhere are shrinking in areas where development occurs. The desire for oceanfront property is so great that coastal beaches and the wetland areas where rivers flow into the ocean are often paved over.

Other human activities in coastal areas alter the habitat of the creatures that live near the ocean. Many species of crustaceans, especially ghost crabs, live in the dunes and provide food for birds such as sea gulls and other terns. When plants that naturally grow and strengthen sand dunes are destroyed, the sand is more easily blown away by wind or washed away by waves. Overuse of a beach by people can remove vegetation when beachgoers climb sand dunes. On some beaches, a popular pastime is to drive dune buggies and all-terrain vehicles over the dunes, both of which destroy dune vegetation and eventually, the dune itself.

**WORDS TO KNOW**

◆**Clearcut:** The total removal of trees and much of the vegetation from a section of forest.

◆**Diversion:** Changing the direction of a water body such as a stream or river by building canals, dams, or channels.

◆**Erosion:** Wearing away of soil, rock, sand or other material by the action of wind and water.

◆**Extinction:** The total disappearance of a species; the irreversible loss of a living species.

◆**Food web:** The predator and prey relationships between animals and plants.

◆**Habitat:** The environment in which a species naturally or normally lives and grows.

◆**Species:** A group of living organisms that share a unique set of characteristics and have the ability to reproduce and produce offspring with the same set of characteristics.

## Fishing and habitat loss

Habitat destruction can also occur underwater. Fishing with dragnets, for example, destroyed underwater habitats in the 1970s. This method involved dragging a huge net along the bottom of the ocean. The front of the net often had a heavy bar attached to it to keep the net open and to deliberately clear out any obstacles that might snag the net, including beneficial plants and coral. The scrapping of the ocean floor completely destroyed habitats of some lobsters, crabs, and fish off the eastern coast of Canada.

In many areas of the United States, the Canadian mid-west, and other countries the small family farm has been largely replaced by farms that are owned and run by large companies. Corporate-owned farms are often thousands of acres (square meters) in size. The plowing under of wetlands to create more land for farming and farming practices such as the use of pesticides has disturbed water habitats. Erosion (wearing away) and the run-off of chemicals from the fields have contaminated both surface and ground waters.

Leatherneck turtles are threatened by a loss of habitat, especially near sensitive breeding areas. © *Kennan Ward/Corbis. Reproduced by permission.*

## Growth of cities

Most of the world's cities are growing in size and population. Often the most rapid growth takes place on the edges of cities where many people live. Roads and other transportation routes are continually being built to bring suburban commuters closer to the working center of the city. This new development turns fields, forests, and wetlands into more expanses of pavement. In some cities earth and rock is dumped into the water to create new land for housing.

All this change can be bad news for a habitat. In California in the 1990s, growth of cities reduced the amount of a plant called the coastal sage shrub by over 90%. One of the creatures that lives in the coastal sage shrub is the California gnatcatcher, an insect that is now threatened with extinction.

## Logging and mining

Logging, or removing trees for wood, can be accomplished in a way that does not harm a habitat. Removing only selected tress and hauling the tress out by horse or small tractor can actually help create more sunlight in a forest, and so encourage growth of new trees. However this does not supply enough trees for the needs of large lumber companies. Instead, often all the trees in an area of a forest are removed and hauled away. This is called clearcutting and it can devastate entire habitats. With no roots left to hold the soil erosion can quickly occur, clogging streams with soil. The biggest threat to the survival of the grizzly bear in Alaska is logging and the building of roads for logging trucks.

Mining, especially where huge pits are dug in the ground, can also destroy natural habitats. The water that runs off from a mine site can contain harmful metals that cause illness if present in the body even in small amounts (heavy metals) and can be so full of acid that it can burn skin and pollute nearby waters. A gold mine located in northern Idaho, for example, is leaking low levels of a toxic (poisonous) chemical called cyanide into a part of the South Fork Salmon River for years. This has contaminated an area of the river where chinook salmon breed, and has threatened the entire salmon population in the South Fork Salmon River.

## Changing waterways

Building dams, constructing channels, and changing the direction of a river or stream (diversion) for flood control will all change water habitats, forcing animals to adapt to the changed habitat or find a new home. In the Pacific Northwest, the building of dams on the Columbia River has reduced the number of chinook, coho, chum, sockeye, and pink salmon populations. Two large river fish that were used by Native Americans for food and fertilizer, the bonytail and the razorback sucker, have suffered from changes to the Colorado River imposed by dams and diversion. The bonytail is nearly extinct and the razorback sucker is threatened. In California the use of water for agriculture has caused a toxic

### Kesterson National Wildlife Refuge and Selenium

The Kesterson National Wildlife Refuge is a system of wetlands, grassy regions and surface water pools that cover almost 11,000 acres (4,452 hectares) in the San Joaquin Valley of central California. The refuge was created in 1969 to provide an area where waters draining from surrounding higher land could gather and be protected. The area was also an important stop on the north-south migration route of some birds.

In the 1970s the agriculture nearby began to affect the water draining into the refuge. The agricultural operations removed large amounts of underground freshwater and the water draining into the refuge consisted of more runoff water from the crop fields. By 1981 almost all the water entering the refuge was the leftover agricultural water. This water contained high amounts of an element called selenium. Selenium naturally exists in some soils. As surface water in the refuge evaporated, the selenium that was left behind accumulated to levels that were poisonous. Before scientists learned of the problem and diverted the water away from the refuge, many birds that nested in the refuge died or hatched with physical defects.

The poisoning that occurred at the Kesterson refuge alerted scientists to the fact that along with pesticides and other chemicals in agricultural runoff, naturally occurring compounds could also pose a problem to habitats if the water flow in an area changed.

compound called selenium to build up in the soil. Runoff (water that flows over ground surface to bodies of water) of selenium into the Kesterson National Wildlife Refuge has caused the deaths of large numbers of birds.

**Preventing species loss**

Some local governments are working to plan development along coastlines in order to preserve wetland, marsh, beach, and dune habitats. The U.S. Environmental Protection Agency monitors water quality in threatened habitats, and private organizations such as the Nature Conservancy create refuges by buying both wetland habitats and saltwater marshes for conserving as natural areas. So far, several sea turtle species have benefited from these efforts, as well as the dwarf seahorse and the Florida manatee.

*Brian Hoyle, Ph.D.*

**For More Information**

**Books**

Davidson, Olsha Gray. *The Enchanted Braid: Coming to Terms with Nature on the Coral Reef.* New York: Wiley, 1998.

Kerley, Barbara. *A Cool Drink of Water.* Washington, DC: National Geographic Society, 2002.

Locker, Thomas. *Water Dance.* New York: Voyager Books, 2002.

**Websites**

"How You Can Help." *National Save the Sea Turtle Foundation.* http://www.savetheseaturtle.org/HowYouCanHelp.htm (accessed on September 1, 2004).

"The State of Disappearing Species and Habitat: A Sierra Club Report." *Sierra Club.* http://www.sierraclub.org/wildlife/species/habitat_report/intro.asp (accessed on September 1, 2004)

# Industrial and Commercial Waste

Many everyday activities create waste. Even cutting the lawn makes grass clippings that can stress water bodies such as streams and rivers if too much washes into the water. This is because the grass is food for in the water. Microorganisms can grow quickly in great numbers, and rob the water of the oxygen that is needed by fish and other living creatures inhabiting the water.

One person alone might not produce enough waste material to contaminate a water source. However, a community of many people and large industries produce large amounts of waste. For example, the city of Halifax, Nova Scotia, on Canada's east coast still directly discharges sewage into the harbor. Even though the city is relatively small (approximately 300,000 people), millions of gallons of raw sewage pour into the water each day. If enough waste gets into a stream, river, pond, lake, or other body of water, the water can become contaminated and unhealthy for animals and humans who use the water as a source of drinking water or for recreation. Some of this waste can also move down through the soil and rock to contaminate water present below the surface (groundwater).

Waste water can carry large numbers of bacteria that normally live in the intestinal tract. Some of these such as Salmonella and Shigella can cause serious diseases if ingested. As well, waste water can carry compounds like mercury, lead and other metals that can be dangerous to health if ingested.

**Commercial waste**

Commercial operations are those that provide a service or sell a product. A feature that is common to most commercial operations is a paved parking lot. Grocery stores, restaurants, shopping malls, movie theatres, office buildings, and libraries, typically have spots where vehicles are parked. Vehicles can leak oil, antifreeze, and other fluids that are used to keep engines running smoothly, brakes operating safely, and windshields clean. These fluids gather on the pavement and are washed away in rains or when accumulated snow melts. If a water body is located nearby, the wastes could flow into the water. Wastes accumulated on concrete are particularly washed away during heavy rainstorms, as drains that are usually placed in the parking lot cannot hold all of the sudden, heavy flow of water.

Excess packaging can also become a source of commercial waste, especially when a careless individual discards it as litter. Paper and plastic products that litter the ground can be blown or carried by runoff (water that flows over ground surface) to a water body. In the water litter can alter or even stop the natural flow of the natural streams that drain larger bodies of water. Litter in the water also harms animals and other organisms. For example, the plastic rings that keep soft drinks and beer together in six or eight-packs can become entwined around the necks or beaks of birds and choke them.

**WORDS TO KNOW**

◆**Groundwater:** Water that moves from the surface down through the soil and rock to gather below the surface.

◆**Superfund:** A program managed by the Environmental Protection Agency that identifies, investigates, and cleans up the worst hazardous waste sites in the United States.

◆**Surface water:** Water that is present on the surface. Examples include rivers, lakes and oceans.

## Love Canal

Hazardous waste contamination closes a school in Love Canal, near Niagara Falls, New York. © *Galen Rowell/Corbis. Reproduced by permission.*

Love Canal is a neighborhood in Niagara Falls, New York, that has become a symbol of the hazards to groundwater from industrial waste. The nickname "Love Canal" honors a man named William Love, who in 1896 attempted to dig a canal linking Lake Ontario and Lake Erie that would be used to generate electrical power. The project was never completed and the canal was left unused.

From 1947 to 1952 the Hooker Chemical Company, which had a plant located next to the canal, dumped the left-over liquids from its chemical making operation into the canal. In time the canal became full of the waste. It was covered up and the land was sold to the city of Niagara Falls for $1.00. A school and houses were built over the buried waste.

By the 1970s, over a thousand families were living in the 15-acre (6 hectares) Love Canal neighborhood. Some began to complain of similar health problems. A high rate of birth defects occurred in the area. Many trees and other vegetation in the Love Canal neighborhood turned unusual colors and died. In 1977 chemicals that were leaking out of the canal were discovered. The same chemicals were also discovered leaking from the groundwater into the basements of some homes. In 1978 President Jimmy Carter declared the Love Canal site a disaster area. Eventually 239 families who lived next to the buried canal were moved out of their homes at government expense. In 1980 the evacuation of over 700 more families was ordered.

In 2004, the canal is still off-limits and the waterway is buried under a plastic liner, clay, and topsoil. After clean-up efforts that took 20 years and over $350 million, some surrounding areas, especially north of the canal, are being rebuilt. The Love Canal environmental disaster triggered the formation of a program called the Superfund, managed by the Environmental Protection Agency. The Superfund program locates, investigates, and cleans up the worst sites of hazardous waste in the United States.

---

Many businesses store liquids near the workplace. Gas stations have large underground tanks to store the gas. Businesses requiring heat during colder winter months may have large storage tanks for oil. Both above ground and underground storage tanks can develop cracks and the chemicals inside can leak. When this happens nearby surface waters are threatened. Groundwater is also at risk for contamination, especially when the leak is from an underground tank. Contaminants in groundwater can flow sideways, spreading for hundreds of yards (meters) away from the site of the spill. Most communities require chemical storage tanks to be regularly checked for leaks to prevent groundwater or surface water sources from contamination by commercial waste.

The sewage from commercial and industrial facilities, as well as water that has been used in the manufacturing processes, usually ends up in a plant that is designed to treat the wastewater before it is released back to the environment. The treatment removes the solid material and many of the microorganisms and chemicals from the water. In large cities, millions of gallons of this wastewater are treated every day. However, there are still some big cities in North America and around the world where untreated wastewater is dumped directly into natural waters.

**Industrial waste**

Industries such as manufacturing often generates large amounts of solid and liquid waste. Water is often used to cool machinery and mixes with the oils, greases, and other chemicals in manufacturing plants. Some, but not all of the water can be treated to remove the chemicals, and some of the wastewater can be released to the environment. Some water is too contaminated to release back to the environment. This water can be retained in storage lagoons. Of course, as time goes by and the volume of this water increases, the storage capacity of such lagoons will be reached.

Some industrial waters, such as those used in various manufacturing processes, contain metals that can make humans ill even if ingested in low amounts. These so-called heavy metals are recognized as a hazard, and many federal, state and municipal governments have rules in place to limit the amount of heavy metals that can be in industrial wastewater. The regulations governing the level of contaminants that are considered acceptable varies from country to country. Some jurisdictions enact regulations that are stricter than found elsewhere. For example, the manufacturing zone in Mexico near the border with the United States has regulations that are relatively lax. Much environmental damage is occurring in this region.

Many industries treat the water that is released from the factory. Water can be treated physically, such as by passing the water through a barrier that contains tiny holes in it (a filter). The filter allows water to pass, but traps larger chemicals. Water can also be passed through materials, which will bind to substances like metals. These and other techniques help ensure that the industrial water is reduced in the amount of harmful molecules.

*Brian Hoyle, Ph.D.*

### For More Information

#### Books

Botkin, Daniel B., and Edward A. Keller. *Environmental Science: Earth as a Living Planet.* New York: Wiley, 2002.

Kerley, Barbara. *A Cool Drink of Water.* Washington, DC: National Geographic Society, 2002.

Smol, John. *Pollution of Lakes and Rivers.* London: Arnold Publishers, 2002.

#### Websites

"About Superfund." *U.S. Environmental Protection Agency.* http://www.epa.gov/superfund/about.htm (accessed on September 1, 2004).

U.S. Geological Survey. "Wastewater Treatment Water Use." *Water Science for Schools.* http://ga.water.usgs.gov/edu/wuwww.html (accessed on September 1, 2004).

## Landfills

Landfills are areas where solid garbage is buried. The construction, use, and maintenance of landfills can impact aquifers and groundwater that lie underneath and around the landfill. Groundwater is fresh water in the rock and soil layers beneath Earth's land surface; aquifers are a type of groundwater source that yields water suitable for drinking. The material inside a landfill can contain harmful chemicals and microorganisms. As some of the material in a landfill decomposes (breaks down), other harmful chemicals can be created and released. One well-known example is methane gas; another is leachate, the acidic liquid that contains water and contaminants from the products of decomposition.

Landfills are a necessary part of life in highly developed countries such as the United States. The United States has over 3,000 landfills that are being filled with trash and over 10,000 landfills that have already been filled, according to the U.S. Environmental Protection Agency. The need for all this garbage storage is because the amount of garbage produced every day in the United States averages four pounds for each American.

**Above:** Waves continually change a beach's shape by moving sand, small rocks, and debris. See "Beach Erosion" entry.
*M. Woodbridge Williams, National Park Service. Reproduced by permission.*

**Right:** A school of fish hovers about a coral reef in the Indian Ocean. Even slight global climate change can affect fragile ecosystems such as coral reefs. See "Global Climate Change" entry.
*© Stephen Frink/Corbis. Reproduced by permission.*

**Above:** A manatee, one of many endangered species of marine mammals, swimming in waters off of Florida. See "Endangered Species Laws" entry. © *Brandon D. Cole/Corbis. Reproduced by permission.*

**Left:** A farmer surveys the parched soil of his drought-stricken south Texas farm. See "Desertification" entry. *Jim Sugar Photography/Corbis-Bettmann. Reproduced by permission.*

**Above:** Plastic material dumped in the water chokes the neck of a royal shroud bird. See "Water Pollution" entry. *Anthony F. Amos. Reproduced by permission.*

**Right:** This river near San Juan, Puerto Rico, carries silt, a form of sediment, into the ocean. Any contaminants in the silt are also deposited in the ocean. See "Sediment Contamination" entry. *William Folsom, National Oceanic and Atmospheric Administration/ Department of Commerce. Reproduced by permission.*

**Right:** Evidence of melting pack ice located in the Canadian Arctic. See "Global Climate Change" entry. © *Eric and David Hosking/Corbis. Reproduced by permission.*

**Below:** A school of bluefin tuna snagged during a mattanza (a mass tuna catch) that periodically occurs off the coast of Sicily, Italy. See "Bioaccumulation of Heavy Metals" entry. © *Jeffrey L. Rotman/Corbis. Reproduced by permission.*

**Right:** Algal blooms, such as the bloom in the Florida Keys viewed from the space shuttle *Discovery*, are often fed by agricultural runoff and other non-point sources of pollution. See "Non-point Sources of Pollution" entry. © *1996 Corbis. Reproduced by permission.*

**Below:** Sediment contamination can adversely impact water quality and the food chain upon which other species such as this bald eagle depend. See "Sediment Contamination" entry. © *John Conrad/CORBIS. Reproduced by permission.*

**Left:** After removing and arresting the crew, U.S. Navy and Coast Guard vessels destroy a vessel filled with illegal drugs. See "International Water Laws and Enforcement" entry. © *Airman Jeffrey/U.S. Navy/ZUMA/Corbis. Reproduced by permission.*

**Below:** Endangered species laws seek to protect animals such as the California sea otter. See "Endangered Species Laws" entry. © *Ron Sanford/Corbis. Reproduced by permission.*

**Above:** In this photo from 1994, sewage is emptied into the ocean near Cornwall, England, where the tide carries it toward beaches. See "Water Pollution" entry.
© Ecoscene/Corbis. Reproduced by permission.

**Below:** Acid rain damage in a German forest. See "Acid Rain" entry. © *Boussu Regis/Corbis Sygma. Reproduced by permission.*

That's over 200 million tons every year, more than twice the trash produced in many other countries. Some of it can be recycled or burned but most, about 150 tons per year in the United States, is left over. While some of these leftovers will break down over time into the basic chemicals that make up the material, without a landfill, the result can be a stinky mess that lies in the open air.

## What is a landfill?

A landfill is a carefully designed structure that is built into the ground or as a pile above the ground. The garbage that is added to the landfill does not contact the surrounding soil and rock. Rather, a layer of pounded-down clay or a film of plastic or other material is used to line the outside of the landfill. The purpose of this liner is to prevent what is inside the landfill from escaping into the nearby soil. A landfill can be thought of as a vault in which trash is locked away forever

Some landfills have only the clay zone barrier. These are known as sanitary landfills. Other landfills use the plastic barrier, and these are called municipal solid waste landfills. There are some landfills that use both barriers, although this process is more expensive. Ideally, the break down of material in a landfill should hardly occur as the inside of the landfill is supposed to be dry, although small amounts of moisture within the garbage itself contributes to the breakdown of some materials, resulting in an acidic solution of water and dissolved chemicals called leachate. Leachate is drained into a collection pond and is eventually treated similar to sewage or other wastewater.

When landfills work properly they are an efficient means to hide trash. They can even be put to some use. In the Canadian city of Toronto, Ontario, one landfill has been turned into a small ski resort that is locally known as "Garbage Hill." However, a badly designed or malfunctioning landfill can result in the escape or runoff (water that flows on the surface) of contaminated material, and can pollute nearby water sources.

## Construction of a landfill

In most areas of the world careful planning and safety rules are in place to spell out how a landfill is constructed. In the United States, before a landfill can be built a survey must demonstrate that the landfill will not disturb the environment in an unacceptable manner (environmental impact study). Some things that an environmental impact study examines include the proposed location for the landfill, nearby animal

### WORDS TO KNOW

**Aquifer:** A underground reservoir of water that is the collection area for the water in a certain geographical area.

**Cell:** Small sections of landfills.

**Environmental impact study:** A survey conducted to determine if a landfill project could have negative effects on the environment.

**Groundwater:** Freshwater that resides in rock and soil layers beneath Earth's land surface.

**Leachate:** An acidic wastewater that contains contaminants from decomposed materials in a landfill.

**Liner:** A sheet of plastic or other material that is put on top of clay on the inside of a landfill to prevent material from leaking out of the landfill.

Landfill seepage and runoff may contaminate groundwaters, nearby streams and rivers. © Terry W. Eggers/Corbis. Reproduced by permission.

habitats, the location of nearby surface water sources, the direction in which material escaping the landfill would flow, and how close to the surface any underground water supply lies.

A properly constructed landfill will include the liner, collection areas to trap any liquid that escapes, and a method of releasing gases such as methane that build up inside the landfill. Efficient landfills are constructed in small sections (cells) that are filled up with trash that is compressed by bulldozers and other equipment, which drive back and forth over it. One cell is sealed off before another cell is filled. Ultimately, a landfill is completely sealed with a plastic layer, and at least 6 inches (15 centimeters) of soil and grass is planted over it.

## Landfill monitoring

It is important to make sure that a landfill is not disturbing the environment, both during its construction, as it is filled, and in the years after the site is closed. Pipes are usually placed into the ground at many sites throughout a landfill and these pipes are connected to a water source for regular testing. If the water temperature is higher than normal, it may indicate that decomposing material is leaking into the water. Additionally, chemical tests are conducted to ensure that harmful chemicals are not leaking into the groundwater. Careful records of landfill sites are also maintained in order to determine which landfill sites can be reused.

*Brian Hoyle, Ph.D.*

### For More Information
**Books**
Riley, Karen. *Landfill Lunchbox.* Indio, CA: S.C.R.A.P. Gallery, 2001.

Strasser, Susan. *Waste and Want: A Social History of Trash.* New York: Owl Books, 2000.

**Websites**
Freudenrich, Craig C. "How Landfills Work." *How Stuff Works.* http://people.howstuffworks.com/landfill.htm (accessed on September 1, 2004).

"MSW Disposal." *U.S. Environmental Protection Agency.* http://www.epa.gov/epaoswer/non-hw/muncpl/disposal.htm (accessed on September 1, 2004).

## Non-point Sources of Pollution

Non-point source pollution is pollution that enters water from many different sites, rather than from just one site. Examples of non-point source pollution are contaminated rain falling from the sky, polluted melting snow, runoff (water flow on land) of polluted water, and impure water draining down into the groundwater from many different sites on the surface. In contrast, an example of point source pollution is a polluted river flowing into a lake.

Because non-point source pollutants enter a water body such as a stream, river, or lake at different locations, the control and prevention of non-point pollution can be much more difficult than when the contaminants are entering at a single site. As the water runs over the land or through the ground on its way to the body of water, it can pick up a variety of pollutants. These chemicals and undesirable microscopic organisms in the water pollute the water into which they flow. The flow of the polluted water can also harm plants and carry soil into the water, which can change the shape and flow of the current (steady flow of water in a prevailing direction) in a water body.

## WORDS TO KNOW

◆**Eutrophication:** A process in which a body of water changes with time as deposits of nutrients and sediments from the surrounding area accumulate.

◆**Heavy metal:** Elements such as lead and mercury that tend to be toxic to plant and animal life, even when present in a low concentration.

◆**Non-point source pollution:** Pollution that enters water from many different sites.

◆**Point-source pollution:** Water pollution that enters the water body from a particular site.

◆**Runoff:** Excess water when the amount of precipitation (water falling to Earth's surface) is greater than the ability of the land to soak up the water.

According to the U.S. Environmental Protection Agency, about 40% of all U.S. freshwater sources that have been surveyed (mapped) have been damaged by non-point source pollution. The damage in many areas is enough that the water is unhealthy for swimming and fish caught from the water should not be eaten.

### Types of non-source pollutants

**Sediment.** Sediment is small particles of soil, rock, or dirt carried and deposited by water. This material can enter water from many sources, such as fields, construction sites, mining or logging operations that scour off surface vegetation, and erosion (wearing away) of riverbanks or other land.

**Nutrients.** A nutrient is a food source and all organisms need these to survive. Non-point source pollution carries a greater flow of nutrients into a water body from croplands, nurseries, orchards, livestock and poultry farms, lawns, and landfills that can disrupt the balance of life in the water. This disruption can change the chemistry of the water so that it is no longer able to sustain fish and plant life.

**Heavy metals.** Heavy metals, such as lead or mercury, are poisonous if present in too high a concentration in the body. Fluids that leak out of vehicles and runoff from mine sites, roads, and parking lots can all contain heavy metals.

**Toxic chemicals.** Toxic (poisonous) chemicals can enter water from the runoff from farmland, nurseries, orchards, construction sites, and lawns and landfills. They can kill or harm organisms in the water, such as fish, and sicken animals and people who eat these organisms. In 2002 scientists found unhealthy levels of mercury in salmon taken from waters off the Pacific Northwest and urged the public to limit consumption of salmon to one serving per week.

**Pathogens.** Pathogens are microorganisms that can cause disease. Examples of pathogens include certain types of bacteria, viruses, and protozoa. Water that is contaminated with human or animal feces (such as sewage, waste from farms, and fluid leaking from landfills) often contains harmful microorganisms. If the microorganisms are not removed from the water then people who drink the water can become ill.

### Origins of non-source pollution

**Urban areas.** Cities and towns contain a lot more people per area than rural areas and many people in one place mean that there are more potential sources of pollution. In urban areas one of these sources is the home. When a lawn is sprayed with pesticide (chemicals to harm pests) to kill weeds, rain or other water can cause of the poison to flow into the sewer pipes, which drain excess water off the streets. In many cities the sewer water runs directly into a nearby water body. Fertilizer that is applied to the lawn to help grass grow can contain nutrients for organisms in the water (such as nitrogen and phosphorus). The pollution of water by fertilizer is also a big problem in agricultural areas.

The waste left behind on the lawn by the family dog can be washed away. This fecal material can contain pathogens. Water that is flushed down toilets or drains from sinks can also contribute to pollution. Even though many communities will treat this wastewater, some contaminants can make it through the treatment process. For example, studies that have been done in the 1990s have found oil, grease, some harmful metals, and even antibiotics (chemicals that kill bacteria) in the water that leaves treatment plants.

Another major source of non-point source pollution in more northern urban areas is the salt that is spread to keep roads free of ice during winter. In the city of Toronto, Canada, the runoff of salt into Lake Ontario was so great one winter in the 1990s that scientists found that portions of the lake contained plants that are normally found along ocean coastlines. Also, oil and gasoline can seep from cars and trucks. These pollutants are washed away and will end up in a nearby water body.

**Rural and industrial areas.** The nitrogen and phosphorus components of many fertilizers, which are food sources for the crops, can also be a rich source of food to microorganisms such as algae. The rapid growth and huge increase in the numbers of the microorganisms can use up much of the oxygen in the water. Creatures such as fish that depend on oxygen for their survival will die. As well, the lack of oxygen disrupts the normal chemical processes that keep the water healthy. This process is called eutrophication.

In some areas of North America farms contain tens of thousands of poultry or pigs. The waste material and huge amounts of water used in the farm operation are typically stored in large lagoons (shallow bodies of water that are separated from the sea by a reef or narrow island). There have been cases where a lagoon wall has ruptured, allowing the contaminated water to pour into a nearby stream or river, or to seep down into the

Algal blooms, such as the bloom in the Florida Keys (viewed from the space shuttle Discovery) are often fed by agricultural runoff and other non-point sources of pollution. © 1996 Corbis. Reproduced by permission.

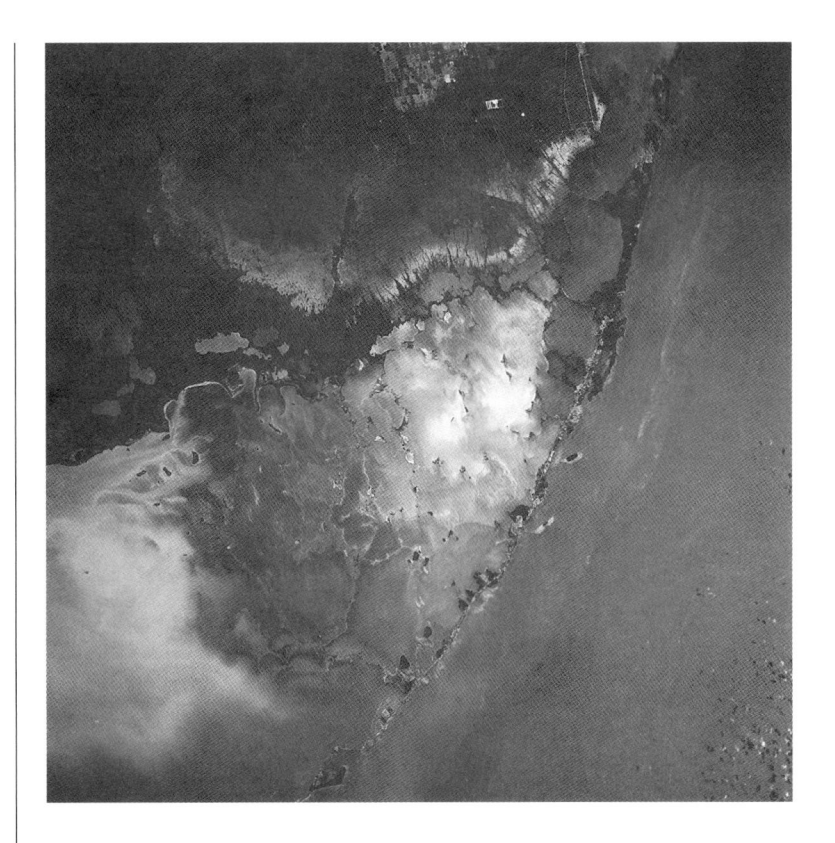

groundwater. Much effort is being directed at trying to find better and safer ways to store and safely dispose of this contaminated water.

### Control of non-point source pollution

Although it is impossible to prevent all runoff from entering water, steps can be taken to reduce the pollutants in the runoff. At a national level the U.S. federal government created water pollution control measures in 1972 known as the Clean Water Act. The regulations of the act help restrict the harmful compounds that enter water, by setting acceptable water quality standards, by making the presence of certain compounds in water illegal and by penalizing polluters. States and communities can also have their own standards and regulations.

In 1990 the federal government also passed legislation known as the Coastal Zone Act Reauthorization Amendments, which was directed at the problem of the non-point source pollution of coastal waters. The regulations help federal and state officials manage the development and use of land that borders the streams, lakes, and rivers that empty into the sea. The intent is to make the freshwater that enters the sea as free of pollution as possible.

There are actions that everyone can take to reduce non-point source pollution. Alternatives can be found to many toxic cleaners and other household chemicals. Lawn care products need not be toxic to water; environmentally friendly weed killers can be used, as can the manual way of pulling weeds by hand. When toxic chemicals need to be disposed of they should be taken to a facility, such as a fire station, that can safely deal with the chemicals rather than dumping the liquid down the drain Picking up after the dog is another way to reduce microorganisms from getting into water bodies. Finally, learning more about water pollution and taking actions both personally and by helping change the behavior of others can help reduce non-point source pollution.

*Brian Hoyle, Ph.D.*

## For More Information

### Books

U.S. Environmental Protection Agency. *EPA 833-K-98-001: Wastewater Primer.* Washington, DC: U.S. EPA Office of Wastewater Management. Also available at http://www.epa.gov/owm/primer.pdf (accessed on September 3, 2004).

Wolverton, B. C., and J. D. Wolverton. *Growing Clean Water: Nature's Solution to Water Pollution.* Picayune, MS: Wolverton Environmental Services, 2001.

### Websites

"Acid Rain." *U.S. Environmental Protection Agency.* http://www.epa.gov/airmarkets/acidrain (accessed on September 3, 2004).

"Agricultural Runoff Management." *Wisconsin Department of Natural Resources.* http://www.dnr.state.wi.us/org/water/wm/nps/animal.htm (accessed on September 3, 2004).

---

### Agricultural Runoff

Agricultural runoff is the main source of pollution in U.S. streams and lakes and is the third leading cause of pollution to the zone where freshwater mixes with saltwater (estuary), according to the U.S. Environmental Protection Agency.

Treating the polluted water once it has entered a stream, river, or lake is ineffective. The best strategy is to try and prevent the pollution in the first place. Agricultural runoff occurs when the amount of precipitation (water falling to Earth's surface) is greater than the ability of the land to soak up the water. The capacity of land to act as a sponge is increased when vegetation (plant life) is present. This is why leaving a border of trees and grass along a watercourse that runs through an agricultural area is a wise idea. Another effective strategy is to reduce the loss of the topsoil, called erosion. Farmlands in North America lose an estimated 10 tons or more of soil per acre every year.

Many regions of the U.S. are affected by agricultural runoff. One well-known example is the Chesapeake Bay in Maryland. Once a thriving place, Chesapeake Bay has long been receiving runoff that contains agricultural fertilizer and manure. The large growth of algae that occurs in the presence of this food source (algal blooms) saps the oxygen, resulting in the death of species like fish and crabs. Concerned residents and politicians are working hard to try to reverse the deterioration of Chesapeake Bay before the water becomes a "dead zone" incapable of supporting plant and animal life.

## WORDS TO KNOW

**Detergent:** A chemical used as a cleaning agent because it encourages the formation of an oil-in-water emulsion.

**Dispersant:** A chemical agent that reduces the surface tension of liquid hydrocarbons, encouraging the formation of an oil-in-water emulsion. This reduces the volume of residual oil on shorelines or the water surface after a spill.

**Mousse:** A water-in-oil emulsion that is formed by turbulence of the surface water after a petroleum spill to the aquatic environment.

**Petroleum:** A naturally occurring, liquid mixture of hydrocarbons that is mined and refined for energy and the manufacturing of chemicals, especially plastics. Also known as crude oil.

Goo, Robert. "Do's and Don'ts Around the Home." *U.S. Environmental Protection Agency.* http://www.epa.gov/owow/nps/dosdont.html (accessed on September 3, 2004).

"Managing Urban Runoff." *United States Environmental Protection Agency.* http://www.epa.gov/OWOW/NPS/facts/point7.htm (accessed on September 3, 2004).

# Oil Spills

Oil is a critical resource for the world. Millions of barrels of oil are shipped from where the oil is taken from the Earth to where it is processed (refined) into substances varying from fuel to plastics. Because the world's demand for crude oil is great, oil must be shipped in large quantities by oceanic tankers, barges on inland waters, and pipelines that run over the land and under the sea. When there is a mistake or accident that causes oil to spill from any of these means of transport, damage to the water, beaches, and economy can be devastating.

Oil (also known as petroleum) is a naturally occurring thick liquid mixture of the elements hydrogen and carbon combined to form chemicals known as hydrocarbons. The oil taken from the ground (or seafloor) is called crude oil. Crude oil is then pumped or shipped to plants (refineries) where the crude oil is converted into fuels such as gasoline and home heating oil, or turned into chemicals that are used in hundreds of other products such as plastic.

In addition to accidental spills, oil can also be spilled during routine processes of cleaning ships and pipelines as well as when loading and unloading ships. Evidence is mounting that the combined effects of these small spills in ports or local waters can cause substantial damage over time. More spectacular and damaging, however, are the sudden spills associated with the sinking or damage to an oil tanker or oil drilling platform at sea.

### Oil pollution of waters

The total spillage of petroleum into the oceans through human activities is estimated to range from one million tons to two million tons of oil every year. Although this is less than about one-thousandth of the amount of oil shipped every year (0.1%), the effects can be very damaging if the concentration of oil (for example, the amount of oil in a liter or gallon of water) in a small area becomes too large.

The most damaging oil spills arise from disabled ocean tankers or drilling platforms, from barges or ships on inland waters, or from blowouts of wells or damaged pipelines. Damage is also caused by the relatively frequent spills and discharges from refineries. Large quantities of oil are also spilled when tankers clean out the petroleum residues from their huge storage compartment, sometimes dumping the oil and water mixture directly into the ocean.

## Accidents and spills

Some the largest oil spills from ocean supertankers include:

- *Amoco Cadiz,* which went aground in the English Channel in 1978, spilling 253,000 tons (230,000 metric tons) of crude oil

- *Torrey Canyon,* which ran aground in 1967 off southern England, spilling about 129,000 tons (117,000 metric tons) of crude oil

- *Braer,* which spilled 93,000 tons (84,000 metric tons) of crude oil off the Shetland Islands of Scotland in 1993

- *Prestige,* which split in half off Galicia, Spain, in November 2002, spilling about 67,000 tons (61,000 metric tons) of crude oil

- *Metula,* which wrecked in 1973 in the Strait of Magellan and spilled 58,000 tons (53,000 metric tons) of petroleum

- *Exxon Valdez,* which ran onto a reef in Prince William Sound in southern Alaska in 1989 and discharged 39,000 tons (35,000 metric tons) of petroleum.

All of the tankers involved in these spills were of the older single hull (the frame or body of a ship) design. New-double hulled tankers are designed to reduce the chances of a spill following an accident.

### *Prestige* Oil Spill Near Spain

Despite rescue efforts, the oil tanker *Prestige* sank off the coast of Spain in November 2002. Oil washed ashore along the coasts of Spain, Portugal, and France. The spill threatened hundreds of miles of wildlife-rich coasts. Scientists and environmentalists compared the damage from the *Prestige* spill to the damage caused by the 1989 *Exxon Valdez* spill in Alaska.

Although the final estimate on the size of the spill is debated, most petroleum engineers estimate that about 67,000 tons (61,000 metric tons) of fuel oil spilled. The tanker broke apart as it was being towed to deeper waters. Engineers initially hoped that most of the oil might solidify (form tar balls) inside the sunken *Prestige* tanker's compartments in the colder and deeper water, but later estimates showed that most of the oil escaped.

The oil spilled was far more toxic (poisonous) than the type of oil carried by the *Exxon Valdez.*

Experts predict that marine and bird life will suffer death and disease caused by the *Prestige* spill well into 2012. In addition to those species directly harmed, other species in the food chain will also suffer, either from lack of food or from eating other poisoned animals.

The preliminary cost for cleanup and lost economic activity is estimated at $42 million.

Significant oil spills have also occurred from offshore drilling or production platforms. In 1979, the *IXTOC-I* exploration well had an uncontrolled blowout that spilled more than 551,000 tons (500,000 metric tons) of petroleum into the Gulf of Mexico. Smaller spills include one that occurred in 1969 off Santa Barbara in southern California, when about 11,000 tons (10,000 metric tons) were discharged, and the Ekofisk blowout in 1977 in the North Sea off Norway, which totaled 33,000 tons (30,000 metric tons) of crude oil.

### Wartime spills

Enormous quantities of petroleum have also been released during warfare. Because petroleum and its refined products are critically important to economies and industry, enemies have commonly targeted tankers and other petroleum-related facilities during wars. For example, during World War II (1939–45), German submarines sank 42 tankers off the east coast of the United States, causing a total spillage of about 460,000 tons (417,000 metric tons) of petroleum and refined products. There were 314 attacks on oil tankers during the Iran-Iraq War of 1981–87, 70% of them by Iraqi forces. The largest individual spill during that war occurred when Iraq damaged five tankers and three production wells at the offshore *Nowruz* complex, resulting in the spillage of more than 287,000 tons (260,000 metric tons) of petroleum into the Gulf of Arabia.

A worker releases a sorbent boom in an attempt to contain an oil slick from the 1989 *Exxon Valdez* oil spill. © *Natalie Fobes/Corbis. Reproduced by permission.*

The largest-ever spill of petroleum into the marine environment occurred during the brief Gulf War of 1991. In that incident, Iraqi forces deliberately released an estimated 0.6–2.2 million tons (0.5–2 million metric tons) of petroleum into the Persian Gulf from several tankers and an offshore tanker-loading facility known as the *Sea Island Terminal*. An additional, extraordinarily large spill of petroleum to the land and atmosphere also occurred as a result of the Gulf War, when more than 700 production wells in Kuwait were sabotaged and ignited by Iraqi forces in January 1991. The total spillage of crude oil was an estimated 46 to 138 million tons (42 to 126 million tons).

> ### *Exxon Valdez*
>
> The most damaging oil spill ever to occur in North American waters was the 1989 *Exxon Valdez* accident.
>
> More than most tanker accidents, this one was very preventable. It was caused when the captain (who was later found to have been drinking alcohol) gave temporary command of the supertanker to an unqualified and inexperienced subordinate, who quickly made a mistake in navigation and ran the ship aground onto a well-known reef. The spilled oil affected about 1,200 miles (1,900 kilometers) of shoreline of Prince William Sound and its vicinity, causing especially great ecological damage.
>
> Large numbers of sea mammals and birds were also affected in offshore waters. An estimated 5,000–10,000 sea otters were present in Prince William Sound, and at least 1,000 of these charismatic mammals were killed by oiling. About 36,000 dead seabirds of various species were collected from beaches and other places, but the actual number of killed birds was probably in the range of 100,000–300,000. At least 153 bald eagles died from poisoning when they consumed the carcasses of oiled seabirds.
>
> Great efforts were expended in cleaning up the oiled shoreline, almost entirely using manual and physical methods, rather than dispersants and detergents. In total, about 11,000 people participated in the cleanup, and about $2.5 billion was spent by the ship owners and $154 million by the U.S. federal government. This was by far the most expensive cleanup ever undertaken after an oil spill. Within a year of the spill, the combined effects of the cleanup and winter storms had removed most of the residues of the *Exxon Valdez* spill from the environment. However, in August 2002, the *Exxon Valdez* Trustee Council released a report stating that many fish and wildlife species injured by the spill had still not fully recovered.

Much of the spilled petroleum burned in spectacular atmospheric infernos, while additional, massive quantities accumulated locally as lakes of oil, which eventually contained 5.5–23 million tons (5–21 million tons) of crude oil. Large quantities of petroleum vapors were dispersed to the atmosphere. About one-half of the free-flowing wells were capped (closed) by May, and the last one in November 1991.

## After the spill

After oil is spilled into the environment, it spreads out or sinks (dissipates) in a number of ways. Spreading refers to the process by which spilled petroleum moves and disperses itself over the surface of water. The resulting slick can then be transported away from the initial site of the spill by currents and winds. The rate and degree of spreading are affected by the thickness (viscosity) of the oil, wind speed, and waves.

If a spill is near enough to land, a mixture of oil and water called a mousse can wash up on the shore. The mousse combines with sand on the shore to form sticky patties that can harden into asphalt like lumps (material similar to that used to make roads).

At sea, the mousse eventually forms tar balls and in the vicinity of frequently traveled tanker routes world-wide, tar balls can be commonly found floating offshore and on beaches.

**Ecological damages of oil spills**

Even small oil spills can cause important change in ecologically sensitive environments. For example, a small discharge of oily bilge (wastewater) washings from the tanker *Stylis* during a routine cleaning of its petroleum-storage compartments caused the deaths of about 30,000 seabirds, because the oil was spilled in a place where the birds were abundant.

Studies made after large oceanic spills have shown that the ecological damage can be severe. After the *Torrey Canyon* spill in 1967, hundreds of miles of the coasts of southern England and the Brittany region of France were polluted by oily mousse. The oil pollution caused severe ecological damage and many different life forms suffered from exposure to petroleum. The ecological damages were made much worse by some of the cleanup methods, because of the highly toxic detergents and dispersants that were used.

The effects of oil spills can be harmful both immediately and over time. For example, the *Torrey Canyon* spill caused the deaths of at least 30,000 birds, but it also resulted in a large population of surviving birds that experienced difficulty in laying eggs for many years after the spill.

The damage caused by detergents and dispersants (chemicals used to break up spills) during the cleanup of shorelines polluted by the *Torrey Canyon* spill provided an important lesson. Subsequent cleanups of oil spills involved the use of less toxic chemicals.

In 1978, the *Amoco Cadiz* was wrecked in the same general area as the *Torrey Canyon*. Considerable ecological damage was also caused by this accident. However, the damage was less intense than that caused by the *Torrey Canyon* because less-toxic detergents and dispersants were used during the cleanup.

*William J. Engle and William Arthur*

## For More Information

### Books
Keeble, John *Out of the Channel: The Exxon Valdez Oil Spill in Prince William Sound.* 2nd ed. Cheney: Eastern Washington University Press, 1999.

### Websites
U.S. Environmental Protection Agency. "Oil Program." http://www.epa.gov/oilspill/ (accessed on September 8, 2004).

# Overuse

In countries like the United States, where some states are dotted with countless lakes and many people live within easy reach of an ocean, it may be easy to assume that drinking and recreational waters are limitless. This is not the case. In many areas of the world, water is a preciously limited resource and in some cases, water scarcity is the result of human activity. In many countries in which the water supply is scare, water is being used faster than it is being renewed, often for agriculture or to supply water for a growing population.

## Agricultural overuse

About 30% of all the freshwater used in the United States and 60% of the world's available supply of freshwater is used to grow crops. Crops require a large volume of water for production. For example, to produce 2.2 pounds (1 kilogram) of rice requires about a bathtub full of water. Only about half of the billions of gallons of water applied to crops each year makes it back to the surface or underground. The rest is lost to the air as evaporation (the change of water from liquid to vapor) and transpiration (evaporation of water from plant leaves), leaks, and spills.

The oldest known method of irrigation (watering crops) is the most wasteful. Flooding fields with water has been used since ancient times, and still is the method of choice for crops like rice. Only about half of all the water added to a field, however, actually reaches the plant. Some modern refinements to flood irrigation have made the process less wasteful, but flood irrigation still contributes to the overuse of water.

## Residential overuse

Flying over a western city like Phoenix, Arizona, can be an eye-opening experience. Sitting in the middle of a desert is an

## WORDS TO KNOW

**Aquifer:** An underground reservoir of water that is the collection area for the water in a certain geographical area.

**Groundwater:** Freshwater that resides in rock and soil layers beneath Earth's land surface.

**Irrigation:** In agriculture, a process where dry land or crops are supplied with water.

## Overfishing

Fishing provides the main food source for 200 million people around the world. In some poorer countries, one in five people lives mainly on fish. But the catching of more fish than is produced, called overfishing, is threatening many of the ocean's stocks of fish.

One example lies in the Grand Banks, which is off the coast of the Canadian province of Newfoundland. The shallower water and nearby warm waters of the Gulf Stream combined to make the Grand Banks home to a huge number of fish. Photographs taken in the 1940s show fishing nets bulging with cod and other fish. This bounty caused many to regard the waters as an endless source of fishing. Wasteful fishing practices and the use of huge factory trawlers capable of harvesting millions of fish in a short time took their toll. By the 1970s, it was apparent that the Grand Banks fishery was in trouble; numbers of fish were dwindling. In the early 1990s, the Canadian government closed the cod fishery. People in Newfoundland whose families had fished the waters for a hundred years lost their jobs.

The fishery closing was intended to be a temporary measure to allow the numbers of cod to rebound to their former numbers. This has not happened, and the cod fishery off the east coast of Canada continues to yield few fish.

In the United States, scientists and citizens groups such as the National Coalition for Marine Conservation (NCMC) are also working to bring the issue of overfishing to the forefront of lawmakers. In 2000, the NCMC convinced congress to outlaw the practice of killing sharks for their fins in an effort to protect shark populations in U.S waters. Many laws that were once designed solely to support the fishing industry have also been redefined to limit catches of threatened species of fish and to regulate fishing techniques that disrupt their habitat.

---

oasis (fertile area) where many houses have the distinctive blue patch in the backyard that is a swimming pool, and where hundreds of streaks of green golf course fairways stand out against the surrounding brown land. None of this would be possible without water. In naturally arid (dry areas with little annual rainfall) cities like Phoenix, the recreational use of water is a concern. Just to the south, the city of Tucson has water police who patrol the city searching for people who break rules that are designed to prevent water waste. Infractions such as aiming a water sprinkler at the sidewalk or watering the lawn in hot periods of the day can cost a homeowner or business hundreds of dollars for a first offense.

The water used around the home in swimming pools, washing the car, washing dishes and laundry, running a lawn sprinkler, taking a bath or shower, and even flushing the toilet all use a tremendous amount of water. Statistics gathered by the government of Canada tell the tale. Canada and the United States top the world list of average daily domestic water use. Canadian

Modern fishing methods often contribute to overfishing. © *Brojan Brecelj/Corbis. Reproduced by permission.*

households use an average of 91 US gallons each day, while American households use just over 100 gallons. Contrast this to Israel, where water supplies are limited, which uses an average of only 36 gallons per household per day.

Overuse in North America is potentially due to the view that water is a plentiful and economical resource. Community fees that people pay to use water in North America are much lower than those in other developed countries. Germans, for example, pay an average of $2.15 per volume of water, while in the U.S., that same volume averages only 80 cents.

## Community overuse

When a community gets its water supply from one or more wells or surface water sources such as a nearby lake, the amount of water that can be withdrawn can be very large. The amount of water taken out can be more than the amount of water that flows back into the source. For example, if wells are placed too close together they can draw water from the same underground fresh water source (aquifer). This can sap water from the area much faster than if the wells are further apart and drawing water from separate aquifers.

The city of Las Vegas, Nevada, has grown from a small desert town to a city of over one million people in only about 60 years, and the population continues to skyrocket. As well, millions of people flock to the city every year for recreation. Water use in Las Vegas has increased to the point where nearby surface and underground sources of water strain to keep up with the demand. The amount of groundwater (freshwater in rock and

**Overuse** | **437**

soil layers beneath the surface) that has been removed has caused some areas of the land near Las Vegas to sink more than 5 feet (1.5 meters) in the past 100 years.

In contrast to the sailors of a few centuries ago, humans now know that the water supply is not endless. Residential and community water use is managed in more communities throughout the developed world with the goal that the water supply is used at a rate that will ensure its availability for future generations, the ultimate goal.

*Brian Hoyle, Ph.D.*

## For More Information

### Books

Glennon, Robert. *Water Follies: Groundwater Pumping and the Fate of America's Fresh Waters.* Washington, DC: Island Press, 2004.

Locker, Thomas. *Water Dance.* New York: Voyager Books, 2002.

### Websites

U.S. Environmental Protection Agency. "How Excessive Water Use Affects Water Quality." *Cleaner Water Through Conservation.* http://www.epa.gov/OW/you/chap2.html (accessed on September 1, 2004).

U.S. Environmental Protection Agency. "How to Conserve Water and Use It Effectively." *Cleaner Water Through Conservation.* http://www.epa.gov/watrhome/you/chap3.html (accessed on September 1, 2004).

# Sediment Contamination

The bottom of streams, rivers, lakes, ponds, mudflats, and even oceans is made up of materials that were deposited there by the natural forces of currents (a constant flow of water in a predominant direction), gravity (attraction between two masses), and flows of incoming streams and rivers. This material, consisting of soil, pebbles, silt, clay and other material, is known as sediment. Sedimentation (the deposit of sediments) becomes a problem if it is contaminated by toxic (poisonous) chemicals or harmful microorganisms. Just as soil and other material is carried to the bottom of water bodies, harmful chemicals or organisms can collect on the sediments.

The problem of sediment contamination is increasing in many areas throughout the world. The United States Environmental Protection Agency (EPA) conducted a survey across the country in 1998 in which they found hundreds of contaminated sites. Many of these were located in coastal areas, which are rich habitats for plant and animal life. According to the EPA, every major harbor in the United States has some degree of contamination in the local sediment.

## Consequences of sediment contamination: bioaccumulation

Sediment is often a rich source of food for the living creatures in fresh or salt water. For example, rivers deposit large amounts of sediment into deltas, the point where the river enters the sea. When the tide goes out, the sediment is uncovered. This muddy region can be home to clams, which in turn become food for animals such as seals.

Toxic materials in the sediment can be taken in by small creatures such as mussels or clams. When many of these smaller animals are eaten by a larger animal (such a seal), the toxins become more concentrated in the larger creature. This pattern can be repeated as predator organisms eat the usually smaller prey organisms (a relationship that is called the food web or food chain), and the concentration of the harmful chemical becomes greater. The increasing concentration of harmful substances accumulated through the food web is known as bioaccumulation. Bioaccumulation of toxic substances can cause illness, birth defects, or death to affected organisms, including humans.

In the 1950s, people in Japan whose diet contained several servings of tuna per week suffered nerve and brain damage from eating tuna that contained high levels of the metal mercury. In 2004 the U.S. Federal Drug Administration published new recommendations about including tuna and other fish in the diets of young children and women who are of childbearing age. The recommendations suggest that persons in these age groups should limit light tuna to two six-ounce (170 grams) servings per week, and that canned albacore tuna and fresh tuna be limited to one six-ounce serving per week.

This river near San Juan, Puerto Rico, carries silt, a form of sediment, into the ocean. Any contaminants in the silt are also deposited in the ocean. *William Folsom, National Oceanic and Atmospheric Administration/Department of Commerce. Reproduced by permission.*

### WORDS TO KNOW

**Bioaccumulation:** Tendency for substances to increase in concentration in living organisms as they take in contaminated air, water, or food.

**Delta:** Sedimentary deposit that forms at the mouth of a river.

**Groundwater:** Freshwater that resides in rock and soil layers beneath Earth's land surface.

**Pesticide:** Chemical that kills a plant or animal pest.

## PCB Effects on Bird Populations

Sediment contamination can adversely impact water quality and the food chain upon which other species such as this Bald Eagle depend. © *John Conrad/Corbis. Reproduced by permission.*

The persistence of PCBs in sediment and in sediment-dwelling creatures is well documented. The effects that these compounds have on birds higher up in the food chain are a concern to scientists, but are less clear.

Studies have shown that female birds that contain higher than normal level of PCBs lay eggs that have thinner and more fragile shells. When the mother bird sits on the eggs to keep them warm, the eggs can break, killing the developing chick. As well, PCBs appear to cause malfunctioning in the structure of the genetic material. Defects that have occurred in offspring of female birds that were exposed to PCB include beaks that cross (making it hard to feed), extra toes, malformed feet, and liver disease. Together, these various defects make survival of the bird species more difficult. Some species affected in the past or currently affected by PCB contamination include the bald eagle, some raptors, some owls, and the kestrel.

Polychlorinated biphenyls (PCBs) were plastic materials made in the United States beginning in 1929 and ending in 1977, although some other countries continue to use PCBs.

### WORDS TO KNOW

**Polychlorinated biphenyls (PCBs):** Group of several hundred compounds once used in U.S. industry that are known to cause a variety of illnesses in humans and wildlife.

**Sediment:** Material such as soil and rock that has been deposited by natural processes.

### Other examples of sediment contamination

By the 1960s pesticides (chemicals designed to kill or harm insects and pests) became more popular and were used in agriculture, on recreational areas such as golf courses, and neighborhood lawns. Correspondingly, pesticides began to appear in water and sediment.

Polycyclic aromatic hydrocarbons (PAH) are harmful chemicals produced when coal, oil and gas, garbage, or other substances such as tobacco or charbroiled meat are burned. Many PAHs are caused by natural events such as forest fires and volcanoes, but most of the PAH particles in the air come from the exhaust of automobiles. PAH compounds have a structure that is difficult to break apart in water. As PAH particles come into contact with surface water, either from the air or through industrial or municipal (community) wastewater, their solid structure causes them to sink and stick to sediment particles. PAH particles can also move through soil layers to contaminate groundwater (freshwater in rock and soil layers beneath Earth's surface)

## Heavy metals

Many heavy metals (metallic elements such as mercury and lead) can cause illness even if present in humans at low levels. Heavy metals including lead, cadmium, cobalt, nickel, and mercury, which can all gather in sediment, can alter blood cell formation. As well, heavy metals can damage the liver, kidneys, blood circulation, nerves, and may also be a trigger of cancer. Heavy metals have been found in sediments downstream from many of the world's major cities, such as the Limmat River downstream from Zürich, Switzerland, and the Pearl River Delta between Hong Kong and Macao, China. Industrial wastes, sewage, litter, marine boat traffic, and runoff from mines are all potential sources for heavy metal contamination of sediment.

## Historical sediment contamination

Because chemicals can stay in sediment for decades or longer, sediment contamination is sometimes due to activities that were ended years ago. For example, the pesticides chlordane and DDT were recognized as a threat to the environment and were banned from use in North America in the 1960s. Yet these chemicals are still recovered in small numbers from some sediments.

The knowledge that sediment contamination can be a long-term problem makes the effort to reduce sediment contamination challenging for scientists. Even though the levels of some toxic compounds are likely to remain high in sediment for some years to come, the outlook is promising. The restricted use of unhealthy pesticides and other chemicals should eventually reduce their levels in the sediment.

*Brian Hoyle, Ph.D.*

## For More Information

### Books

Miller, Benjamin. *Fat of the Land: The Garbage of New York: The Last Two Hundred Years.* New York: Four Walls Eight Windows, 2000.

Postel, Sandra, and Brian Richter. *Rivers for Life: Managing Water for People and Nature.* Washington, DC: Island Press, 2003.

## WORDS TO KNOW

**Ballast water:** Water that is pumped into the hull of a ship to keep the ship balanced correctly in the water when it is empty.

**Biodiversity:** The vast range and number of different species that usually occurs in a healthy environment.

**Native species:** A species naturally-occurring in an environment.

**Species:** Classification of related organisms that can interbreed to produce like, fertile offspring.

### Websites

"Contaminated Sediment." *U.S. Environmental Protection Agency.* http://www.epa.gov/waterscience/cs (accessed on September 1, 2004).

U.S. Department of Health and Human Services and U.S. Environmental Protection Agency. "EPA-823-R-04-005: What You Need to Know About Mercury in Fish and Shellfish." *U.S. Food and Drug Administration Center for Food Safety and Applied Nutrition.* http://www.cfsan.fda.gov/~dms/admehg3.html (accessed on September 1, 2004).

## Species Introduction

Daily life in most environments, including the watery environments of salty oceans and freshwater streams, rivers, lakes, ponds, and wetlands is a balance between all the living things in the particular environment (ecosystem). Changing the mix of these living things can upset the ecosystem and have undesirable consequences.

Sometimes the change is accidental. A new species (a classification of related organisms that can reproduce) can happen to find its way into a new environment where the conditions include plenty of food, few enemies, and an ideal temperature. The change can also be deliberate, due to humans' attempts to control one undesirable species by adding another. Sometimes, the introduced species thrives in the environment and becomes the dominant species. This can reduce the biodiversity (the vast range and number of different species) of the environment, as the introduced species outcompetes other species. But, this is not always the case. Species that are already present can adapt to the introduced species, survive, and even thrive.

### The problem of species introduction

Introducing one organism into a new environment can often lead to disastrous results. For example, rice farmers in the Philippines have had their crops chewed up by the water-loving golden apple snail. The appetite of this snail, which was not native (natural to an environment) to the area, but which has taken over, has cost the farmers an estimated $1 billion. Some water-loving plants can also disturb the biodiversity of an area. For example, the water hyacinth and water lettuce are two plants (normally considered weeds) that grow well in water. Their growth crowds out other plants that are being grown for food. In Africa, about $60 million is spent each year battling these two plants.

A century ago, the problem of species introduction was more of a local issue. An undesirable plant could have flowed downstream in the river to come ashore and take root, for example. Spread of organisms could occur over a wider area, such as on logs drifting in an ocean current. Natural barriers, however, such as oceans, differing climates, and soil conditions often prevented a new species from widespread drift. The world remained mostly distinctive in its distribution of life from place to place (think of all the exotic creatures that are found in Australia and nowhere else).

In today's world of rapid international travel, the spread of unwanted species occurs all over the globe. When a foreign species enters a new environment, there may be few other creatures that can outgrow it or find it a good source of food. So there may be little to stop the explosive growth of the new species.

## A major cause of species introduction: ballast water

Water is the perfect container to transport many organisms from one environment to another. Ocean-going ships use water to weigh down and balance the weight of the ship. This water (ballast) is typically pumped into a ship in one harbor after the ship unloads its cargo. When cargo is loaded at a new harbor, the ballast water is pumped out to reduce the weight of the ship, which reduces the amount of fuel needed to power the ship through the ocean water. This practice of filling up with water in one harbor and dumping the water in another harbor means that water, and the living things in that water, can be moved all over the world from one environment to an entirely different environment.

Huge amounts of ballast water can be shifted from place to place. Big ocean-going tankers and cargo ships can hold millions of pounds of ballast water. In the water, a wide variety of creatures (anything small enough to make it through the pumps) can travel with the ship. Scientists have estimated that a typical load of ballast water can carry at least 7,000 different species of

Scientists form the Untied States Fish and Wildlife Service monitor lake trout and other fish near Ludington, Michigan to measure the impact of sea lamprey infestation. © *James L. Amos/Corbis. Reproduced by permission.*

Species Introduction 443

microorganisms, plants, and other living things! While all do not survive the journey, many species do survive.

The spread of species in ballast water is now recognized by agencies such as the United Nations as being a threat to the health of the oceans, freshwaters, and to the economy of many countries. Unlike an oil spill that can be quickly detected and whose damage can be at least partly reversed, the spread of species in water is often invisible until the problem is already difficult to treat. Sometimes, an introduced species reproduces so successfully in its new environment that the resulting problems are irreversible.

## Examples of species introduction

Studies have shown that ballast water can transport a type of bacteria called *Vibrio cholera* from place to place. If this microorganism sounds familiar, it is because of its last name. *Vibrio cholera* is the cause of cholera, a serious disease of the intestines that can cause loss of body fluids in the form of diarrhea and lead to death in severe cases. Cholera is still a big problem in some areas of the world, such as India. People around the world are susceptible to the bacteria (the bacteria can cause disease in everyone), but are not exposed to the bacteria, as it is not found in local waters in numbers large enough to cause disease. When *Vibrio cholera* is introduced and reproduces in new waters, a cholera outbreak among the local population can result.

Of course, ballast water is not the sole means of transport of the bacterium. In the developing world, where the bacterium exists naturally in the warm water, cholera remains a big problem. The disease can also be spread through contaminated food such as fish and shellfish, and via feces.

Another example of troublesome species introduction involves the Japanese shore crab. While the nature of its introduction is not known, the outcome of its presence has been dis-

---

### Zebra Mussels in the Great Lakes

Zebra mussels are a type of shellfish related to clams and oysters that were normally found in the Caspian Sea area of Asia. Scientists hypothesize that in the mid 1980s some of the mussels got into ballast water of a ship that sailed from that area of the world to a port in the Great Lakes. That port was likely the city of Detroit, Michigan, since the zebra mussel was first discovered nearby in 1988 in Lake St. Clair (a relatively small lake that is located in between Lake Erie and Lake Huron).

In the new environment, where there were no natural competitors to control the numbers of the zebra mussels, their population exploded very quickly. In about a decade, the mussels spread to all of the Great Lakes, as well as into waterways that connect to the lakes.

A big reason for the spread of zebra mussels is their remarkable ability to latch onto surfaces. They can attach so tightly that they can clog up the intake of water into pipes and can slow down the rotation of ship propellers.

The huge numbers of zebra mussels in the Great Lakes has reduced the numbers of microscopic plants and animals that are the main food source of other creatures. As well, the mussels can produce a toxin (poison) that sickens fish and wildlife that eats them. The result has been a drastic and undesirable change in the balance of life in the Great Lakes. Numbers of some native species have dwindled, while the zebra mussel continue to thrive.

turbing for the natural population in the coastal waters. This species of crab is rapidly growing in numbers along the Atlantic coast of the United States around Cape Cod, Massachusetts. This is bad news for the crabs and other creatures that naturally live in the area, as they must now compete with a growing new population for the same amount of available food.

*Brian Hoyle, Ph.D.*

### For More Information

#### Books
McNeely, Jeffrey, ed. *Great Reshuffling: Human Dimensions of Invasive Alien Species.* Gland, Switzerland: IUCN, 2001.

Mooney, Harold A, and Richard J. Hobbs, eds. *Invasive Species in a Changing World.* Washington, DC: Island Press, 2000.

#### Websites
"Alien Species." *Secretariat of the Convention on Biological Diversity, United Nations Environment Programme.* http://www.biodiv.org/programmes/cross-cutting/alien (accessed on September 8, 2004).

"Ships' Ballast Water and Invasive Marine Species." *UN Atlas of the Oceans.* http://www.oceansatlas.org/servlet/CDSServlet?status=ND0yMzU0Jjc9ZW4mNjE9KiY2NT1rb3M¯ (accessed on September 8, 2004).

## Water Conservation

Conservation is the philosophy that natural resources should be used cautiously so that they will remain available for future generations of people. In practice, conservation is the act of protecting, managing, and restoring shared earth resources such as soil, air, forests, minerals, petroleum, wildlife, and water—one of humans' most essential resources. Water conservation can be as simple as one person using water sparingly during a drought (prolonged period of dry weather), or as complex as a multi-national committee developing a long-term water distribution plan for an entire continent.

The word conservation means different things to different people, and a workable conservation plan for a particular region or resource usually involves a compromise between several interest groups. Consider, for example, a forest. To a log-

## WORDS TO KNOW

**Conservation:** Protection, management, or restoration of natural resources such as soil, forests, wetlands, minerals, and water.

**Natural resources:** Economically valuable materials that humans extract from the Earth; water is one of humans' most essential natural resource.

**Preservationist:** One who argues for the protection of wilderness, historical sites, or endangered species against human exploitation and development.

**Sustainable development:** Resource and social management scheme that balances short-term needs with long-term environmental and economic interests of future generations.

ging company, forest conservation means developing a system of cutting and replanting healthy, fast-growing trees that ensures continuing profits. To a forest ecologist (a person who studies relationship between organisms and their environment) it means restoring a forest to a more natural state that supports a healthy community of plants and animals, along with protecting its most fragile areas and species. To a homeowner conservation means preserving the natural beauty of the forest and safeguarding property from forest fires. And to a preservationist it means letting nature manage the forest with little or no human intervention.

Conservation generally involves managing natural resources to serve people, whether by providing materials for essential needs (water, food, shelter, and energy) and consumer products (cars, clothing, computers, furniture), or simply by protecting wild areas where people can enjoy nature and outdoor recreation. While most scientists do not argue with using Earth's natural resources to meet human needs, most scientists also agree with the general idea that shared natural resources should be protected from overuse and pollution, and wisely managed using sound scientific information.

### Need for water conservation

Water is Earth's most plentiful natural resource. It covers almost three-quarters of our planet's surface. Astronauts say Earth looks like a "blue marble" from space with its blue oceans and white swirls of water droplets (clouds) in the atmosphere (mass of air surrounding Earth). Water is also a renewable resource. Water moves endlessly within the hydrologic cycle, and is almost never destroyed in the process. When humans draw water from lakes, rivers, oceans, or groundwater reservoirs (aquifers), new water replaces it. Water is even self-cleansing. When it evaporates, it leaves pollution and salts behind and forms clouds that produce fresh rainwater. New water that flows into polluted lakes and rivers acts to dilute (lower the concentration or amount) and disperse (spread out) pollutants.

Why then, if water is so abundant and easily replenished, do people need to conserve it? First, fresh, liquid water that is suitable for human use only makes up a small percentage of Earth's total water supply. Almost all (97%) of Earth's water is undrinkable salt water that resides in the oceans. In addition to being too salty to drink, seawater corrodes (wears away) metals and gums up machinery, making it unsuitable for most other human uses. Much of the remaining 3% is frozen in glaciers (slow moving mass of ice) and ice in the North and South Poles. Second, fresh water is distributed unevenly on Earth's surface. Some regions have abundant freshwater resources and others are arid (dry) deserts where water is scarce. Third, though water is a renewable resource in a general sense, local and even regional water supplies can run dry from overuse. Finally, human activities that add chemical substances to surface water, groundwater and the oceans can pollute water to the extent that it is unsafe for human use and damages the larger ecosystem. For all these reasons, water conservation and management are extremely important, especially in places where a large human population depends on a limited water supply.

**Water conservation in history**

Humans have shared public water resources since they first settled in permanent villages thousands of years ago. Early peoples however, usually solved water supply or contamination problems by simply moving their villages. When wells ran dry from overuse, or rivers became polluted with human waste, they just relocated to a new, unspoiled location. Ancient civilizations in the arid Middle East, Africa, and China, who needed to supply water to the residents of large cities and to permanent agricultural lands were the first true water conservationists.

Throughout history societies have succeeded, in part, because of water management plans that ensured a steady supply of unpolluted water through periods of drought (prolonged shortage of rain) and flood. The desert empires of Mesopotamia and Egypt flourished by using elaborate irrigation (crop watering) and plumbing systems to distribute water from the rivers Tigris, Euphrates, and Nile to cities and croplands. The Ancient Greeks constructed drainage systems and huge stone sewers at the palace of King Minos at Knossos on the island of Crete almost 5,000 years ago. Water engineering was one of the great hallmarks of the Roman Empire. The Romans built aqueducts, canals, irrigation systems, city sewers, and indoor plumbing throughout their vast empire. (The modern English word plumber comes from the Latin word for lead, *plumbus*, and the ingenious Roman lead workers, *plumberium*, who engineered the world's first reliable indoor plumbing.)

Civilizations and empires have also failed because of poor water conservation practices or water management. Populations that have overused their water supplies or have allowed their water to become polluted have suffered serious consequences. Many archeologists attribute the mysterious disappearance of the Anasazi people from the American Southwest to inadequate water supply. Diseases caused by poor sanitation and poisoning from lead pipes were ironically, two factors that contributed to the fall of the Roman Empire. Improper waste management has also played a major role in the spread of diseases such as the bubonic plague that killed millions of Europeans during the Middle Ages. Waterborne diseases such as cholera, typhoid, typhus, and dysentery thrive where sewers bearing waste from infected persons empty into a public water supply. Scientists only began to understand the dangers of microscopic bacteria in sewage-polluted water after an epidemic of cholera killed thousands of people in Europe and the United States in the 1830s.

**History of the American conservation movement.** The idea of conservation only began to gain popularity in the United States at the end of the 1800s. Until then the North American frontier had provided seemingly inexhaustible natural resources, including abundant fresh water. By the 1890s however, European settlement had reached across the entire continent, and the census of 1890 declared the American frontier closed. Unrestricted sport hunting had slaughtered the bison herds of the Great Plains and killed off the flocks of passenger pigeons that once migrated (traveled periodically) down the Atlantic coast. Logging, grazing, mining, and hydropower (power from water energy) development threatened America's most dramatic national landmarks. Niagara Falls, for example, nearly lost its untamed water flow.

The Gilded Age at the end of the nineteenth century was also a time of unregulated resource exploitation and social inequality that made conservation an appealing idea to the general American public and to government leaders. Powerful businessmen of the mining, timber, railroad, and ranching industries became immensely wealthy as they laid waste to America's pristine forests, prairies, wetlands and waterways. At the same time, most Americans saw their living standards decline. Without government oversight, laborers, owners of small businesses, and independent settlers were at the mercy of the economically and politically powerful industrialists. While the powerful of the gilded age enjoyed luxurious estates and the diversions of high society, average Americans received low wages, worked in poor conditions, and lived in crowded cities and towns.

Gifford Pinchot (1865–1946) founded the conservation movement in the United States in the late 1890s. Pinchot argued that the best use of nature was to improve the life of common citizens. Pinchot's ideas were inspired by his observations of environmental destruction and social inequality that resulted from unregulated wilderness exploitation during the 1800s. He was also influenced by the writings of other nineteenth century explorers and naturalists including George Perkins Marsh and John Wesley Powell. Pinchot had great influence during the presidency of Theodore Roosevelt (1901–9), and he helped to steer conservation policies from the turn of the century until the 1940s. (Roosevelt was an avid hunter and an ardent conservationist in his own right.) Pinchot became the first head of the U.S. National Forest Service when it was established in 1905. Its motto, "The Land of Many Uses" reflects Pinchot's philosophy.

Conservation efforts have continued in the United States since the era of Roosevelt and Pinchot. Government agencies, groups of private citizens, and even business leaders have developed strategies to protect America's natural resources. The U.S. government has set aside millions of acres of public land as national forests and parks, and a large group of agencies now manage the nation's natural resources in a scientifically and economically reasonable manner. Universities and professional schools offer courses in resource management and natural sciences such as biology and geology. The discipline of ecology, the study of communities of plants and animals that live and interact in a specific environment, blossomed as scientists, engineers, and policy makers sought to understand the natural environments they were charged to protect.

Some early conservation strategies may seem strange by modern standards, and have had unintended negative consequences. For example, extreme flood control measures along the Mississippi river system exposed a large human population to catastrophic mega-floods. However early environmental policies were based on the science of the time, and were unquestionably fairer and less destructive than the unchecked industrial development they replaced.

Water conservation programs and projects played a major role in President Franklin D. Roosevelt's (1882–1945) "New Deal" plan to revive the United States economy during and after the Great Depression of the 1930s. Government-sponsored hydroelectric projects such as the Tennessee Valley Authority (TVA), which dammed the Tennessee River for flood control and electricity generation, provided work for thousands of unemployed engineers and laborers. The Bureau of

Reclamation, a government agency that manages the surface water west of the Rocky Mountains, constructed more than 600 dams during 1920s and 1930s, including Hoover Dam on the Colorado River, and Grand Coulee Dam on the Columbia River. East of the Rockies, the Army Corps of Engineers helped put the American public back to work by building dams and other water control structures in the Mississippi River system. The Soil Conservation Service was established to advise farmers in maintaining and developing their farmland.

**Conservation or preservation?** Pinchot and other early conservationists fundamentally disagreed with early preservationists who thought that some wilderness should be protected solely to preserve its beauty or its natural ecosystem. John Muir, an eloquent writer who worked to protect Yosemite Valley in California, led the early preservationist movement. He bitterly opposed Pinchot's vision of the nation's wilderness and waterways as warehouses of useful materials. Because of its more moderate stance, Pinchot's conservation became the more popular position and it has since guided U.S. environmental policy. The preservationists did however, strike a chord with the American public and some of their ideas were incorporated into a mainstream conservation movement. In the 1960s, environmentalists echoed Muir's arguments when they raised objections to conservation's anthropocentric (human-centered) emphasis. Late twentieth century naturalists such as Rachel Carson (1907–1964), Edward Abbey (1927–1989), Aldo Leopold (1913–1983), as well as more radical environmental groups, including Greenpeace and Earth First!, owe much of their legacy to the turn of the century preservationists.

### Water conservation in the United States

Water is by far the most carefully managed natural resource in the United States today. The average American uses about 100 gallons (378.5 liters) of water each day for direct purposes such as drinking, cooking, bathing, washing clothes and dishes, watering lawns, and washing cars. Per person water use is even greater when including indirect uses such as irrigation for a person's food and water used to manufacture consumer products. A complex system of local, state, and national water boards and agencies manages the U.S. water supply to ensure that all 280 million Americans have access to a steady supply of fresh water.

It is only a slight exaggeration to say that every drop of river water in the United States encounters a human water control structure or system of some sort before eventually reaching the ocean or evaporating into the atmosphere. All of the nation's

## The Hetch-Hetchy debate: What Use Is the Use of Wilderness?

Rafting the Tuolumne River below Yosemite National Park, California is one of many tourist activities that environmentalists fear might endanger conservation efforts in sensitive habitats. © *Galen Rowell/Corbis. Reproduced by permission.*

The Hetch-Hetchy valley of the Tuolumne River in California's Yosemite National Park was the subject of one of America's first and fiercest environmental debates. James Phelan (1861–1930), the mayor of San Francisco, and Pinchot, at that time head of the U.S. Forest Service, stood on one side of the bargaining table. Muir, founder of the Sierra Club, stood on the other.

In 1901, Mayor Phelan proposed damming the Tuolumne River to create a reservoir in the Hetch-Hetchy valley that would supply San Francisco with much-needed fresh water. To Pinchot and other early conservationists, the project was an example of the wise use of natural resources to improve the lives of common citizens. Most of the common citizens of San Francisco had never heard of Hetch-Hetchy, let alone made the 150-mile (241-kilometer) trip by carriage to enjoy its natural beauty. They were however, very interested in ending the perpetual water shortages and outbreaks of waterborne illness that plagued their booming city.

To Muir, the Hetch-Hetchy dam was heresy. He wrote, in a 1908 Sierra Club bulletin, "Hetch-Hetchy valley, far from being a plain, common, rock-bound meadow ... is a grand landscape garden, one of Nature's rarest and most precious mountain mansions.... Dam Hetch-Hetchy! As well dam for water-tanks the people's cathedrals and churches, for no holier temple has ever been consecrated by the heart of man." Muir campaigned tirelessly against the Hetch-Hetchy project. He wrote passionately in defense of Yosemite's natural beauty and spiritual worth. He took his appeal to lawmakers in Sacramento and Washington, D.C., and enlisted thousands of supporters.

To Mayor Phelan, John Muir was insensitive to the needs of people, and a thorn in the side of reasonable progress. Phelan's Hetch-Hetchy 1901 proposal was turned down, and Muir's campaign stalled the plan again in 1903, 1905, and 1907. Phelan wrote of Muir, "He [John Muir] is a poetical gentleman. I am sure he would sacrifice his own family for the sake of beauty. He considers human life very cheap." Phelan eventually triumphed in the aftermath of the 1906 San Francisco earthquake. The quake ruptured gas lines and fuel tanks and fires raged throughout the city. Residents assumed that city firefighters' inadequate water supply was one of the reasons for the total destruction.

Hetch-Hetchy reservoir was filled in 1913. Muir died, disappointed, a year later. Muir's legacy, however, remained. His book and essays continue to inspire new generations of nature lovers and environmental activists. John Muir was America's first environmentalists.

major rivers and most of its smaller rivers and streams are dammed, constricted by levees, or both to protect humans from floods, provide hydroelectric power, and hold back reservoirs (artificial lakes) that contain local water supplies. Engineers and water managers control river flows in the United States to such an extent that many floods and shortages are today an act of man as well as nature.

Water is one of the most economically valuable resources. In the bone-dry American West and Southwest, booming cities such as Phoenix, Las Vegas, and Los Angeles share scarce water supplies with large-scale agricultural regions such as California's San Joaquin Valley. Central California receives only a few inches (centimeters) of rain each year, but with irrigation water imported from the Sierra Mountains and the Colorado River, it has become "America's salad bowl." Much of the produce (lettuce, tomatoes, avocadoes) stocking the grocery store shelves in the United States comes from irrigated fields in the deserts of California and Texas. The Colorado River is so heavily used by the states along its path (Colorado, Utah, Arizona, Nevada, and California) that it contains only a trickle of water where it crosses the Mexican border and it no longer reaches the ocean. (In fact, because the Colorado River water distribution plan was agreed upon during a relatively wet period, the river actually contains less water than was promised to its various human users.)

Water use is strictly regulated according to local, state, and national laws. With the exception of small lakes and streams on private property, bodies of surface water are public property. In most states private landowners must allow the general public to use water from rivers or lakes on their property. Furthermore, they must abide by the same water quality and withdrawal guidelines as the rest of their water district.

Unlike surface water groundwater usually belongs legally to the owner of the overlying land. Most groundwater laws were written before scientists understood groundwater moves in underground reservoirs, and that single users can overuse or pollute shared groundwater resources. Individuals, industries, and communities that abuse groundwater usually face few legal consequences, especially compared to users who pollute or overuse surface water. If for example, a city's water reservoir runs low during a dry spell the regional water district can legally purchase water from other sources, and can require the whole community to take water-saving measures like restricting summertime lawn irrigation and car washing. If on the other hand, a farm's well goes dry after the farmer's neighbor lowers the water table (level below which rocks and soils are saturated with water) by over pumping, no legal action could be taken against the neighbor and the farmers would likely need to drill a deeper well.

### International water conservation

Although water shortages, floods, pollution, and water-related legal conflicts are relatively common in the United States, water conservation policies generally ensure that Americans can trust their water supply. People in other parts of the world are not so fortunate, particularly in the developing nations of Africa, South America, and Asia. In many regions arid climate, rapid population growth, poverty, and political instability are a recipe for water shortages and pollution. Two-thirds of the world's population lives on less than 13 gallons (49 liters) of water per day. (Remember that an average American uses about eight times that much water.) When political tension becomes war or an already dry climate gets drier, people who were surviving with limited freshwater are faced with famine (food shortages leading to starvation) and disease.

In recent decades conservation has become a critical issue for the international community. Organizations such as the United Nations Environment Program (UNEP), the International Union for the Conservation of Nature and Natural Resources (IUCN), and the World Wildlife Fund (WWF) are working to help individual countries plan for the maintenance and protection of their resources. Their strategy, called sustainable development, is based on a philosophy that is very similar to Pinchot's original conservation ideal. Earlier international programs viewed environmental protection and economic development as an "either-or" decision between preserving nature and human prosperity. Sustainable development schemes aim to address humans' most pressing social issues like poverty, famine, and disease by solving environmental problems such as water scarcity and pollution. New strategies for coping with environmental issues also involve providing economic incentives that encourage economically powerful nations and industries to act for the common good.

*Laurie Duncan, Ph.D.*

## For More Information

### Books

Bixler, Patricia E. *Gifford Pinchot*. Historic Pennsylvania Leaflet No. 39. Edited by Harold L. Myers. Harrisburg, PA: Pennsylvania Historical & Museum Commission, 1976. Also available at http://www.dep.state.pa.us/dep/PA_Env-Her/pinchot_bio.htm (accessed on September 3, 2004).

McPhee, John. *The Control of Nature*. New York: Farrar, Straus and Giroux, 1989.

Muir, John. *The Yosemite*. New York: The Century Company, 1912.

Pipkin, Bernard, W. and D. D. Trent. "Fresh-water Resources." In *Geology and the Environment*. Pacific Grove, CA: Brooks/Cole, 2001.

### Websites

"Conservation: Fresh Water." *National Geographic.com*. http://magma.nationalgeographic.com/education/gaw/frwater (accessed on September 3, 2004).

Daughtry, Hill. *Theplumber.com*. http://www.theplumber.com (accessed on September 3, 2004).

"Hetch Hetchy." *The Sierra Club*. http://www.sierraclub.org/ca/hetchhetchy/history.asp (accessed on September 3, 2004).

*United Nations Environment Programme*. http://www.unep.org (accessed on September 3, 2004).

*United States Department of Agriculture Forest Service*. http://www.fs.fed.us (accessed on September 3, 2004).

United States Geological Survey. "Earth's Water." *Water Science for Schools*. http://ga.water.usgs.gov/edu/mearth.html (accessed on September 3, 2004).

# Water Politics: Issues of Use and Abuse

All communities are based around a source of water, whether an ocean, lake, river, stream, or well. Individuals need water for drinking, bathing, cooking, cleaning, and aiding the disposal of waste. Agriculture uses water for irrigation (water crops), aiding the production of a plentiful harvest even when rainfall is less than normal. Industry uses water for the production of electricity and the manufacturing of goods. Because water is so essential, nations, states, cities, and even individuals that share a water source must cooperate to protect their water from pollution and overuse, while ensuring a useable supply of water.

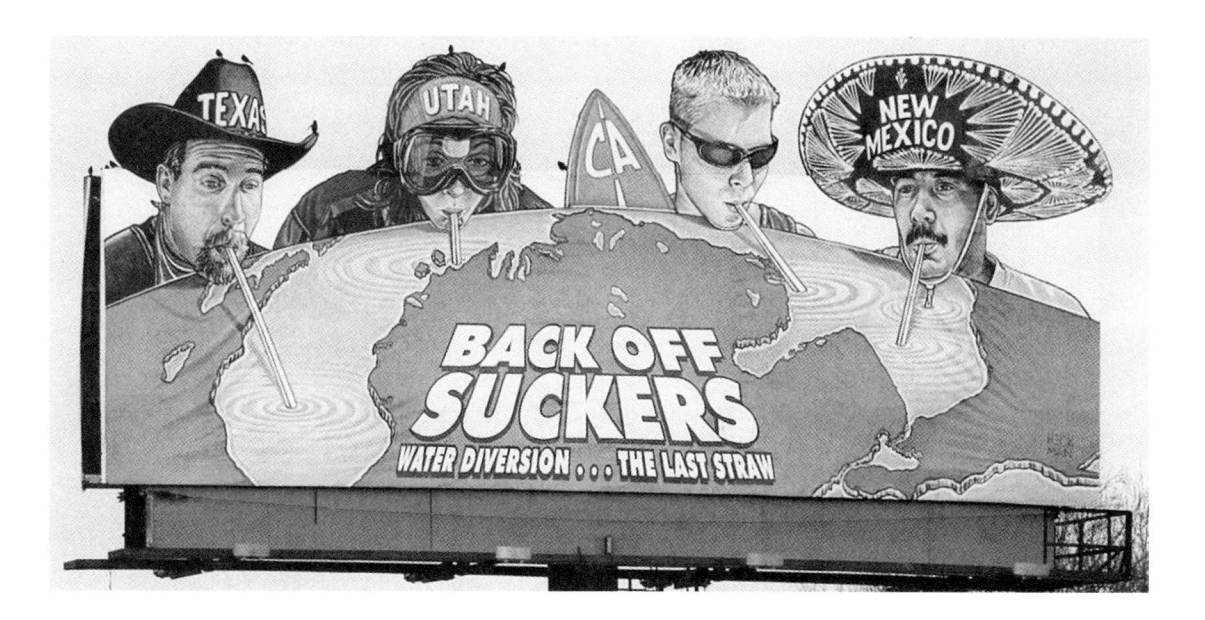

How much fresh water communities or nations consume or use is known as their water footprint. Individuals and communities in different parts of the world use different amounts of water. For example, communities in the United States are some of the world's largets consumers of water, while communities in Northern Africa are among those who consume the least. Studying water footprints helps scientists see how communities use water. Studying water footprints also shows where water is wasted, helping communities conserve water. Sustainability, or using a natural resource in a manner that satisfies the immediate need while preserving the resource for future generations, is the ultimate goal for maintaining water resources.

In developed nations, fresh, clean water is supplied by a municipal (local) water works or individual well. A large network of pipes carries clean water to its destination for use, while another network of pipes carries wastewater away. Wastewater is cleaned and treated before being released back into the environment.

For some people, getting water may be easy as turning on a faucet; expelling wastewater as simple as lifting the stopper on a bathtub drain. However nearly 1 out of every 3 people in the

A billboard along I-94 in Michigan depicts four stereotypical characters from other parts of America all sucking water from Michigan's Great Lakes through straws to emphasize that Michigan's water was shared and used by other parts of the country. © 2002 Mark D. Heckman. Reproduced by permission.

### WORDS TO KNOW

◆**Aquifer:** An underground rock formation that contains water.

◆**Wastewater:** Water left over after it has been used; for example, any water that empties into a drain or sewer is wastewater.

◆**Water footprint:** The amount of water used by an individual, business, community, or nation.

◆**Water mining:** The appearance of a cone-shaped depression at the base of an aquifer when too much water is pumped from the aquifer at too rapid a rate.

world do not have access to clean drinking water on a daily basis Many more do not have a sanitary and safe way of disposing of waste and wastewater without polluting nearby water sources. Unsafe and unclean water can transmit diseases. Polluted water used for irrigation can ruin crops. Several international organizations, including the United Nations work to increase access to clean, safe, freshwater around the world.

### Using and protecting surface waters

Surface waters include rivers, lakes, streams, wetlands, ponds, and the oceans. Oceans, rivers, and lakes that touch or flow through several nations require international cooperation to protect them from pollution and overuse. International agreements keep one nation from polluting or overusing a water source, such as a river, before it flows into another nation that is also dependent on the river as a water source.

In the United States, the Colorado River is a major source of freshwater for many arid (extremely dry) western states. The Colorado River also flows into Mexico. Parts of Arizona, California, Colorado, Nevada, New Mexico, Utah, and Wyoming currently depend on some water from the Colorado River, its headwaters (source) or one of the tributaries (small rivers that flow from the main river). Use of water from the river sustains agriculture, provides water for use in peoples home (residential water use), and produces electricity.

The Colorado River is an example of a water source that is stretched to its limits. The growth of large cities, especially in California, demands an ever-increasing supply of water for residential use. Recent laws state that California must find another source of water for its southern cities. By 2015, California is scheduled to lose much of its access to Colorado River water. Agriculture in the dry region requires significant assistance from irrigation, which also uses river water. So much water is diverted from the river for residential, industrial, and agricultural use that the large river is the size of a stream by the time it reaches the national border with Mexico.

Shrinking river volume and diminishing supply is not the only problem facing the Colorado river. The low volume of flow has made the water in the river more saline. Saline water has a high amount of minerals, the most common of which is salt. As the water become more saline it requires more treatment before being used for drinking water. Towards the end of the river, the mineral content of the water makes it unsuitable for irrigating some types of crops.

## Using and protecting groundwater

Groundwater is also a source of water for residents, businesses, and agriculture. Large, underground, water-bearing rock formations are called aquifers. Aquifers are a source of clean, freshwater that replenishes when surface water from rain and snow seeps into the ground. This rate may be very slow, however. Fossil aquifers cannot replenish themselves or only do so after tens of thousands of years. Some of the largest and most used aquifers in the world are fossil aquifers, such as the Artesian Basin in Australia and the Ogallala aquifer in the United States. Other fossil aquifers lie beneath the surface of Africa's Sahara and Kalahari deserts.

In many parts of the world aquifers are endangered by over-use. The supply of water in an aquifer lowers when water is pumped out of an aquifer at a faster rater than it is replenished. If water is taken rapidly from an aquifer, then a cone-shaped trench may form at its bottom. As this depression grows and more water is drawn from the aquifer, the water level inside the aquifer will drop faster than it would with pumping alone. This is known as mining or water mining.

Taking too much water from an aquifer causes the water table to drop. The water table is the level underground at which water fills every space in the underlying rock. As the water table drops, surface soil often becomes drier. A low water table can kill tress and vegetation whose roots can no longer reach enough water. People who depend on a well for water may have to dig new wells or deepen their existing wells. Aquifer depletion also affects the level of local streams, springs, and rivers fed by the aquifer. Water for household, industrial, and recreational use could become scarce if the aquifer is the only local source of water. The system of water rights decides who gets to pump what amount of groundwater from an aquifer and what uses of water are most important for the community as a whole.

*Adrienne Lerner*

### Ogallala Water Mining

The Ogallala aquifer is one of the world's largest fossil aquifers. Located on the American high plains in Nebraska, it provides irrigation for some of the most productive farmland in the United States. Water from the aquifer sustains 25% of the nation's cotton crop, 15% of its corn and wheat, and nearly half of all cattle raised for food. As more residents move into the region water is increasingly mined from the aquifer. The Aquifer is a key source of water, but people are pumping water from the aquifer eight times faster then the aquifer can refill itself. By the year 2050, half of the Ogallala aquifer's supply of fresh water will have been pumped out of the ground.

Eventually the aquifer could be pumped completely dry, depriving the region around the aquifer without the water necessary to sustain large farms or cities. Recent laws have set out to better govern the pumping and use of Ogallala aquifer water, but because it is the main source of clean, freshwater in the region, pumping cannot be stopped. Scientists are experimenting with a system to artificially recharge the aquifer by pumping in rainwater. While this will aid the overall water level it is unlikely to replace most of the water mined from the Ogallala aquifer.

### For More Information

**Books**

Fradkin, Philip L. *A River No More: The Colorado River and the West*. Berkeley: University of California Press, 1996.

Opie, John. *Ogallala: Water for Dry Land (Our Sustainable Future Series)*. Lincoln: University of Nebraska Press, 2001.

**Websites**

UNESCO. *Water Footprint Project*. http://www.waterfootprint.org (accessed on September 8, 2004).

USGS. "Special Topics." *Water Science for Schools*. http://ga.water.usgs.gov/edu/specials.html (accessed on September 8, 2004).

# Water Pollution

Pollution is defined as the addition of harmful substances into the ecosystem (the network of interactions between living organisms and their environment). Pollutants might be slightly harmful to humans, but very harmful to aquatic life. For instance, in certain lakes and rivers when acid rain (rain polluted with acidic chemicals) falls upon them, toxic (poisonous) metals that cause fish to die are released from sediments (particles of soil, sand, and minerals, and animal or plant matter washed from land into water). These metals—chromium, aluminum, and mercury are just a few—are harmful to fish. But humans would have to ingest much larger quantities than the aquatic or marine life. The toxins also accumulate in the tissues of fish as they eat other fish (ingest) or plants containing toxins. If one were to catch and eat a fish that has a high content of toxins in them the human is affected too. Metals are not the only pollutants that are of concern, as evidenced by oil spills that kill marine life in large quantities and persist on beaches and in sediments for a long time. Industrial processes produce harmful waste, and often this is discharged into a nearby stream, river, or ocean. There are many ways to cause pollution and many types of pollutants.

### Levels of pollution

Transportation is a leading source of pollution, both in the atmosphere (mass of air surrounding Earth) and in water reserves. Every time oil or gasoline is spilled on the roadway, it eventually is transported to the nearest water reserve. Many of these reserves are groundwater. Groundwater is freshwater that resides in rock and soil layers beneath Earth's land surface, and groundwater can eventually transport pollutants into rivers, streams, and the sea. Thus, pollutants can come from large areas or specific areas. These are referred to as non-point source and point-source pollution, respectively.

If the source of pollution is able to be identified and "pointed" to, the source of pollution is point-source. Point sources include drainage pipes from factories, leaky underground gasoline tanks, and places where people discard used motor oil. Non-point sources are far more reaching, such as the transportation example. Not only do toxic chemicals come from leaky automobiles and gasoline spills, they come from exhaust fumes that are taken into the atmosphere and then are brought back down to earth in rain. A smokestack that releases hazardous gasses into the air might very well be responsible for acid rain many miles away, but it would be hard to identify the source if the factory was a sufficient distance from the site of the rainfall event.

How do pollutants affect the world around us? An oil spill renders seabirds flightless, because the oil coats their feathers. Oil makes areas of waterfront land uninhabitable, and some animals (turtles) bury eggs in the sand and thus they are affected too. Metal contamination from industrial processes—like the ones mentioned above as well as lead, arsenic, antimony, and cadmium—are by-products of the manufacturing of many types of goods. It turns out that chemicals contained in oil and gasoline are carcinogenic, which means they can cause cancer. The metals, known as heavy metals, can cause damage to many organs in one's body, most notably the liver and the brain.

Even "land based" pollutants eventually make their way into groundwater, streams, and rivers. Many older houses were painted with paint that contained lead, and that anyone who eats paint chips from these older homes can develop mental difficulties because lead is very toxic. Mercury is used in thermostats in many homes, in thermometers, and in industry. It is

Young children play near a stream of sewage on a beach in Gaza. © *Ed Kashi/Corbis. Reproduced by permission.*

### WORDS TO KNOW

◆ **Acid rain:** The result of acidic chemicals reacting in the atmosphere with water and returning to earth as contaminated rain, fog, or snow.

◆ **Ecosystem:** The network of interactions between living organisms and their environment.

◆ **Groundwater:** Freshwater that resides in rock and soil layers beneath Earth's land surface.

## Sewage

*In this photo from 1994, sewage is emptied into the ocean near Cornwall, England, where the tide carries it toward beaches. © Ecoscene/Corbis. Reproduced by permission.*

Untreated sewage from humans and animals poses a problem to water sources. Because of limited facilities in developing countries to handle the processing of this waste, many times it is simply dumped into rivers or oceans untreated. These substances contain disease-causing organisms and present a danger to the health of humans and animals.

Sewage disposal is not only a problem in developing countries; in May 2004, the city of Milwaukee, Wisconsin, dumped 1.5 billion gallons (5.6 million liters) of untreated sewage into Lake Michigan, enough sewage to fill 5,000 Olympic-sized swimming pools. The problem stems from Milwaukee's storm drainage system, which is interconnected with the sewer system. After a heavy rain, the storm drainage pipes and sewer pipes both fill with runoff and the sewers cannot handle the extra load. The result is an overflow and Milwaukee water officials were forced to dump the sewage rather than allow it to back up directly into people's bathrooms and basements. Milwaukee officials are studying different plans in order to choose the best method of separating the city's storm and sewer systems.

## WORDS TO KNOW

**Non-point source pollution:** Water pollution that comes from several unidentified sources, such as contaminated rain, runoff, or groundwater.

**Point-source pollution:** Water pollution that comes from a directly observable source, such as a drainpipe.

**Sediment:** Particles of soil, sand, minerals, and animal or plant matter washed from land into water.

also used in batteries, but to a limited extent. Mercury can combine with other elements to form one of the most dangerous chemicals known to man, dimethyl mercury. A single drop can kill a person in less than one month. Arsenic is used, among other things, to make lumber resist rotting. However, the arsenic gets soaked from the wood eventually and ends up in the ecosystem.

## Sources and types of pollutants

The population of Earth is over six billion people, and not all countries adhere to the same regulations about protecting the environment. Before the industrial revolution in the late nineteenth century, pollution of sea water and surface waters was largely attributable to natural causes, such as drought (prolonged below-normal levels of rain) conditions that in turn, led to increased concentrations of various compounds in the water supply. When automobiles and gasoline-powered

Plastic material dumped in the water chokes the neck of a Royal shroud bird. *Anthony F. Amos. Reproduced by permission.*

machinery became available, pollution surged, due to increased output of consumer goods and machinery. Conservation laws in many developed countries have helped to correct pollution in many air and water sources since the time of the industrial revolution. Some developing countries still use highly-polluting products such as fuel with lead components, and environmental scientists are now concentrating their efforts in studying the long-term effects of water and air pollution on a worldwide scope.

Not all pollution is attributed to oil spills, industry, and transportation. Humans contribute to pollution in the course of everyday activities. Washing automobiles, lawn fertilizers, cleaning products eventually end up in the water supply. The soap and shampoo from bathing, disinfectants for cleaning the kitchen and bathroom, nail polish, and the waxes and oils for cleaning floors are just a few examples of home products that contribute to the pollution of the water supply. Lawnmowers are very inefficient when it comes to cleaning exhaust, so the gasses end up in the atmosphere and fall to Earth in rain. Medical products, such as antibiotics contain substances that are helpful to some organisms but not to others, and the introduction of these substances can result in the killing of aquatic life or altering the reproductive cycles of various species.

Based on many years of scientific studies, there are regulations from the U.S. government as to acceptable levels of particular pollutants. For instance, the human body needs chromium, but very little of it, and a person gets it automatically from eating a balanced diet. Iron is critical for making sure

## Ocean Dumping

A major concern of the damage of the quality of ocean waters is the dumping of garbage. It is a common practice to load barges with millions of pounds of refuse every day and sail offshore for several miles, then dump the contents into the sea. Many items in these garbage barges are toxic, such as metals from old batteries and medical waste. Other items, such as decaying foodstuffs, are dangerous sources of bacteria that are harmful for all life. Although dumping garbage far out to sea is supposed to result in natural degradation (breaking apart), various currents, storms, and other physical events often lead to garbage washing back to shore, where it again enters the pollution cycle.

Cholera infested garbage and chemical waste covers a beach in Lima, Peru. © *Gustavo Gilabert/Corbis SABA. Reproduced by permission.*

---

oxygen gets transported with blood cells but too much iron is dangerous. The Environmental Protection Agency (EPA) is a U.S. government division that monitors the levels of contaminants (pollutants) in the ecosystem. Based on studies with animals, plants, and humans, the EPA has determined what levels of many pollutants can be ingested with no proven risk of health trouble. Adhering to these standards is expensive because industries that produce pollutants must buy expensive equipment to filter the harmful chemicals (as well as gasses) from the waters they discharge. The price is passed along to the consumer by raising product prices. This was the case in the early 1980s with gasoline, when adding a lead-based compound to gasoline prolonged engine life. The risks of the added lead outweighed the benefits, and the government decided to ban lead-products in gasoline and replace them with a chemical that essentially does the same job, but is non-toxic.

*Laurie Duncan, Ph.D.*

### For More Information

**Books**

Maclean, Norman. *A River Runs Through it*. Washington, DC: Island Press, 2003.

Postel, Sandra, and Brian Richter. *Rivers for Life: Managing Water for People and Nature.* Washington, DC: Island Press, 2003.

Vigil, Kenneth M. *Clean Water: An Introduction to Water Quality and Pollution Control.* 2nd ed. Corvallis: Oregon State University Press, 2003.

**Websites**

"Facts About Water Pollution." *Project Clean Water, County of Santa Barbara.* http://www.countyofsb.org/project_cleanwater/facts.htm (accessed on September 8, 2004).

United States Geological Survey. "Acid Rain: Do You Need to Start Wearing a Rainhat?" *Water Science for Schools.* http://ga.water.usgs.gov/edu/acidrain.html (accessed on September 8, 2004).

# Watersheds

A watershed is a connected series of streams, rivers, and lakes that collects water from a specific area of land. Watersheds are important habitats for animals and plants, and offer a source of drinking and recreational water for many communities. The quality of the water in a watershed, also sometimes referred to as the health of the watershed, is important to preserve or remediate (to repair after damage). Water quality generally refers to the appearance, smell, and, above all, ability to serve as drinking water (a quality known as potability).

At the beginning of the twentieth century, most watersheds were unaffected by man-made pollution; pollution occurred only from natural sources such as animal waste. Before increased levels of man-made contamination, most watersheds were able to dilute pollutants or filter them out through surrounding wetlands (grassy areas that hold water throughout most of the year). Today, pristine and uncontaminated watersheds are rarely observed. Pressures from modern urban development, mainly runoff of pollution and decreased air quality, make monitoring water quality a necessity.

## Water quality

A number of factors determine water quality. Scientists measure levels of chemicals and observe living creatures whose presence (or in some cases, absence) in water indicates that the

## WORDS TO KNOW

**Deforestation:** Large-scale removal of trees form a woodland.

**Erosion:** Wearing away by water and wind.

**Potability:** Water quality that makes it suitable for drinking.

**Riparian zone:** Narrow strip of vegetation that is found bounding the edge of a natural water body such as a stream or river.

**Wetlands:** Grassy areas that hold water most of the year.

water is contaminated. A well-known example of a contamination is from the bacterium *Escherichia coli*.

*Escherichia coli* (commonly referred to as *E. coli*) lives in the digestive tract of humans and other warm-blooded animals. The bacteria do not usually survive or thrive (exist in high numbers) in other environments, such as fresh water. High numbers of the bacteria in water is usually evidence of contamination by human or animal intestinal waste. Because the detection of *E. coli* requires simple and relatively inexpensive tests, such testing is a fundamental part of programs that monitor fresh water quality.

In addition to the detection of *E. coli*, there are other ways to determine water quality exist. For example, determining the number of species in a certain area of a stream can provide information on upstream water quality, especially if the species do not live and reproduce in contaminated water.

Tests to measure water quality are performed at different sites along the watershed at different times. Repeated test sites and test times are necessary to develop a watershed history. Also, results can vary according to location. For example, a low level of *E. coli* at one point in a stream does not necessarily guarantee that another area is uncontaminated.

Inorganic, or non-living, indicators of water quality (for example, amounts of certain chemicals) tend to be easier to measure throughout the course of the watershed. Scientists often used a combination of tests to determine water quality.

One important inorganic measurement determines the level of nitrates in the water. Nitrate ($NO_3$) is a chemical form of the element nitrogen. Another chemical form of nitrogen, nitrites ($NO_2$), form important compounds that permit the growth of algae and some plants. Nitrate is hard to measure directly, but can be determined from nitrite levels. Too much nitrate leads to the explosive growth of algae, which overuses the available oxygen in the water, crippling the survival of other water species.

The dissolved oxygen level is another chemical indicator of water quality. The level of oxygen in the water can be lowered by chemical conditions or the presence of biological material such as sewage. If maintained, the low amount of oxygen makes the watershed incapable of supporting life.

Other measurement tools measure the presence of other important chemicals in the watershed such as salt (the salinity of the water) and phosphorus (a component of agricultural fertilizers that can enter watersheds via runoff from lawns, golf courses, and agricultural land). Phosphorus is another nutrient that can stimulate the explosive growth of algae.

Some tests are performed because of the location of the watershed. For example, if the watershed is near a mine, then monitoring to detect the acid that can flow from mining activities may be warranted. Alternatively, if the watershed is near a nuclear power plant or uranium facility, testing for the presence of radioactive compounds is often warranted. Watersheds that incorporate urban areas are often monitored for the presence of petroleum. Watersheds in rural areas are monitored for the presence of farm fertilizer and pesticides.

Historically, local, regional, and federal governments conducted most watershed quality monitoring. Increasingly, however, citizens groups and committees are seeking funding to conduct tests. Governments generally support such civic efforts, and training is available in many areas for those desiring to learn proper sampling techniques. The quality of freshwater in watershed areas is often improved with civic awareness and involvement.

## Restoring watersheds

Restoration of a watershed returns the ecosystem to as close as possible to its state prior to a specific incident or period of deterioration. If a watershed has deteriorated abruptly due to a sewage spill, restoration may consist of only a few procedures. When deterioration of a watershed occurs gradually, however, restoration can require lengthy, complicated, and costly operations.

The restorative process includes the remediation of the water quality, repairing the source of the water damage, and repopulating the watershed with animal, fish, or bird species. In some cases, it is sufficient to make the restored habitat attractive to native species and to allow natural repopulation.

Watershed restoration is important, not only for the benefit of the species living in the area, but also for those who will use the water that emerges from the watershed. A contaminated watershed affects all the watersheds downstream from the contamination site. Communities that are miles away from a contaminated watershed can be adversely affected.

Restoration can be divided into two broad categories, reestablishment and rehabilitation. Reestablishment is the

Former loggers on the Olympic Peninsula in Washington work to repair damaged watersheds for salmon runs. © Macduff Everton/Corbis. Reproduced by permission.

alteration of the various characteristics of a watershed in order to restore the site's former function. Reestablishment can involve construction to rebuild physical parts of the watershed. Often, reestablishment results in the enlargement of the total area of the watershed, as acreage that has fallen into disuse is reutilized to restore the former dimensions of the watershed.

Rehabilitation seeks to repair the watershed, not necessarily to restore its original function. Correcting the damage from a sewage spill, for example, is considered watershed rehabilitation. The rehabilitated portion of the watershed does not necessarily function at its previous best (optimum) level. Nonetheless, the short-term damage is repaired.

The restoration of watershed ecosystems is increasing, as the realization grows of the importance of the watersheds to the health of animals and plants that are part of the ecosystem and to the communities that depend on the watershed for their drinking water. For example, the U.S. government has committed to improve or restore 100,000 acres of wetlands each year and 25,000 miles of stream shoreline.

### Risks in restoration

Scientists are increasingly aware of the dangers of not using native plant and animal species during restoration efforts. In many places around the world, the introduction of a non-indigenous (nonnative) species has caused trouble. The foreign species, which may not have any competition or natural enemies, can grow explosively and out-compete the native species. The fast-growing kudzu plant, for example, was planted in the southeastern United States during the 1930s as a means to prevent soil erosion (wearing away). Native to China and Japan, and without its natural controls, the kudzu proved hardier than expected and by 2002, kudzu occupied an estimated two million acres of forest and watershed land in the United States. Kudzu can grow up to one foot per day, and densely covers trees and other vegetation, eventually causing their death from lack of sunlight. Kudzu eradication efforts remain an ongoing concern in southern states.

### Impact of fire and logging on watersheds

The presence of forests in a watershed enhances the capability of a watershed to acquire and retain water. Conversely, the loss of trees, whether naturally due to fire, or deliberately such as the removal of trees for lumber or to permit construction of a road, can have adverse impacts on a watershed.

The presence of trees and other vegetation contributes to the water-bearing capacity of the watershed. The roots of the trees and other plants stabilize the soil. Roots also help retain moisture. Additionally, watershed vegetation shades and cools the ground, minimizing the loss of moisture. Moisture in the form of rainfall is gathered on the leaves of trees and trickles slowly to the soil. The slow addition of moisture to the soil allows the soil to retain more water because the soil does not become saturated (holding the maximum amount of water), as would happen if it were deluged with water.

### The riparian zone

An example of the importance of forests to a watershed is the riparian zone. The riparian zone is a narrow strip of vegetation that is found bounding the edge of a natural water body such as a stream or river. The riparian zone enhances watershed stability and quality because plant roots minimize erosion of the shoreline. A water body that is clear of mud is better able to support fish and other life. The riparian vegetation is also the source of wood and larger debris that helps create pools in the water body. Such pools enhance the ability of the water to support life.

The loss of the riparian vegetation can be detrimental to a water body. Erosion of the shoreline is increased because there is no supporting network of roots to stabilize the bank. Large sections of the shoreline may give way in a landslide. Runoff of material into the water is also increased. The cloudier water will contain less oxygen; therefore, sunlight cannot penetrate as far into the water. The result is a habitat that is less suitable for life. Torrential rains can also lead to flooding because the floodwaters are not held back by vegetation.

**Deforestation**

An event such as a forest fire represents a natural means of deforestation (the large-scale removal of trees from a woodland). Typically, a forest fire does not removal all the vegetation. Rather, the effect is to thin out the forest, which can lead to promotion of future growth by the opening up of space and the nutrient supply created by the decomposition of the tree remains. A natural removal of forests by fire can actually have beneficial results for a watershed.

In contrast, the unnatural deforestation and loss of vegetation associated with clear cut lumbering (removing all trees from an area for their wood) is never beneficial for a watershed. The mass loss of vegetation often lowers. Loss of surrounding forest can also alter the movement of water through the watershed. A healthy watershed will have a fairly constant rate of water movement. Without the water retention provided by forests, rainfall can result in flooding.

A fluctuating water supply can also be a serious concern when a watershed supplies drinking water for communities. As a result, many communities are passing legislation to protect their watersheds. Development, logging and road construction are restricted or kept to a minimum in the watershed zone. If houses are built, often barriers to minimize erosion and runoff (excess water that does not soak into the soil) must be maintained. Some communities require riparian zones to remain undisturbed before and after construction.

*Brian D. Hoyle, Ph.D.*

## For More Information

### Books
United States Department of the Interior. *Wetlands and Groundwater in the US.* Washington, DC: Library of Congress, 1994.

### Websites
"Monitoring and Assessing Water Quality." *United States Environmental Protection Agency.* http://www.epa.gov/owow/monitoring (accessed on September 8, 2004).

"What is Restoration?" *United States Environmental Protection Agency.* http://www.epa.gov/owow/wetlands/restore/defs.html (accessed on September 8, 2004).

Wheeling Jesuit University/NASA Classroom of the Future. "Water Quality: Methods for Monitoring." *Exploring the Environment.* http://www.cotf.edu/ete/modules/waterq/methods.html (accessed on September 8, 2004).

# Chapter 13
# Legal and Political Issues

## Endangered Species Laws

A species (group of like organisms that can reproduce) is listed as endangered if it is in immediate danger of extinction throughout all or a significant part of its habitat. Fossils show that many plants and animals have become extinct over millions of years. As of 2004, there are about 400 animals and 600 plants that are native to the United States listed as endangered. Over 125 animals and nearly 150 plants are currently listed as threatened. A species is listed as threatened if that species is likely to become endangered in the foreseeable future.

Many species of plants and animals become endangered and extinct naturally, usually due to changes in climate or loss of food sources. However, over the last several centuries, humans have posed a new threat to plants and animals. Human activities have resulted in the extinction of thousands of species. Human activities, such as hunting and pollution, continued to endanger many species. Worldwide, over 1,500 species of plants and animals are listed as endangered. Nearly 200 of these endangered species are fish or other aquatic animals.

### Causes of species' extinction

The rapid growth of the human population over the last several centuries led humans to develop more land. The development of land for farming often leads to clearing native forests and jungles. Clearing these lands leads to the destruction of the habitats of many species. The destruction of a species' habitat may lead to their endangerment and extinction due to the loss of food and shelter.

## WORDS TO KNOW

**Convention on International Trade in Endangered Species of Wild Fauna and Flora (CITES):** A 1973 treaty that restricts international commerce between participating nations for plant and animal species that are believed to be harmed by trade.

**Endangered:** A species that is in danger of becoming extinct within the foreseeable future throughout all or a significant portion of its natural habitat.

**Endangered Species Act:** Law passed in 1973 that identifies species that face possible extinction and implements measures to prevent extinction; species may be listed as either endangered or threatened under the act.

**Extinction:** The total disappearance of a species.

**Habitat:** The environment in which a species naturally or normally lives and grows, consisting of climate, food, and shelter.

**Industrial Revolution:** Period of rapid industrial growth, usually dated from 1750 to 1900, that resulted in a shift from economies based on agriculture and small businesses to economies based on industry and large corporations.

**Marine Mammal Protection Act:** Law that seeks to increase the population of marine mammal species by prohibiting the hunting, capture, or killing of marine mammals.

Human activities that have caused pollution have also led to loss of habitat and the endangerment and extinction of species. Human advancements in technology have increased greatly from the mid-eighteenth century. During the Industrial Revolution (1750–1900) humans shifted from economies based on agriculture and small businesses to industry and large corporations. Coal and petroleum, which cause pollution, powered the machines of the Industrial Revolution and today. Pollution can cause the extinction and endangerment of species by harming that species' shelter, food source, and water supply.

Whether for food or sport, humans have also hunted several species into endangerment and extinction. The dodo, a flightless bird, was hunted into extinction by humans and nonnative animals that invaded its habitat. Between 1850 and 1910, settlers in the western United States hunted the American bison until it was endangered. In the twentieth century, poachers threaten the survival of the African elephant and rhinoceros. Poachers are hunters who illegally kill wild animals in order to profit from the sale of the furs, hides, tusks, or other parts of the animals.

Humans have had an even more severe impact on marine wildlife. Pollution, in particular, has taken a great toll on aquatic animals, because these species are often more sensitive to changes in habitat than plants and animals on land. Commercial fishing and whaling also threatened the existence of fish and whale species. The survival of the Atlantic salmon for example, is threatened in the wild today. Fishing and whaling were some of the first areas to face strict government controls and laws to protect species from further endangerment.

## Endangered Species Protection Act of 1966

By the mid-twentieth century, the negative influence of humans on plants and animals became apparent. With thousands of species facing extinction, many nations passed laws to save these species. The United States Congress passed the Endangered Species Preservation Act in 1966 and the Endangered Species Conservation Act in 1969. These two laws were a major step towards recognizing the need for humans to act in order to prevent the extinction of plants and animals.

Despite the positive step forward of the Endangered Species Preservation Act and the Endangered Species Conservation Act, the two acts did little to prevent the extinction of species. The Endangered Species Preservation Act of 1966 only allowed for

> ## Marine Mammal Protection Act of 1972
>
> A manatee, one of many endangered species of marine mammals, swimming in waters off of Florida. © Brandon D. Cole/Corbis. Reproduced by permission.
>
> By the mid-twentieth century, human activity threatened the existence of numerous marine mammals. Familiar marine mammals include otters, walruses, dolphins, manatees, and seals. In 1972, Congress passed the Marine Mammal Protection Act, a law designed to protect marine mammal populations.
>
> The Marine Mammal Protection Act established a halt on the hunting, capturing, and killing of marine mammals by anyone in United States waters. The Act also prevents United States' citizens from hunting, capturing, and killing marine mammals anywhere in the world, not just in United States waters. The Marine Mammal Protection Act also prohibits the import of marine mammals or marine mammal products into the United States. Marine mammal products include walrus tusks and seal furs.
>
> Two government agencies, the Department of the Interior and the Department of Commerce's National Marine Fisheries Service, share the responsibility of enforcing the Marine Mammal Protection Act. These agencies also measure the number of marine mammals in U.S. waters. If the population of a particular species of marine mammal is too low, then steps are taken to increase that species' population.

animals native to the United States to be listed as endangered. Once a species was identified as endangered, the Endangered Species Preservation Act offered little protection for that species. The Endangered Species Conservation Act of 1969 allowed for species around the world to be listed as endangered. The law also prohibited the import of endangered species into the United States.

## Heightened need for protection of endangered species

Realizing the need for increased protection of endangered species, Congress passed the Endangered Species Act of 1973. After signing the Endangered Species Act into law, President Richard Nixon (1913–1994) stated, "Nothing is more priceless and worthy of preservation than the rich array of animal life with which our country has been blessed."

### WORDS TO KNOW

**Species:** Group of living organisms that share a unique set of characteristics and have the ability to reproduce.

**Threatened:** A species that is likely to become endangered in the foreseeable future.

> ### Endangered Species Act of 1973
>
> The Endangered Species Act is administered by both the United States Department of the Interior and the United States Department of Commerce. The Department of the Interior's United States Fish and Wildlife Service enforces the Endangered Species Act to preserve all land and freshwater species, including the California condor, gray wolf, and southern river otter. The Department of Commerce's National Marine Fisheries Service enforces the Endangered Species Act for all marine species, including Atlantic salmon, blue whale, humpback whale, and the leatherback sea turtle.
>
> The government also works with private landowners to conserve the habitat of endangered and threatened species. The Fish and Wildlife Service and National Marine Fisheries Service use the best scientific and commercial data available when determining whether to list a species as endangered or threatened. This is often a difficult process. Years of study are often required to identify a group of animals as a distinct species.
>
> Once the Fish and Wildlife Service or the National Marine Fisheries Service lists a species as endangered or threatened, they work to create a plan to preserve the species. Recovery of the species' population is the ultimate goal. These preservation plans are the most controversial part of the Endangered Species Act. The most important part of these plans is the preservation of the species' natural habitat. Habitat conservation plans often involve preventing the construction of buildings or roadways that would destroy the habitat of the species.

Under the Endangered Species Act, species may be listed as endangered or threatened. Once a species is listed as endangered or threatened, the Endangered Species Act provides for strict protective action to be taken in order to preserve that species. Recovery plans prevent hunters and fishers from killing an endangered species or threatened species. Landowners are also required to avoid taking any action that would threaten the survival of an endangered or threatened species. Landowners may not clear land or remove water from an area that is a natural habitat for the endangered or threatened species.

One of the primary goals of the Endangered Species Act is to provide protection that allows the population of a species to recover. Once the population of the species has rebounded, it is removed from the list of endangered or threatened species. An endangered species may also be downgraded to threatened as its numbers increase.

The Endangered Species Act has been successful in preventing the extinction of species in the United States. However it has had limited success in population recovery and removal from the list of endangered or threatened species. Over 1,300 species

> ## CITES
>
> Every year, billions of dollars worth of plants and animals are traded. Most of this trade involves the shipment of food, leather goods, and wood. Much of this trade is "harmless," or not related to endangered species. CITES ensures that the trade of these goods is conducted in a way that will not reduce the number of the plant or animal too quickly.
>
> CITES has been relatively successful. Over 30,000 species of plants and animals are protected under CITES. Since CITES went into effect in 1975, no species listed under CITES has become extinct. CITES has not been able to stop the illegal trade of plants and animals. In 2004, nearly one-fourth of all plant and animal trade was illegal. Stopping the illegal trade of plants and animals requires the cooperation that participate with CITES. In 2004, 166 nations were members of CITES. Customs agents for each CITES member are responsible for preventing illegal plants and animals from entering or leaving that country.
>
> Endangered species laws seek to protect animals such as the California Sea Otter. © *Ron Sanford/Corbis. Reproduced by permission.*
>
> In 1963 The World Conservation Union called for an international meeting to discuss the trade of endangered species, and The Endangered Species Conservation Act of 1969 repeated this call. In 1973 eighty nations met in Washington, D.C. and wrote the Convention on International Trade in Endangered Species of Wild Fauna and Flora (CITES). CITES went into effect in 1975.

have been listed on the Endangered Species Act's list of endangered or threatened species. Only 30 species as of 2004 have had population recoveries that allowed their removal from the list.

The Endangered Species Act also signals the United States' participation in the Convention on International Trade in Endangered Species of Wild Fauna and Flora, or CITES. Also passed in 1973, CITES restricts international trade of plant and animal species that are endangered or threatened by such trading. Perhaps the best-known example is a ban on the trade of elephant ivory. The Endangered Species Act lists nearly 600 endangered or threatened plants and animals that are not native to the United States. Under the Endangered Species Act and CITES, it is illegal for anyone in the United States to buy, sell, or trade these plants and animals or any product that contains them.

*Joseph P. Hyder*

### For More Information

**Websites**

*Convention on International Trade in Endangered Species of Wild Fauna and Flora.* http://www.cites.org (accessed on September 8, 2004).

"Endangered Species Related Laws, Regulations, Policies & Notices." *U.S. Fish and Wildlife Service.* http://endangered.fws.gov/policies (accessed on September 8, 2004).

"Legislation." *NOAA Fisheries.* http://www.nmfs.noaa.gov/legislation.htm (accessed on September 8, 2004).

## Exclusive Economic Zones

For centuries, coastal nations have sought control over the oceans near their shores. These countries have also sought the right to control the ocean's valuable resources as coastal nations have long valued coastal waters with large amounts of fish. Fishing is important for food and trade. Coastal nations quickly realized that they must control and defend their coastal waters in order to protect their ocean resources. In modern day, countries have established exclusive economic zones, or EEZs. An EEZ gives a coastal nation the sole right to explore and extract all natural resources from the ocean for 200 miles (322 kilometers) off its shores. That nation also has the duty to conserve and responsibly use the ocean resources within its EEZ.

### Establishing territorial waters

By the seventeenth century, laws governing the ocean began to develop. The ocean was divided into two categories: territorial waters and the open ocean. Territorial waters are the part of the ocean just off a nation's coast over which that nation may exercise any right. The nation in control of the territorial waters may defend those waters from other nations. Only the nation in control of its territorial waters could remove resources from those waters. The open ocean, or high seas, is the expansive, deep part of the ocean. Every nation had the right to travel over the open ocean and remove any resources.

From the seventeenth century until the mid-twentieth century, territorial waters extended for 3 miles (4.8 kilometers) off of a nation's coastline. There were two main reasons for this 3-mile (4.8-kilometer) limit. First, a nation could not claim an area larger than it could protect. Some scholars theorize that this 3-mile (4.8-kilometer) limit developed because a seventeenth century cannon mounted on land could only fire a cannonball that far. Therefore even nations without a strong navy could easily defend the ocean for 3 miles (4.8 kilometers). Second, the 3-mile (4.8-kilometer) limit supplied most coastal nations with all of the ocean resources that they needed. Until the twentieth century, the main resources that nations took from the oceans were fish and whales. Usually an abundant supply of fish could be found within 3 miles (4.8 kilometers) of the coast. If a sufficient supply of fish or whales were not within that limit, that nation's fishermen or whales could easily travel out into the open ocean.

By the mid-twentieth century, new technology allowed fishing vessels to travel thousands of miles and remain at sea for months. This led to overfishing (catching fish at a greater rate than they can breed) and overwhaling in many areas. With fish stocks dwindling, coastal nations sought protection beyond the traditional 3 miles (4.8 kilometers) limit.

Oil and natural gas exploration on the seabed also led many nations to look beyond their territorial waters. New technology allowed nations to extract oil and gas from the seabed. Most of this oil and gas lay under the continental shelf and beyond the 3-mile (4.8 kilometer) limit. In 1945, the United States became the first country to abandon the 3-mile (4.8 kilometer) limit. President Harry S. Truman (1884–1972) declared that the United States had the right to all of the ocean resources that existed on the continental shelf. A continental shelf is a gently sloping, underwater plain that quickly drops off to the deep open ocean sea floor.

Many nations followed the United States' lead and abandoned the traditional 3-mile (4.8 kilometer) limit. Like the United States, some nations claimed all resources on their continental shelves. Some nations extended their territorial waters to 12 miles (19.3 kilometers), and others claimed a 200-mile (322-kilometer) zone.

## United Nations and the Law of the Sea

By the 1960s it was apparent that nations would not give up their claims to additional ocean resources. Demand now outpaced supply for fish, minerals, oil, and gas. The United Nations stepped in to help establish a consistent system of ocean resource management. The United Nations is an international organization of nations established in 1945 designed to promote peace and security.

### WORDS TO KNOW

**Continental shelf:** The edge of a continent that gently slopes in relatively shallow water before dropping off steeply to the great depths of the open ocean.

**Territorial waters:** Ocean waters governed by a nation; territorial waters in most countries extend for 12 miles from a nation's coastline.

**United Nations:** Established in 1945, the United Nations is an organization of most of the countries of the world designed to promote peace and security.

In 1973 the United Nations held the Third United Nations Conference on the Law of the Sea. The conference aimed to settle issues of navigation rights and dividing the ocean's resources. In 1982 the conference resulted in the United Nations Convention on the Law of the Sea, which set laws for how nations could use the oceans. Perhaps the most groundbreaking part of the United Nations Convention of the Law of the Sea was its establishment of EEZs.

Some ocean resources lie in the open ocean. Open ocean resources are resources that do not lie within any nation's EEZ. Resources in the open ocean are considered to belong to every nation. Therefore any nation may extract resources from the open ocean.Occasionally, two nations will have EEZs that overlap. When this occurs, those nations may enter into agreements on sharing the resources within that EEZ, or the United Nations may redraw the lines for those nations' EEZs.

The Law of the Seas also allows for transit passage of naval ships through the territorial waters of another country. Transit passage means that a naval vessel may pass through the territorial water of another country if the ship does so innocently and quickly. Without the right of transit passage, naval and even merchant ships could be forced to travel thousands of miles (kilometers) as a detour to avoid another country's territorial waters.

Many nations that claim all of the resources found on their continental shelves opposed the 200-mile (322-kilometer) EEZ limit. The continental shelf extended beyond 200 miles (322 kilometers) from the shore in some places. A compromise was made at the Third United Nations Conference on the Law of the Sea that allowed a nation to extend its EEZ up to 350 miles (563 kilometers) to the edge of its continental shelf.

Exclusive economic zones benefit coastal nations. Most of the ocean's resources lie on continental shelves and an estimated 87% of undersea oil and gas reserves fall under the EEZ of some nation. Almost all of the world's fishing grounds also fall within an EEZ, but some nations, including the United States, have not ratified (approved and adopted) the Law of the Sea. Opponents argue that the Law of the Sea could provide the United Nations with authority over waters that a nation considers in its domain. Nevertheless, the United States in 1983 enacted its own exclusive economic zone proclamation similar to those under the Law of the Sea, establishing a 200-mile (322 kilometer) economic zone in most coastal waters.

*Joseph P. Hyder*

## For More Information

### Books
Birnie, Patricia W. and Alan E. Boyle. *International Law and the Environment.* New York: Oxford University Press, 2002.

### Websites
"Exclusive Economic Zones." *United Nations Atlas of the Oceans.* http://www.oceansatlas.org/servlet/CDSServlet?status=ND0xMjI3MSY3PWVuJjYxPSomNjU9a29z (accessed on September 1, 2004).

United Nations. "United Nations Convention on the Law of the Sea." *United Nations Division for Ocean Affairs and the Law of the Sea.* http://www.un.org/Depts/los/convention_agreements/convention_overview_convention.htm (accessed on September 1, 2004).

# Fishing, Commercial Regulation (Fresh and Salt Water)

Fishing regulations are government restrictions on where and how fish may be caught. Typically fishing regulations address the time of year, place, and how many fish of a certain type of fish may be caught. Commercial fishers have to follow many fishing regulations. A commercial fisher is a company that seeks to make a profit from the sale of fish.

## Commercial fishing regulations are necessary

Worldwide, one out of every five people relies on fish as their primary source of protein. A decrease in fish populations could lead to malnutrition in human populations. Fishing is also economically important, as over 200 million people work in the fishing industry. Fishing regulation seek to minimize the decrease in fish populations and harm done to the ocean environment.

**Overfishing.** Until the mid-1800s humans did not have the ability or the need to catch extremely large numbers of fish. Advancements in fishing capabilities and technology changed this situation. In the mid-nineteenth century, steam powered ships began to replace sailboats. Steam ships could travel faster and remain at sea for long periods, catching more fish than sailboats. In the twentieth century, diesel powered ships replaced steam ships. Diesel ships could travel faster and farther than steam ships. Steel and iron replaced wood as the primary build-

## WORDS TO KNOW

**Biodiversity:** The variety of living organisms and the ecosystems in which they occur.

**Coral reef:** Tropical marine feature created by numerous colonies of tiny coral animals; coral reefs contain a great diversity of marine animals

**Ecosystem:** Community of plants, animals, and other organisms that interact with each other and with their physical environment

**Fishing regulation:** Restrictions placed on where, when, and how fish may be caught.

**Food chain:** Relationship of organisms in an ecosystem in which each member species feeds on other species.

**Overfishing:** Catching a species of fish faster than it can naturally reproduce resulting in a decline in the overall population of that species.

**Species:** Group of organisms that have a unique set of characteristics, such as body shape and behavior, and are capable of reproducing with each other and producing offspring.

**United Nations:** An association of countries founded in 1945 that is devoted to the promotion of peace, security, and cooperation between nations.

ing material for ships after about 1850. The use of steel and iron allowed ship builders to make larger ships capable of storing more catch. By 1950 fishing ships had become large, fast ships that could remain at sea for months at a time. These fishing ships used refrigeration to keep their enormous catches fresh for the voyage home. The invention of refrigeration and freezing units also allowed fish to be sent to areas far inland. Before refrigeration, only people who lived close to the coast could eat fish.

The ability to catch larger numbers of fish and the increased market proved to be an unfortunate combination for many species of fish. In the 1990s the populations of cod, haddock, and flounder in the North Atlantic Ocean fell by over 90%. Cod fishing off the Canadian waters was restricted by law in order to encourage the species to rebound in numbers but as of 2004, the cod population had not recovered.

Overfishing is one of the largest threats to the ocean ecosystem in the twenty-first century. An ecosystem is a community of plants, animals, and other organisms that interact with each other and with their physical environment. Overfishing occurs when fish are caught faster than they can reproduce. Overfishing results in a loss in number of fish and threatens many species of fish with extinction (disappearance). A species is a group of organisms that have a unique set of characteristics, such as body shape and behavior, and that can reproduce. Around the world, scientists estimate that more than half of all fish species that humans use for food are overfished.

Overfishing also contributes to the destruction of habitat. Many fishing methods destroy coral reefs. A coral reef is a tropical marine feature created by numerous colonies of tiny coral animals. Many different species of fish live in coral reefs. Once a coral reef is destroyed many marine animals die.

**Pollution.** Pollution also threaten many species of fish with extinction. Pollution destroys or alters the habitats of many species of fish. This kills fish, because they lose their sources of food, shelter, and protection.

Despite regulations to control ocean pollution adopted by most developing countries, pollution still threatens the survival of many species of fish. Pollution usually does not directly kill most species of fish. Pollution destroys food sources that the fish rely on for survival. When the primary food source for a species decreases, the population of that fish species will also decrease. The decrease in food supply also forces the surviving members of that species to look for food in new areas. This may put that species in competition with other fish species for the same food supply.

## Destruction of coral reefs

Coral reefs are an important habitat for many marine species. Coral reefs abound with many different species of marine plants and animals. Coral reefs only cover about 0.2% of the world's oceans, yet they contain 25% of the marine plant and animal species. Most of the world's large coral reefs lie near Australia, the United States, and in the Caribbean.

Overfishing has had a major impact on coral reefs. Commercial fishing operations naturally want to go to the places where they can catch the most fish, and often choose to fish near coral reefs. Coral reef ecosystems evolved over millions of years to achieve a balance within the food chain. When overfishing upsets this ecosystem, the entire coral reef ecosystem could collapse. Some of the world's most sensitive coral reefs are in developing nations with few fishing regulations. In these nations, commercial fishers often use dynamite to create an explosion on the bottom of the reef, stunning vast numbers of fish and causing them to float to the water surface for an easy catch. Dynamite fishing destroys plants and coral, as well as fish.

## Fishing regulations

Overfishing, pollution, and loss of habitat all contribute to a dangerously quick decrease in fish populations. A population decrease of a particular species may strain the population (reduce the numbers) of other fish species. Each marine animal plays an important part in the food chain, which is an important factor for biodiversity (variety of living organisms). The food chain is a sequence of organisms in an ecosystem in which each member feeds on the member below it. The animals near the top of the food chain rely on the animals near the middle of the food chain for food.

In order to prevent overfishing, in the 1990s, the United Nations and individual nations began to take action. The United Nations is an association of countries founded in 1945 that is devoted to the promotion of peace, security, and cooperation between nations. The United Nations and many countries began to pass two types of commercial fishing resolutions: no-take zones and fishing limits.

**No-take zones.** A no-take zone is an area of the sea where no fishing may take place. No-take zones are usually created to protect a certain species of fish in its natural habitat. The

United Nations has had limited success in establishing no-take zones, also called marine protection areas, due to the numbers of countries who oppose them because the country's citizens depend on fishing for their living. As a result of this opposition, less than 1% of the world's oceans are included in a United Nations Marine Protection Area.

In some areas where no-take zones have been established, certain fish populations have recovered quickly. In the Florida Keys National Marine Sanctuary, no-takes zones were established in 1997 for the spiny lobster, and for the yellowtail snapper and grouper, both reef fish. By the end of 1998, all three species had shown significant increases in their populations, and the coral reef in which they live showed increased vitality.

**Fishing limits.** The creation of fishing limits has been a more popular solution to overfishing than no-take zones. Unlike no-take zones, limits do not completely ban fishing within a certain area, but seek to conserve fish populations by restricting when a species of fish may be caught and limiting the size of the catch. Fishing limits also prohibit catching a fish before it reaches a targeted size. This provides the fish an opportunity to reproduce before being caught.

In order for fishing limits to be effective, the governing agency must rely on accurate scientific data. Fish populations are closely monitored and if the population of a certain species shrinks, additional limits may be placed for that species. If populations recover, catch limits may be raised for the monitored species. Limits often restrict the time of year when a certain species can be caught, creating a season for the fishing of monitored species. These restrictions are usually based on the breeding season for that species of fish. Fishing limit regulations also create a total weight limit that may be harvested within a season. When calculating the weight, all of the fish caught by all fishers is taken into account. Once the weight limit is met, the season on that species is closed.

While fishing limits are usually set by individual nations, fish do not remain in one place. Large schools (groups) of fish can migrate (periodically travel) over great distances that might take them from the waters of one nation to the waters of another. Overfishing by one country can affect fishing in other nations. The United Nations addressed this issue by passing the Agreement on Straddling Fish Stocks and Highly Migratory Fish Stocks. This treaty, which went into effect December 2001, limits the amount of fish that nations can take from large schools of fish that may travel to the waters of other countries.

In order to prevent pollution and habitat loss from commercial fishing, in 1982, the International Maritime Organization put into practice an agreement known as MARPOL 73/78. Part of the MARPOL agreement banned fishing boats from discharging sewage, garbage, and other substances identified as noxious (harmful) into the sea. Broken and used fishing gear are classified as garbage and cannot be dumped into the sea, where they could hook untargeted fish species or, in the case of some nets, become entangled and damage an entire local habitat such as coral.

### Freshwater fishing regulations

Commercial fishing regulations on species of freshwater fish are not as common as regulation on marine fish. Freshwater fish are usually not overfished by commercial fishers, as freshwater fish usually do not travel in huge schools and large fishing boats cannot travel easily on rivers. Most regulations to protect freshwater fish involve pollution control, destruction of habitat, and limiting catches in specific lakes or rivers by individuals.

*Joseph P. Hyder*

### For More Information

#### Websites

Jason Education Project at Texas A&M University. "Coral Reef Destruction and Conservation." *Ocean World.* http://ocean-world.tamu.edu/students/coral/coral5.htm (accessed on September 8, 2004).

"Overfishing." *The Ocean Conservancy.* http://www.oceanconservancy.org/site/PageServer?pagename=issues_overfishing (accessed on September 8, 2004).

United Nations. "Overfishing: A Threat to Marine Diversity." *Ten Stories the World Should Hear More About.* http://www.un.org/events/tenstories/story.asp?storyID=800 (accessed on September 8, 2004).

# Nonprofit International Organizations

An international organization is a group that includes two or more countries and that operates in more than one country. Non-profit organizations operate for the public good, rather than for monetary gain. Many international non-profit organi-

## WORDS TO KNOW

**Drought:** A temporary but extended period of abnormally low rainfall.

**International organization:** A group that includes two or more countries and that operates in more than one country.

**Karst:** Landscapes and geologic layers that have been chemically eroded by rainwater.

**Pathogen:** Organism capable of causing disease.

**Sustainability:** The use of a natural resource in a manner where it can be maintained and renewed for future generations.

**Wastewater:** Water that must be cleaned after it is used.

zations share the latest techniques and knowledge about managing the water resources of the world. These international organizations focus mainly on improving the water supply, preventing and treating water pollution, and educating the public about conserving water.

A significant part of humanity, especially in developing countries, lives in areas where water is in short supply. Over 1 billion people in the world are without access to enough water, and over one-third of all people on Earth lack proper sanitation facilities, including the means to purify water and wastewater (water used by humans, animals, or industry). As a result, more than 3 million people die each year from diseases caused by contaminated water.

### Reasons for water shortages

In large portions of Africa, Asia, and the Americas, the climate is usually arid (dry). Human life in desert and semi-desert regions of the world can be difficult due to lack of rain. Some regions of the Atacama Desert in Chile, for example, have not had rain for over 400 years! Although few, if any, people live in the Atacama Desert, the overall dry climate affects regions nearby where people live. When rain does fall in some desert areas, such as in many parts of Arizona, the soil cannot absorb the rainwater quickly enough to contribute to the water supply. This results in fast-moving floods that further erode (wear away) the soil surface, contributing to desert conditions. Lakes in arid areas, such as the Great Salt Lake in Utah, sometimes contain water that is too salty to drink or water crops. Because water evaporates faster in dryer conditions, the concentration of salt increases in the water that remains in the lake.

Regions that are not arid can also experience shortages of fresh water due to natural and man-made causes. In karst (areas of soluable rocks) regions, rainwater often does not have the chance to accumulate on the surface, as it sinks into porous (leaky) beds of rock such as limestone and gypsum. Limestone and gypsum can partially dissolve in water, and the water that seeps into these rocks often forms channels (passages for flowing water) and caves. Little water remains on the surface in karst regions, and although stores of water remain deep inside the rocks, technology must be used to reach the water. Other areas of the world with sufficient rainfall do not have suitable technology to purify their water. In some remote areas of India and Indonesia, for example, surface waters naturally contain enough pathogens (disease-causing organisms) to be deadly to some people. Some of these organisms can survive at extreme conditions (such as high temperatures) and it is difficult to disinfect the water containing them.

Besides climate, the most common reasons for water shortages are caused primarily by human activity. Water pollution can occur from both industry and leaking of septic (waste) water into the water supply system. In both cases, the water may become dangerous for the health of the people and unusable for industry. Purification of industrial waste is expensive, and sometimes, economic interests may conflict with protecting the environment. Many developing countries cannot afford proper water purification because their main concern is survival rather than the quality of the environment. Pollution, however, is a global concern and affects people in other countries besides the source of the pollution. People everywhere hope to secure a clean and safe environment for their children, therefore international efforts are underway to reduce pollution in the world's waters.

## Working for sustainable water supplies

The goal of any international water-relief agency is to help to achieve sustainable (able to be replenished or workable for the long term) water projects in the community. International organizations such as the International Water and Sanitation Center, Water and Sanitation Program, Water Supply and Sanitation Collaborative Council, and WaterPartners International help to solve problems in countries where water is in short supply. Other organizations receive the help of the United Nations (UN), an international organization dedicated to promoting peace and security, to aid in water supply efforts. The United Nations Development Program and the United Nations International Children's Fund are two examples of UN agencies that deal with providing relief from water shortages.

## Managing the water supply

In order to achieve a sustainable water supply, it is necessary to carefully manage the water resources that are available. Purifying wastewater is important so that available water can be reused. Systems for irrigating (watering) crops must also be efficient in arid (dry) areas to prevent salts from building up in the soil and local waters.

International organizations such as the United Nations Environment Program- Fresh Water Unit, the International Water Management Institute, the Global Water Partnership, the International Institute for Land Reclamation and Improvement,

## Nature Conservancy

The Nature Conservancy uses different strategies to protect lands and waters than most other international organizations. By working with local communities and businesses, the Nature Conservancy purchases fragile lands in order to preserve the natural environment. As of mid-2004, the Nature Conservancy has protected more than 117 million acres around the world. Scientists then work in the preserved areas to restore native plants and animals, and protect the land and water that they need to survive.

The Nature Conservancy also promotes ecotourism (vacationing without harming the environment) and education about protecting the land and water. Some everyday things people can do to help protect the quality of their local rivers and waters, according to the Nature Conservancy, include:

- Reduce the amount of water used in each toilet flush by placing a jar or container filled with water in the toilet tank. This displaces water and reduces the amount of water that fills the tank.

- Collect rainwater by placing containers where gutters meet the ground. Use the rainwater for watering gardens.

- Install low-flow heads in showers and low-flow spigots in sinks. Some water companies in the United States provide them without cost.

- Use brooms or blowers to sweep patios and sidewalks instead of water and the water hose.

- Inspect home for leaky faucets. One leaky faucet can waste up to 50 gallons of water in one day!

- Encourage family and community to landscape with native plants rather than grass. This reduces the amount of water needed for the garden, and attracts butterflies and birds.

- Encourage family and community to limit the use of pesticides (chemicals that control pests), which can be carried into the water supply by precipitation.

---

the International Hydrological Program, and the International Commission on Irrigation and Drainage help to manage water resources by bringing new technologies for building a water supply, reusing it, and keeping the water clean. Additionally, the Water Resources Program of the World Meteorological Organization predicts upcoming floods and droughts (extended periods of dry weather), allowing scientists to respond before the water becomes contaminated or in short supply.

When irrigation, drainage, and flood control systems are improved in developing countries, then land can be used more efficiently. Farmers can grow more crops, and the food supply is increased. This, in turn, reduces poverty and allows farmers to devote more resources to maintaining a clean and efficient water supply.

Pierce Island, in Oregon, is a Nature Conservancy Preserve. © Gary Braasch/Corbis. Reproduced by permission.

**Pollution prevention and conservation**

Many international organizations are focus on water quality throughout the water cycle, causes of water contamination, and preventing water pollution. Their goal is to protect and conserve the environment by controlling pollution at its source, and to development new treatment processes. These organizations promote environmental cleanup and help restore the natural balance of plant and animal life to lakes, rivers, and the oceans, along with preventing further pollution. Such organizations include the United Nations Environment Program-Water Branch, the International Water Association, the International Association for Environmental Hydrology, the International Commission on Water Quality, the Worldwatch Institute, the World Water Council, and the World Conservation Union.

Water that has been contaminated with pathogens can cause major outbreaks of illnesses such as cholera and typhoid. Organizations such as the U.S. Centers for Disease Control, the World Health Organization, and Médecins sans Frontières (Doctors Without Borders) quickly send teams of scientists and physicians worldwide to care for the sick, identify the cause of the outbreak, and stop the spread of disease, often by treating the water.

When efforts to manage the world's fresh or salt water supplies and environments are questioned or politically charged, international citizen groups such as Greenpeace have sometimes become involved. On occasion, one or more of these citizen groups has resisted beyond established laws, by actions such as blockading other ships or entering unauthorized waters.

## Education

Some international organizations provide education, training, and share research in the fields of water and the water environment. The International Water Resources Association, UNESCO-IHE Institute for Water Education, Water Environment Federation, and Global Water all develop public education programs in classrooms, forums, and businesses to publicize water problems and encourage the public to invest in resolving the world's water needs. WaterWeb also seeks to create a global community, bringing together educational, governmental, nonprofit, and commercial groups interested in water research, conservation, and management.

*Yavor Shopov, Ph.D.*

### For More Information

**Books**

Gleick, Peter H. *The World's Water 2002–2003: The Biennial Report on Freshwater Resources.* Washington, DC: Island Press, 2003.

**Websites**

"Water, Sanitation and Health." *World Health Organization.* http://www.who.int/water_sanitation_health/en (accessed on September 8, 2004).

*WaterWeb Consortium.* http://www.waterweb.org (accessed on September 8, 2004).

*The World's Water.* http://www.worldwater.org (accessed on September 8, 2004).

# International Water Laws and Enforcement

An international water law is an agreement between two or more nations that regulates activity on the seas. Most international laws come into effect after the participating nations sign a treaty. A treaty is an international agreement between two or more nations in written form and governed by international law.

## United Nations Law of the Sea

Until the twentieth century, nations did not have the ability to protect their coastlines and waters for a great distance. Nations also did not require or have the ability to use vast amounts of ocean resources, such as fish or crude oil. For these reasons nations observed only a 3-mile (4.8-kilometer) territorial water zone until 1900. A territorial water zone is an area off the coast or on a nation's border in which a nation can defend and enforce its laws.

By 1850, military progress enabled nations to defend waters far beyond the traditional 3 mile (4.8 kilometer) territorial waters. Modern fishing ships also had the ability to remain at sea for months at a time and catch tons of fish. These developments led many nations to consider extending their territorial waters. After the discovery of oil and natural gas deposits under the ocean floor, the United States, in 1945, became the first nation to abandon the 3-mile (4.8 kilometer) territorial waters limit. Other nations soon joined the race to claim as much of the ocean and its resources as they could.

For several decades nations made different claims on their water laws and how they would enforce those laws. This multitude of laws caused confusion among cargo ships and naval vessels. Realizing the need for standard laws, the United Nations held the Third United Nations Conference on the Law of the Sea in 1973. The United Nations is an international organization of nations designed to promote peace and security. The goals of this conference were to define a modern limit for territorial waters and develop international laws of navigation rights. Navigation rights involve whether or not a country will allow ships from another country to pass through its territorial waters.

After nearly a decade of debate the conference produced the United Nations Law of the Sea in 1982. The United Nations Law of the Sea established a structure within which all maritime activities may occur. The Law of the Sea defined territorial waters as extending for 12 miles (19.3 kilometers) from a coastal nation's shoreline. Nations are free to enforce their laws within their territorial waters. Essentially territorial waters are part of that nation. The Law of the Sea also contained a provision for "exclusive economic zones." An exclusive economic zone is an area that extends for 200 miles (322 kilometers) from a nation's coast. A nation has the right to all of the natural resources contained within its exclusive economic zone, including fishing rights, and oil and gas rights.

### WORDS TO KNOW

**Exclusive economic zone:** A 200-mile (322 kilometers) area extending from a nation's coastline that permits that nation to extract resources such as oil, gas, and fish and to pass laws to protect those resources.

**Navigation rights:** The right of the ships from one nation to pass through certain waters, particularly the territorial waters of another nation.

**Territorial water:** Ocean waters governed by a nation; most territorial waters extend for 12 miles (19.3 kilometers) from a nation's coastline.

**Treaty:** An international agreement between two or more nations in written form and governed by international law.

**United Nations:** Established on October 24, 1945 as an organization of most of the countries of the world designed to promote peace and security.

**United Nations Law of the Sea:** International law that governs the rights and responsibilities of nations and their approach to the oceans.

"Boat people"—Haitian refugees from economic and political oppression—sail on a rickety boat in Biscayne Bay, Florida, as they seek asylum in the United States © *Nathan Benn/Corbis. Reproduced by permission.*

The United Nations Law of the Seas also addressed the right of ships to navigate the seas. Nations with large navies were concerned that an increase of territorial waters to 12 miles (19.3 kilometers) would limit the free movement of naval ships. A 12-mile (19.3-kilometer) territorial jurisdiction zone would have allowed many smaller nations to block ships from passing through strategically important straits, forcing the vessels to travel hundreds or thousands of miles (kilometers) as a detour. A strait is a narrow body of water that connects two larger bodies of water. For example, either Spain or Morocco could have blocked access to the Mediterranean Sea from the Atlantic by preventing ships from passing through the Strait of Gibraltar, which is only 8 miles (13 kilometers) wide. Also, nations made up of many islands, such as the Philippines or Indonesia, could have forced ships to travel thousands of miles (kilometers) to go around all of their islands. Each island would have had its own 12-mile (19.3-kilometer) territorial water zone. To avoid such divisive issues the Convention allows for transit passage through another country's territorial waters with few restrictions.

## U.S. Coast Guard

U.S. Coast Guard vessels patrol U.S. territorial waters and supply homeland security service, law enforcement, and rescue services. © *Joel W. Rogers/Corbis. Reproduced by permission.*

Founded in 1790, the U.S. Coast Guard is one of the five branches of America's military. Besides performing the familiar search and rescue missions, the Coast Guard protects America's waterways and enforces America's laws near the coast. In 2001 the Coast Guard assumed a major role in homeland security. The Coast Guard is responsible for inspecting ships entering the United States to make sure they are not carrying dangerous cargo.

Another Coast Guard mission is to prevent illegal drugs from being brought into the United States on boats and airplanes. The Coast Guard uses aircraft and ships to stop the flow of drugs. The center of most of the Coast Guard's anti-drug efforts lies in the "transit zone." The transit zone is a 6 million square mile area in the Gulf of Mexico, Caribbean Sea, and Atlantic Ocean. The Coast Guard seizes about $10 million of illegal drugs every day.

Another mission of the Coast Guard is to enforce all of the United States' laws at sea. The Coast Guard prevents illegal migrants from entering the United States by boat. The Coast Guard stops these migrants and returns them to their country of origin, unless they are political refugees. Most of the migrants stopped by the Coast Guard come from the Caribbean, especially from Cuba, Haiti, and the Dominican Republic. The Coast Guard also enforces international treaties that the United States has signed. The Coast Guard ensures that other nations do not fish or drill for oil in America's waters.

The Law of the Sea has been modified several times. These changes speak to new issues as they arise. Perhaps the most important change to the Law of the Sea was the Convention relating to the Conservation and Management of Straddling Fish Stocks and Highly Migratory Fish Stocks in 1995. This law addressed one of the major holes in the original Law of the Sea. Large groups, or schools, of fish migrate. Migration is seasonal travel over great distances. The actions of one country could greatly affect another country. If one country overfished (caught too many fish) a large school of fish, then other countries would be affected when the fish moved into their waters. The Convention relating to the Conservation and Management of Straddling Fish Stocks and Highly Migratory Fish Stocks set limits on how much fish a country could take from schools of fish.

The Law of the Sea set up a unique method of enforcement, which is a way of making sure that everyone obeys the law. Every nation that participates in the Law of the Sea agrees to a process called arbitration. During arbitration the nations that have a disagreement go before an independent party, who presides like a judge. After hearing from the disagreeing nations, the independent party decides what to do about the situation. Under the terms of the Law of the Sea, the disagreeing nations are then bound by this decision. As of mid-2004, 144 nations have ratified (approved and adopted) the Law of the Sea. The United States announced a proclamation in 1982 containing some similarities to the Law of the Sea, including a 200-mile exclusive economic zone, but has not ratified the Law of the Sea. Opponents question the practicality of giving the United Nations authority to make laws in a sovereign (independent) country's territorial waters.

After removing and arresting the crew, U.S. Navy and Coast Guard vessels destroy a vessel filled with illegal drugs. © *Airman Jeffrey/US Navy/ZUMA/Corbis. Reproduced by permission.*

### United Nations Environment Program

In 1973 the United Nations Environment Program began to seek ways to prevent destruction of the ocean environment. The United Nations Environment Program helps nations within a particular region of the world solve problems that are unique to that area. The United Nations Environment Program formed the Regional Seas Conventions. The Regional Seas Conventions are a series of agreements between nations. Each agreement has two or more participating nations. Each agreement addresses environmental problems that are of major concern in that particular part of the world.

### Other international water laws

The United Nations has passed numerous other international water laws. The International Convention for the Regulation of Whaling addresses the issue of killing whales. Whales migrate over vast areas of the ocean. Overwhaling in the past 200 years brought many species of whales near extinction. The International Convention for the Regulation of Whaling prohibits whaling, except in limited circumstances. Other international laws under the United Nations include the Convention on the Transboundary Movement of Hazardous Wastes (Basel Convention), and the Convention on the Prevention of Marine

Pollution by Dumping of Wastes and Other Matters (London Dumping Convention). The Basel Convention addresses the safety of dangerous cargo that is transported over the seas. The London Dumping Convention seeks to prevent nations from dumping their trash and chemicals into the oceans.

Another major focus of international water laws is the right to use rivers. Freshwater is rare in many parts of the world. An important river might flow through several countries, providing people with water for drinking and irrigation (watering crops). Over the last century increases in population and economic development have led nations to use more freshwater. If a country upstream uses too much water from a river, then that river might only be a trickle when it reaches a country downstream.

India and Pakistan for instance, have been at odds for over 50 years regarding the use of the Indus River, which flows from India to Pakistan. In 1960, India and Pakistan signed the Indus Water Treaty. Problems have continued however, with Pakistan claiming violations of the treaty by India.

*Joseph P. Hyder*

## For More Information

### Websites

"Regional Seas." *United Nations Environment Programme.* http://www.unep.ch/seas (accessed on September 3, 2004).

*United Nations Division for Ocean Affairs and the Law of the Sea.* http://www.un.org/Depts/los/index.htm (accessed on September 3, 2004).

*United States Coast Guard.* http://www.uscg.mil (accessed on September 3, 2004).

# Strategies for Sustainable Water Development

In a time when water supplies are being contaminated and overused, the need to guarantee that future water demands will be met is very important. One approach to this challenge is to work towards setting up a balance in the use and supply of water. The amount of water used should be less or about the same as the amount of water that is returning to the water source. This approach is an example of sustainability, the use of a natural resource in a manner that it can be renewed or preserved for future generations.

## WORDS TO KNOW

**Aquifer:** Underground rock or sediment layer that yields water of adequate quantity and purity for human use.

**Desertification:** Gradual changes that take place over a region or area of land that ultimately result in the formation of a desert.

**Gray water:** Water that has been used for bathing, in the kitchen, or other purposes that do not generate highly-contaminated wastewater.

**Groundwater:** Freshwater that resides in rock and soil layers beneath Earth's land surface.

**Irrigation:** In agriculture, a process where dry land or crops are supplied with water.

**Sustainability:** The use of a natural resource in a manner where it can be maintained and renewed for future generations.

Strategies for sustainable water development that can be used by communities, businesses, or people in their own homes include conservation, re-directing excess water, and desalination.

## Conservation

Conservation involves using less of a resource. By decreasing the amount of water used, the amount of water that is removed from a surface water or groundwater source is reduced. While this does not guarantee that the amount of water flowing back into the sources is more than is being removed, conservation is a first step in managing a limited water supply. Strategies for water conservation around the home include a person turning off the faucet while brushing his teeth, which can save gallons of water each day, and repairing leaking faucets. A tap that is dripping at a rate of 1 drop every 30 seconds will waste almost a gallon of water every month. Low-flush toilets can save a great deal of water. Putting a brick or container of water in a regular toilet tank will reduce the amount of water used in each flush by reducing the amount of water that the tank can hold.

Bath or shower water can also be reused. This so-called "gray water" is suitable to water lawns or plants. The plumbing from a bathtub is redesigned so it does not drain to the pipe leading from the building into the municipal system. New houses in many parts of the world are being built this way. For now, those in an older home can put pails at the base of the outside drains; collected rainwater is another good source of garden water.

Industry and municipalities are also employing strategies to conserve water. Many industries that use water in their manufacturing processes are cooling and recycling water that would normally be put into the municipal sewer system early during the manufacturing process. Most textile (cloth goods) industries, for example, now use filters to remove large quantities of salt and other materials from water used during the manufacturing process, enabling the reuse of some of the water. Irrigation systems used in agriculture have been improved to reduce evaporation while watering crops. Municipalities educate the public about water conservation methods and enforce laws designed to promote water conservation, such as requiring low-flush toilets in new construction.

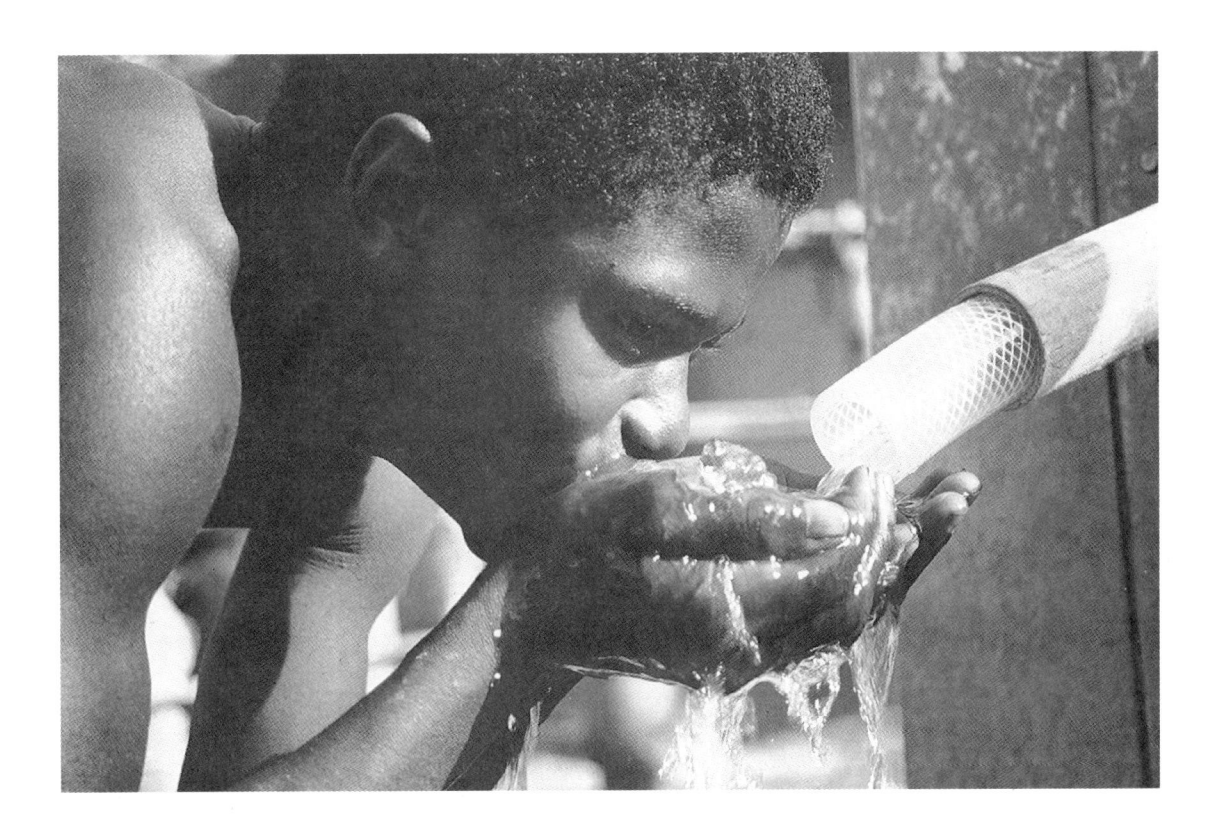

### Re-directing excess water

On a larger scale there are steps that can be taken to help replenish the water that moves from the surrounding area to its final underground location (aquifer). During the rainy time of year water is often taken from a river or other surface water source and deliberately stored underground for use during drier times. In southwest Florida this strategy has been successful. After surface water is treated to remove harmful chemicals and microorganisms it is pumped into an area of the aquifer that is kept separate from the rest of the underground water. This is a safety measure that protects the rest of the underground water in case the added water proves to be contaminated. When needed, this added water can be pumped out and used.

In a similar move water is often taken from surface water sources during the times of year when there is more rain and water levels are higher. Instead of pumping the water underground however, the water is stored above ground in tanks, holding ponds, and other storage areas. Again, the water will be available in times of need.

A man drinks from a well dug with United Nations Children's Fund (UNICEF) funds. © *Liba Taylor/Corbis. Reproduced by permission.*

## UN Role in Sub-Saharan Africa

Forty-seven countries make up the sub-Saharan region (generally defined as the area below the Sahara desert) of Africa. Two-thirds of the people live outside cities and rely on the land and the natural water supplies for their survival. The population is one of the fastest growing in the world, and is predicted to be over a billion people by 2025. Ensuring a plentiful and continuing water supply is a great challenge and priority for sub-Saharan Africa.

As part of this effort, every sub-Saharan country except South Africa has pledged to work towards meeting the goals set out in the United Nations UN Framework Convention on Climate Change, which will encourage environmental issues such as water conservation and protection to be a fundamental part of a country's future policies.

The UN has long been involved with water issues in the sub-Saharan region through the UN Educational Scientific and Cultural Organization (UNESCO). The agency is active in assisting the region battle drought (prolonged shortage of rain), loss of land due to erosion (wearing away due to wind or water), and reducing the destruction of forests by humans. In the sub-Saharan region, poor farmers often burn forestland in order to grow crops for food and trade. In an already dry climate, the loss of forest trees and plants leads to desertification (the process of desert formation). The loss of trees and other vegetation whose root systems hold topsoil in place also results in less water being held in the ground. Areas that were once dry but that could still support the growth of some crops or the grazing of animals become barren as the desertification progresses. The loss of farmland to deserts in Sub-Saharan Africa could soon threaten the water supply for an estimated 135 million people.

### Desalination

Another strategy that is proving valuable in areas located near salt water is the removal of minerals such as salt from the water (desalination). There are more than 7,500 desalination plants operating in the world, with some 4,500 in the Middle East alone. The technique used for desalination can produce water that is near drinking-water quality from sewage water. Although people may not wish to drink this water it is fit for use on crops, which saves water from surface and underground freshwater supplies.

The technique of desalination uses a material that contains many tiny holes to filter the water. Water molecules are small enough to pass through the filter but molecules of sodium (salt) are too big, and so pile up on one side of the filter. Powerful pumps force the water through the holes of the filter, producing water that is almost free from salt.

## Additional strategies for water supply sustainability

A great deal of water is used to put on fields of crops (irrigation). A popular means of irrigation is to spray the water onto the fields. However this method wastes water as leakage and evaporation remove almost half of the water before it reaches the ground. The wasting of freshwater in irrigation can be reduced by burying the water pipe at the roots of the plants. As water oozes out of the pipe, the liquid can be soaked up by the roots. If spraying is necessary, directing the sprayer closer to the crop or dripping water onto the crop can reduce water loss due to the change of liquid water-to-water vapor (evaporation). If channels of water (a passage for water dug into the earth) are used in a field, covering the channels from sunlight also reduces evaporation.

In Chile, a project has adapted a centuries-old technique that uses the plentiful clouds of water vapor (fog) in the mountainous villages to supply water for drinking and irrigation. The villagers string up mesh nets between two posts. As the clouds pass through what look like big volleyball nets, water forms beads on the mesh. The droplets drain down to gutters that empty into a storage tank. This simple system naturally produces up to 4,000 gallons (15,141 liters) of water per day, enough water to fill over 100 bathtubs.

Some public water suppliers reduce the use of water and help pay for keeping surface and groundwater supplies clean and plentiful by charging extra fees for increased water use. This encourages industry and people in their homes to conserve water. Many communities also work to educate citizens about the importance of a sustainable water supply.

*Brian Hoyle, Ph.D.*

## For More Information

### Books
Hunt, Constance Elizabeth. *Thirsty Planet: Strategies for Sustainable Water Management*. London: Zed Books, 2004.

Locker, Thomas. *Water Dance*. New York: Voyager Books, 2002.

### Websites
Napier, David. "Foggy Weather, Bright Future." *Sustainable Times*. http://www.sustainabletimes.ca/articles/fog.htm (accessed on September 8, 2004).

"A Sustainable Water Supply." *Southwest Florida Water Management District.* http://www.swfwmd.state.fl.us/about/isspapers/watersupply.html (accessed on September 8, 2004).

## Surface and Groundwater Rights

Imagine that a group of friends are camping in a hot and dry place with one container of water. The water is necessary for drinking, cooking, and washing. The group must decide the how much each person will receive and for what purposes the water will be used. The individual portion of water is called a water allotment. The laws that govern to whom water allotments are given, and for what purposes water allotments are used, are called water rights. A water right is a use of water or a water source. Everyday, large nations and small communities alike must decide how to allocate their available sources of water. Negotiations similar to those in the camping example are conducted between individuals, cities, and countries to decide who has rights to water on a nation's land or within its borders.

In the United States, all navigable waterways, waterways upon which vessels are able to travel, are considered public. No individual or business can own a river or large stream. Water rights permit use of the water without granting ownership of the waterway. Water rights distribute water in an organized manner, according to international agreements or national, state, and local laws. Water rights allow communities, businesses, and individuals to use a certain amount of water (their allotment). Water rights may restrict where people obtain water, how much they use, and for what purpose they use the water. The goal of water rights is to ensure that many people have access to sources of fresh water and to ensure the sources are protected from pollution or overuse.

The two main sources of freshwater (non-salty water) on Earth are surface water and groundwater. Surface water is water found above ground. Rivers, lakes, streams, ponds, and wetlands are all sources of fresh surface water. Groundwater is freshwater that resides in rock and soil layers beneath Earth's land surface. Surface and groundwater rights cover both the storage and active use of these waters.

## Types of water rights

Just as water is used in different ways by nations, cities, businesses, and individuals, there are different kinds of water rights. These types of water rights are called doctrines. A doctrine is a set of basic rules that is the foundation for laws. Environmental and human factors influence which water rights doctrine a certain area follows. For example, a hot, dry area that is far from a major river will have restrictive water right laws. These laws will usually allow people to take, store, and use less water than areas with abundant rainfall and many streams.

**Riparian doctrine.** The riparian doctrine is most commonly used in places with abundant surface and groundwater supplies. Riparian rights are laws that grant individuals who own the land upon which a water source is located unlimited use of the water. Even in places with a plentiful water supply, riparian water rights can cause conflicts. Examples of riparian doctrine conflicts include water sources located on the land of several individuals in conflict, and people who are granted riparian water rights and exhaust their source of water.

**Reasonable use doctrine.** The reasonable use doctrine is similar to the riparian doctrine. It tries to avoid the problems resulting from competition among owners or overuse of a water source. There are no limits on water use when the supply of water is abundant for landowners under a reasonable use doctrine. However, reasonable use rights limit certain uses of water when water is scarce. Specific laws state how much water should be stored or used for certain purposes. Reasonable use laws consider environmental and human factors when deciding the most important uses for water. For example, during a drought (an extended, but temporary period with less than normal rainfall) water rights under a reasonable use doctrine may limit the amount of water that can be used for watering plants, washing cars, or filling swimming pools.

**Prior appropriation doctrine.** Under the prior appropriation doctrine, the first person to use a water source and claim the water rights, has first use of the water when the supply is limited. The prior appropriation doctrine is also called "first in time, first in right." Usually, the person with the first right (prior appropriation) can use as much of the water as he needs. This may mean that to protect a source from overuse, other people will not be allowed to use the source. For exam-

## WORDS TO KNOW

**Aquifer:** Underground rock formations that contain water.

**Doctrine:** Set of basic rules that are the foundation for laws.

**Groundwater:** Freshwater that resides in rock and soil layers beneath Earth's land surface.

**Riparian:** Pertaining to the banks of a river, stream, or waterway.

**Surface water:** All water above ground, including rivers, lakes, streams, ponds, wetlands, seas, and oceans.

**Water allotment:** An individual portion of water granted by a water right.

**Water right:** Grants a right to use water but not ownership of the waterway.

Groundwater supplies a large-scale aquifer in Arizona that supplies water to many communities. © *Andrew Brown; Ecoscene/Corbis. Reproduced by permission.*

ple, cities or states may prohibit people from drilling wells into a source of groundwater if more water users would deplete the source.

The prior appropriation doctrine is the oldest type of individual water right. It also can cause many problems among landowners. Returning to the camping example, what if the oldest person in the group was permitted to use as much of the water as she wished? Would there be enough water for everyone else?

**Combination of water rights.** Some locations seek to balance water use with water conservation by combining water rights doctrines. Landowners may have rights to the water on their land, but the whole area surrounding and contributing to the water source is also protected. This area is called a watershed. Watersheds are the areas of land drained by a river or stream. Watersheds are protected because use and abuse of water in a local stream watershed can affect other people's use and enjoyment of the river into which it drains. For example, if a business has a water right over a stream and dumps chemicals into that stream, then those chemicals would eventually end up in the river. The river water may become unsafe for drinking or kill plants and other wildlife. Draining and over-use of small, local water sources also can also influence larger watersheds. Due to the movement of water in watersheds, these effects can be felt hundreds of miles (kilometers) away and has made the combination of water rights doctrines necessary.

Areas that govern water usage with a combination of water rights doctrines may allow individuals and businesses to claim water rights under the prior appropriation doctrine when water is plentiful. When water is scarce governments may pass laws that limit water use and water storage. This is called shortage sharing. People may be restricted from using certain water sources or using too much water. Laws may prohibit certain water uses, such as watering lawns or golf courses so that more water is available for irrigation (watering crops).

## Ensuring a water supply

Because assessing the availability of water and assigning water rights is a complex issue, many national and local governments have developed special agencies that administer water rights. In local areas a water commissioner may oversee water rights and regulate water use. National governments may also employ agents like water commissioners but also may have scientists who study, test, and monitor water sources. Sometimes, nations that share a surface water or groundwater source may form an agreement or treaty about how to best use and protect that water source.

In times of shortage some uses of water are preferred. Water rights help make sure that water is put to the best, most necessary uses, but that people have sufficient water. Drinking water and water for crop irrigation are favored uses when water supplies are low. Watering lawns, filling pools, and washing cars are disfavored. When water is abundant, water rights protect the water source while permitting free use of the water by many people.

*Adrienne Wilmoth Lerner*

## For More Information

### Books

De Villers, Marq. *Water: The Fate of Our Most Precious Resource*. Boston: Mariner Books, 2001.

### Websites

"Right to Water." *World Health Organization, Water, Sanitation and Health*. http://www.who.int/water_sanitation_health/rightowater/en (accessed on September 3, 2004).

United States Geological Service. "Ground Water Use in the United States." *Water Science for Schools*. http://ga.water.usgs.gov/edu/wugw.html (accessed on September 3, 2004).

Radioactive wastes and pollution are a long term threat to water quality. The United States and former Soviet Union banned such testing in 1962. In 1996, France conducted the last underwater test near a South Pacific atoll. *UPI/Corbis-Bettmann. Reproduced by permission.*

## WORDS TO KNOW

**Acid rain:** The result of sulfur dioxide and nitrogen oxides reacting in the atmosphere with water and returning to earth as contaminated rain, fog, or snow.

**Environmental Protection Agency:** Federal agency responsible for enforcing laws designed to protect the environment, including air quality, water quality, wetlands, hazardous wastes, and other environmental matters.

**Irrigation** Diverting freshwater from lakes and rivers for use in agriculture to provide water for crops.

**Potable:** Water that is safe to drink.

# U.S. Agencies and Water Issues

Water is among Earth's most important natural resources. All life depends upon water. Humans require water for drinking, food production, and sanitation. People also use water for power production, industry, and recreation, and often people compete for water use. Because water is a limited resource, there sometimes is not enough water to satisfy all of these demands. This problem is complicated by pollution, which can make water unusable for almost any purpose. In the United States, the government has founded agencies that work to protect and conserve water supplies.

## Pollution

Water pollution is one of the most serious problems with the water supply in the United States. Excessive levels of pollution in water make water non-potable (undrinkable) for humans and other animals. Pollution kills aquatic plants and animals, and could eventually threaten plants and animals with extinction (no longer living). High levels of pollutants in fish and shellfish pose a health risk to humans. Fish or shellfish may absorb pollutants, such as mercury. These pollutants can make the fish unsafe for consumption by humans, who could be harmed by the effects of mercury or other toxins in the fish. In addition to health risks, the fishing industry is also harmed by pollution. Fishing is restricted if contaminants are discovered in a fish population.

Additionally, water pollution threatens crops. Many farmers rely on surface water (sources of water above ground such as river or lakes) to irrigate (water) their crops. The water used for irrigation is often pumped directly out of rivers or lakes. If this water contains too many salts or other pollutants, then the water can kill the crops. The pollution can remain in the ground for several years. This may prevent farmers from growing crops in contaminated fields while the pollution remains in the ground.

## Acid rain

Air pollution may get into the water supply and cause many of the same problems as pollutants that run directly into water. Certain types of air pollution can join with water droplets in the air. These water droplets then bring the pollutants to the earth in the form of acid rain. The pH scale is a standard in chemistry used to measure the acidity of a substance. Most lakes and rivers naturally have a fairly neutral pH between 6 and 8. On the pH scale, a pH of 7 is neutral. A pH below 7 indicates that a substance is acidic. Most fish eggs cannot hatch in water that has a pH of 5 or below. Acid rain has reduced the pH of some lakes to nearly a pH of 4.

Most acid rain is produced by the existence of sulfur dioxide and nitrous oxide gases in the air, which mainly come from burning fossil fuels such as gasoline. After falling to the ground, acid rain contaminates the water supply by running into rivers or soaking into the water table (level below the land surface at which spaces in the soil and rock become saturated with water). Acid rain then increases the level of acid in rivers and lakes. Aquatic plants and animals may die if the water becomes too acidic.

Most water systems (including groundwater that seps through soil and porus rock) have the ability to absorb a certain amount acid. Acid is removed as water filters through the soil. If acid rain flows into a river quickly after falling, then the soil has little time to decrease the level of acid. Also, if the acid rain is very acidic then the soil cannot remove all of the acid. When this happens,

### U.S. Geological Survey

The U.S. Geological Survey (U.S.G.S.) conducts scientific research on issues involving natural resources in the United States. The Department of the Interior, parent agency of the U.S.G.S., and other government agencies use the information gathered by the U.S. Geological Survey to make decisions regarding the use of natural resources and the environment. Scientific information gathered by the U.S. Geological Survey focuses on several areas, including natural disasters, the environment, and natural resources.

The U.S. Geological Survey analyzes the likely occurrence of several forms of natural disasters including earthquakes, floods, hurricanes, droughts, and diseases of aquatic species. It then attempts to find solutions to lessen or eliminate the impact of these natural disasters.

The U.S. Geological Survey also analyzes the availability of natural resources including fresh water and aquatic plants and animals. It then recommends ways to properly use these resources.

### WORDS TO KNOW

♦ **U.S. Department of the Interior:** Department in the U.S. government that is responsible for the conservation of natural resources and the administration of government owned land.

♦ **U.S. Geological Survey:** Division of the U.S. Department of the Interior that is responsible for the scientific analysis of natural resources, the environment, and natural disasters.

the acid rain dissolves aluminum in the soil. The aluminum then flows into rivers and lakes. Aluminum is highly poisonous to many aquatic plants and animals.

**Water supply shortages**

In some parts of the United States, the water supply cannot meet the demands for freshwater imposed by people for personal and industrial use. There are relatively few major river systems in the western United States. The rapid population increase in the western United States has placed a tremendous demand on several water systems, including the Colorado River and Snake River.

Industry and citizen demand for water in the western United States has drained the Colorado River to where it no longer flows to its previous outlet at the Sea of Cortez on a regular basis. In 1929 California agreed to limit its use of water from the Colorado River. Growth in population, agriculture, and industry led California to exceed its promised water withdrawal for several decades. In 2003 California agreed to limit its dependence on the Colorado River. California hopes to develop new water supply sources and comply with its 1929 agreement by the year 2015.

U.S. president George W. Bush (right), EPA administrator Christie Whitman (center) and homeland security director Tom Ridge (left) tour a water treatment plant in Kansas City, Missouri, June 2002.
© *Reuters/Corbis*

Many western states are developing new water supply sources. Desalinization (the process of removing salt from water) and new reservoirs will relieve some demand on water systems in the western United States. Many areas still face severe water shortages even with these new water systems. In 2004, the U.S. Department of the Interior projected major water supply problems in parts of Arizona, California, Colorado, Nevada, New Mexico, Texas, and Utah over the next twenty years.

**Water agencies**

Several government agencies work to relieve the water issues facing the United States. The Environmental Protection Agency (EPA) regulates pollution of the environment. The

## Environmental Protection Agency (EPA)

Environmental Protection Agency (EPA) officials employed innovative technologies to tackle the clean up of hazardous waste at the French Limited site in Texas. © Greg Smith/Corbis SABA. Reproduced by permission.

If someone breaks an environmental protection law of the United States, then the Environmental Protection Agency (EPA) may impose sanctions. Sanctions are fines or restrictions that are used to make a violator obey the law. If the violator does not obey the law in a timely manner the EPA may impose additional sanctions including closing down a business or imposing clean-up costs.

The EPA is responsible for enforcing the Clean Water Act. The Clean Water Act sets the level of pollution that water can contain. This protects the environment and human drinking water from water pollution.

The EPA also conducts scientific research to determine current and future environmental concerns such as acid rain and maintaining an adequate supply of fresh water for a growing population. The EPA works to eliminate threats to the environment and find a solution under existing laws. The EPA may push for a new law if current laws prove inadequate to address the issue.

---

EPA enforces laws that protect the environment and seeks to improve the quality of water and air in the United States. The EPA works closely with state environmental agencies to improve local environmental problems. About 40–50% of the EPA's budget is given to state and local environmental agencies.

The U.S. Department of the Interior administers all land owned by the United States. The federal government owns about 15% of all land in the United States. The Department of the Interior manages much of this land as national parks or national wildlife refuges. National parks and national wildlife refuges are areas designed to preserve the environment. Laws limit pollution in these areas and protect wildlife. The Department of the Interior also administers water supply issues in the United States. The Department of the Interior's Water 2025 project aims to relieve some of the water supply issues in the western United States.

*Joseph P. Hyder*

## U.S. Department of the Interior

Nearly one-fifth of all land in the United States is owned by the U.S. government. The Department of the Interior manages and enforces all laws within these lands. The Department of the Interior manages 388 national parks and 544 national wildlife refuges.

The Department of the Interior also protects endangered animals through the U.S. Fish and Wildlife Service, a division of the Department of the Interior. The Fish and Wildlife Service enforces the Endangered Species Act. The Endangered Species Act is a law that lists plants or animals as endangered species if they are in danger of becoming extinct. The Endangered Species Act provides strict protection for plants and animals that are endangered.

The Department of the Interior controls much of the water supply in the United States. The Department of the Interior manages 824 dams that supply water to 31 million Americans. The Department of the Interior also manages water resources for the generation of nearly a third of America's electricity.

## For More Information

### Books
Graham, Ian. *Water: A Resource Our World Depends On.* Burlington, MA: Heinemann, 2004.

### Websites
"Environmental Kids Club." *United States Environmental Protection Agency.* http://www.epa.gov/kids (accessed on September 8, 2004).

"United States Department of the Interior." http://www.doi.gov (accessed on September 8, 2004).

*United States Environmental Protection Agency.* http://www.epa.gov (accessed on September 8, 2004).

*United States Fish and Wildlife Service.* http://www.fws.gov (accessed on September 8, 2004).

"United States Geological Survey." http://www.usgs.gov (accessed on September 8, 2004).

# Water Quality and Contamination Cleanup

For some purposes, it is not necessary for water to be potable (drinkable). For example, the water that is pumped down oil wells to help recover the hard-to-reach oil can have chemicals and microorganisms present. However, drinking water that comes from underground (groundwater) or from sources on the surface (surface water) must meet a higher standard of cleanliness. When harmful chemicals and microorganisms get into the water it is considered contaminated. Contaminants that cause disease must be taken out of the water that humans drink in order for the water to be potable. If not, drinking the water can cause intestinal upsets such as diarrhea if the water contains harmful bacteria, protozoa or viruses. If

Environmental cleanup specialists take readings of air and water near the Rocky Mountain Arsenal, located near Denver, Colorado. © *John Olson/Corbis. Reproduced by permission.*

## WORDS TO KNOW

**Bioremediation:** The cleanup of a contaminated site using microorganisms, usually bacteria, which take in the contaminants.

**Contamination:** Polluted or containing unwanted substances.

**Groundwater:** Freshwater that resides in rock and soil layers beneath Earth's land surface.

**In situ:** In place.

**Potable** Water that is safe to drink.

the contaminant is a compound such as mercury or lead, then the water can be poisonous. For example, mercury-laden water can cause nervous system difficulties.

## Water contamination

Because many different types of chemicals can dissolve in water, water is easily contaminated. Many communities have monitoring programs in place, where the surface and groundwater sources that supply the community with water are checked for contamination on a regular basis. Usually the water is checked for microorganisms more often than for chemicals. This is because microorganisms can quickly enter the water through human and animal body waste. As chemicals generally must move down through the soil and rock to reach the groundwater, chemical contamination may appear in water over a longer period time. Often, chemicals will be filtered by the layers of rock and soil and will be removed before reaching the groundwater level.

Water scientists consider chemical contamination detected in groundwater a significant problem, as groundwater makes up 22% of Earth's total freshwater supply. Breaks in the soil-rock barrier sometimes allow chemicals and microorganisms to rapidly move down to the groundwater layer, where they collect and remain.

Groundwater contamination can occur naturally or as a result of man-made processes. For example, if a cavity (or sinkhole) collapses in the rocky limestone layer beneath a cow pas-

> **CERCLIS Superfund**
>
> Just a few decades ago most people were unaware that a variety of industrial and agricultural chemicals were seeping into water sources and soil. Incidents such as Love Canal in Niagara Falls, New York, when a community that lived over a chemical dump site had to be evacuated because of health problems that developed among many residents, alerted people to the threat of chemical contamination.
>
> In the United States alone, there are thousands of abandoned sites that contain toxic chemicals. Mounting concern over these sites in the 1980s led the Congress to pass an act called the Comprehensive Environmental Response, Compensation and Liability Act (CERCLA). It is more popularly known as the Superfund Program.
>
> The program was designed to seek out and identify toxic sites and rapidly clean up the most harmful sites. The identification process created a database that was called the Comprehensive Environmental Response, Contamination and Liability Information System (CERCLIS). This list of the worst sites is used to decide which sites got priority in the cleanup schedule. The CERCLIS list contains more than 40,000 sites.

ture, then the microorganisms accompanying the animal waste can contaminate the groundwater below. The cavity creates a more direct route for fluids to move down to the groundwater. In a man-made process, an underground tank such as the gas storage tank below a local gas station, can develop a leak. As the gasoline or oil leaks out of the tank, it moves down to the groundwater. Because the tank is below the surface, a slow leak may not be detected until it has contaminated the groundwater. As water moves downward to the groundwater, any contaminant that is on the surface, such as pesticides, road salt, or toxic (poisonous) chemicals buried in a landfill can also threaten the nearby groundwater.

## Contamination cleanup

Several technologies exist to clean up sites that have been contaminated with gas, oil, or other chemicals. Some of these methods attempt to fix the problem without removing the contaminated soil or groundwater. This is an "in place" or *in situ* cleanup. Other cleanup methods require the contaminated soil to be dug up, removed, and the groundwater pumped out of the ground. Treatment is then done at another site. The method that is selected often depends upon the nature of the problem, how urgently the cleanup is needed, the characteristics of the site, and the amount of money available for the clean up project.

Generally contaminated groundwater is pumped to the surface, treated to remove the harmful chemicals and then pumped into a nearby surface water body. The treatment can involve a process where the contaminants are transferred from the water to the air, or passed through filters that remove the harmful chemicals. In some cases, contaminated water can be sent through the normal wastewater treatment process at a treatment plant.

Surface water is more accessible, and so is easier to clean than groundwater. Nevertheless, if the surface water contamination originates from the surrounding land, then clean up can be complicated, and can involve correcting the problem from this surrounding territory.

***In situ* cleanup of soil.** *In situ* methods are usually less expensive than the methods that truck the contaminated soil and water away for treatment. On the other hand, *in situ* treatment is usually a lengthy process.

In one *in situ* method, known as soil venting, wells are drilled and air is injected in the soil. The air evaporates the liquid that contains the contaminated chemicals, making the chemicals easier to remove.

Another method uses microorganisms that occur naturally in the soil or which have been specially designed. These microorganisms (usually bacteria) can use the contaminating chemical as a food. Even radioactive compounds can be chewed up by certain bacteria. This approach is known as bioremediation, and has also been used in some oil spills.

Bioremediation can also occur naturally. If the bacteria necessary for bioremediation live naturally in the soil, the contaminated area may be sealed off and left undisturbed, giving the bacteria time to act. In other cases, bacteria may need to be added to the contaminated site. In these cases, bacteria that have been grown in a watery solution are pumped into the contaminated soil. Over time, samples of the contaminated site are taken to check that the level of the contaminating chemicals is dropping.

**Off-site cleanup of soil.** When soil is taken from the ground to another site to be treated, several methods are used to clean it. Sometimes the soil is mixed with asphalt to encase it. Other times, the soil is spread out in a thin layer on pavement or plastic to let the toxic chemicals pass off into the air. Both methods are accomplished at specially qualified sites, and the processes are monitored to make sure that surrounding air, water, and soil is not being harmed. Another off-site clean-up method involves heating the soil to cause the contaminating chemicals to move from the soil into the air. The air is collected in a device where the contaminants are burned. The remaining soil can be re-used or returned to the original contamination site. Contaminated soil may also be disposed of by burying it in a landfill. This is an expensive option and is not frequently used.

**Ground- and surfacewater treatment by isolation.** When current methods are not sufficient to clean contaminated groundwater, surface waters, or soil, it is sometimes necessary to seal the site off from the surrounding area. This is a measure of last resort, as the area is lost to other uses for generations.

*Brian Hoyle, Ph.D.*

## For More Information

### Books

Hunt, Constance Elizabeth. *Thirsty Planet: Strategies for Sustainable Water Management.* London: Zed Books, 2004.

Locker, Thomas. *Water Dance.* New York: Voyager Books, 2002.

### Websites

Napier, David. "Foggy Weather, Bright Future." *Sustainable Times.* http://www.sustainabletimes.ca/articles/fog.htm (accessed on September 8, 2004).

"A Sustainable Water Supply." *Southwest Florida Water Management District.* http://www.swfwmd.state.fl.us/about/isspapers/watersupply.html (accessed on September 8, 2004).

# Where to Learn More

**Books**

Barry, Roger, et. al. *Atmosphere, Weather, and Climate.* 8th ed. New York: Routledge, 2003.

Bauer, K. Jack. *A Maritime History of the United States: The Role of America's Seas and Waterways.* Columbia: University of South Carolina Press, 1988.

Berger, Melvin, and Berger, Gilda. *What Makes an Ocean Wave?: Questions and Answers About Oceans and Ocean Life.* New York: Scholastic Reference, 2001.

Birnie, Patricia W., and Alan E. Boyle. *International Law and the Environment.* New York: Oxford University Press, 2002.

Burroughs, William, ed. *Climate: Into the 21st Century.* New York: Cambridge University Press, 2003.

Bush, Mark B. *Ecology of a Changing Planet.* Upper Saddle River, NJ: Prentice Hall, 1997.

Byatt, Andrew, et al. *Blue Planet.* London: DK Publishing, 2002.

Cousteau, Jacques. *Jacques Cousteau: The Ocean World.* New York: Harry N. Abrams, 1985.

Cousteau, Jacques-Yves. *The Living Sea.* New York: HarperCollins, 1963.

Cronkite, Walter. *Around America: A Tour of Our Magnificent Coastline.* New York: W. W. Norton, 2001.

Cunningham, William P., and Barbara Woodworth Saigo. *Environmental Science: A Global Concern.* Boston: WCB/McGraw-Hill, 1999.

Davenport, John, et al. *Aquaculture: The Ecological Issues.* Malden, MA: Blackwell Publishers, 2003.

Day, John A., et al. *Peterson First Guide to Clouds and Weather.* Boston: Houghton Mifflin, 1999.

Doris, Helen. *Marine Biology (Real Kids, Real Science).* New York: Thames & Hudson, 1999.

Earle, Sylvia. *Atlas of the Ocean: The Deep Frontier (National Geographic).* Washington, DC: National Geographic, 2001.

Farndon, John. *Water (Science Experiments).* Salt Lake City, UT: Benchmark Books, 2000.

Garrison, Tom. *Oceanography.* 3rd ed. New York: Wadsworth, 1999.

Gemmell, Kathy, et al. *Storms and Hurricanes.* Tulsa, OK: E.D.C. Publishing, 1996.

Gleick, Peter H. *The World's Water 2002–2003: The Biennial Report on Freshwater Resources.* Washington, DC: Island Press, 2003.

Graham, Ian. *Water: A Resource Our World Depends On.* Burlington, MA: Heinemann, 2004.

Graves, Don. *The Oceans: A Book of Questions and Answers.* New York: Wiley, 1989.

Gross, Grant M. *Oceanography: A View of the Earth.* 5th ed. Englewood Cliffs, NJ: Prentice-Hall, 1990.

Haslett, Simon K. *Coastal Systems.* New York: Routledge, 2000.

Josephs, David. *Lakes, Ponds, and Temporary Pools.* New York: Franklin Watts, 2000.

Kennett, James. *Marine Geology.* Upper Saddle River, NJ: Prentice-Hall, 1981.

Kozloff, Eugene. *Invertebrates.* Philadelphia: Saunders College Publishing, 1990.

Levinton, Jeffrey S. *Marine Biology: Function, Biodiversity, Ecology.* 2nd ed. New York: Oxford University Press, 2001.

Marek, Lee, and Lynn Brunelle. *Soakin' Science.* Toronto: Somerville House, 2000.

Marx, Robert F. *The Underwater Dig: An Introduction to Marine Archaeology.* 2nd ed. Oakland, CA: Pisces Books, 1990.

McLeish, Ewan. *Wetlands.* New York: Thomson Learning, 1996.

McManners, Hugh. *Water Sports: An Outdoor Adventure Handbook.* New York: DK Publishers, 1997.

McPhee, John. *The Control of Nature.* New York: Farrar, Straus and Giroux, 1989.

Morgan, Sally, and Pauline Lalor. *Ocean Life.* New York: PRC Publishing Ltd., 2000.

National Audubon Society. *National Audubon Society Pocket Guide to Clouds and Storms.* New York: Knopf, 1995.

Pielou, E.C. *A Naturalist's Guide to the Arctic.* Chicago: University of Chicago Press, 1995.

Pipkin, Bernard W. *Geology and the Environment.* St. Paul, MN: West Publishing Company, 1994.

Postel, Sandra, and Brian Richter. *Rivers for Life: Managing Water for People and Nature.* Washington, DC: Island Press, 2003.

Raven, Peter H., Linda R. Berg, and George B. Johnson. *Environment.* 2nd ed. Fort Worth, TX: Saunders College Publishing, 1998.

Rowland-Entwistle, Theodore. *Rivers and Lakes.* Morristown, NJ: Silver Burdett Press, 1987.

Sayre, April Pulley. *Lake and Pond.* New York: Twenty-First Century Books, 1996.

Sayre, April Pulley. *River and Stream.* New York: Twenty-First Century Books, 1996.

Sayre, April Pulley. *Wetland.* New York: Twenty-First Century Books, 1996.

Steele, Philip W. *Changing Coastlines (Earth's Changing Landscape).* Minneapolis: Smart Apple Media, 2004.

*Sunk! Exploring Underwater Archaeology.* Minneapolis: Runestone Press, 1994.

Taylor, Leighton. *Aquariums: Windows to Nature.* New York: Prentice Hall, 1993.

U.S. Department of the Interior. *Wetlands and Groundwater in the U.S.* Washington, DC: Library of Congress, 1994.

U.S. Environmental Protection Agency. *The Water Sourcebooks: K-12.* Washington, DC: USEPA, 2000.

Vasquez, Tim. *Weather Forecasting Handbook.* 5th ed. Austin, TX: Weather Graphics Technologies, 2002.

**Websites**

"About Ecology." *Ecology.com.* http://www.ecology.com (accessed on October 7, 2004).

"About Water Levels, Tides and Currents." *NOAA/NOS Center for Operational Oceanographic Products and Services* http://www.co-ops.nos.noaa.gov/about2.html (accessed on October 7, 2004).

"Boston Museum of Science. Water on the Move." *Oceans Alive.* http://www.mos.org/oceans/motion/index.html (accessed on October 7, 2004).

"Chapter 8a. Physical Properties of Water." *PhysicalGeography.net.* http://www.physicalgeography.net/fundamentals/8a.html (accessed on October 7, 2004).

"Chemistry Tutorial. The Chemistry of Water." *Biology Project. University of Arizona.* http://www.biology.arizona.edu/biochemistry/tutorials/chemistry/page3.html (accessed on October 7, 2004).

"Conservation: Fresh Water." *National Geographic.com.* http://magma.nationalgeographic.com/education/gaw/frwater (accessed on October 7, 2004).

"The Hydrologic Cycle: Online Meteorology Guide." *WW2010 Department of Atmospheric Sciences. University of Illinois at Urbana-Champagne.* http://ww2010.atmos.uiuc.edu/(Gh)/guides/mtr/hyd/home.rxml (accessed on October 7, 2004).

"Meteorology, the Online Guides." *Weather World 2010, University of Illinois at Urbana-Champagne Department of Atmospheric Sciences.* http://ww2010.atmos.uiuc.edu/(Gh)/guides/mtr/home.rxml (accessed on October 7, 2004).

"National Weather Service Climate Prediction Center." National Oceanic and Atmospheric Administration. http://www.cpc.ncep.noaa.gov/ (accessed on October 7, 2004).

"National Weather Service." *National Oceanic and Atmospheric Administration.* http://www.nws.noaa.gov/ (accessed on October 7, 2004).

"National Weather Service, Tropical Prediction Center." *National Hurricane Center.* http://www.nhc.noaa.gov (accessed on October 7, 2004).

"NOAA National Ocean Service. Marine Navigation." *National Oceanic and Atmospheric Administration.* http://oceanservice.noaa.gov/topics/navops/marinenav/welcome.html (accessed on October 7, 2004).

"An Ocean of Sound." *Oceanlink.* http://oceanlink.island.net/oinfo/acoustics/acoustics.html (accessed on October 7, 2004).

Shaner, Stephen W. "A Brief History of Marine Biology and Oceanography." *University of California Extension Center for*

*Media and Independent Learning.* http://www.meer.org/mbhist.htm (accessed on October 7, 2004).

"This Dynamic Earth: The Story of Plate Tectonics." *U.S. Geological Survey (USGS).* http://pubs.usgs.gov/publications/text/dynamic.html (accessed on October 7, 2004).

U.S. Environmental Protection Agency. "How to Conserve Water and Use It Effectively." *Cleaner Water Through Conservation.* http://www.epa.gov/watrhome/you/chap3.html (accessed on October 7, 2004).

U.S. Geological Survey. "Water Basics." *Water Science for Schools.* http://ga.water.usgs.gov/edu/mwater.html (accessed on October 7, 2004).

"Water Resources of the United States." *U.S. Geological Survey.* http://water.usgs.gov (accessed on October 7, 2004).

# Index

*Italic type indicates volume number;* **boldface** *indicates main entries and their page numbers; illustrations are marked by (ill.).*

## A

Abalone, *1:* 71
Abbey, Edward, *3:* 450
Abiotic part, *2:* 237
Abyssal plains, *1:* 52
Abyssopelagic zone, *1:* 66, 68–69
Acid deposition, *3:* **377.** *See also* Acid rain
　corrosion due to, *3:* 379 (ill.), 382
　in forests, *3:* 381, 382 (ill.)
　in lakes and rivers, *3:* 379–80
　in oceans, *3:* 380–81
　sources of, *3:* 378–79
Acid mine drainage, *2:* 228–29
**Acid rain,** *3:* **377–83,** 458, 503–4 (ill.). *See also* Acid deposition
　art and, *3:* 378, 379 (ill.)
　pH scale and, *3:* 377–78
Acid Rain Program (EPA), *3:* 382
Acidic substances, *3:* 377
Acoustic tomography, *2:* 272
Active volcanoes, *1:* 55
Adirondack Mountains, acid deposition in, *3:* 380

Advanced Marine Biological Systems (AMBS) program, *1:* 75
Aeration systems, *2:* 234
Africa
　rivers in, *1:* 128
　savannah in, *1:* 175
Agar, *1:* 64
Agricultural runoff, *2:* 228
**Agriculture**
　overuse in, *3:* 435
　runoff in, *3:* 429
　**water use in,** *2:* **275–78,** 320; *3:* 454–55
Aguellas Current, *1:* 36
Aircraft, danger of ice on, *1:* 180
Air currents, *1:* 194, 196
Air mass, *1:* 197
Air pollution, *1:* 118, 146; *2:* 325
Alaskan gold rush, *1:* 129–30
Aleutian Islands, *1:* 55
Alexandria (Egypt), *2:* 220, 252, 252 (ill.), 363, 368
Algae
　blue-green, *3:* 395
　brown, *1:* 62; *2:* 280
　defined, *2:* 257
　in estuaries, *1:* 143

　in lakes and ponds, *1:* 106, 123
　red, *1:* 63–64
　in rivers, *1:* 102
　size of, *1:* 62
Algae blooms, *3:* 395–96, 397, 428 (ill.)
Alkaline substances, *3:* 377–78
Alpine glaciers, *1:* 159
Alternating current (AC), *2:* 215
Altocumulus castellanus clouds, *1:* 181
Altocumulus clouds, *1:* 178–79, 180, 181
Altostratus clouds, *1:* 178–79, 180, 181
Aluminum in water pollution, *3:* 458
*Alvin* (submersible), *1:* 26; *2:* 263
Amazon basin, *1:* 130, 175
Amazon River, *1:* 126, 128, 130, 131; *2:* 243
Ambergris, *2:* 329
American bittern, *1:* 148
American Falls, *2:* 345–46
America's Cup, *2:* 348
Amictic lakes, *1:* 115
*Amoco Cadiz* (ship), *3:* 431, 434

lvii

Amoeba, *1:* 84
Amsterdam, *2:* 370
Amundsen, Roald, *1:* 170
Amur River, *1:* 129
Anadromous fish, *1:* 103
Anasazi people, *2:* 366; *3:* 448
Ancient world, inventions and discoveries in, *2:* 364–65
Andes Mountains, *1:* 52
Aneroid barometer, *1:* 195 (ill.)
Angel Falls, *1:* 138
Angler fish, *1:* 47
Animal Feeding Operations (AFOS), *2:* 228
Animals
  in arid climates, *2:* 352–54
  in estuaries, *1:* 143–44
  impact of sound on marine, *2:* 273
  in lakes and ponds, *1:* 107–8, 124
  in rivers and streams, *1:* 103–4
  in the seas, *2:* 339
  on the tundra, *1:* 156–57
Annapolis Royal (Nova Scotia), *2:* 223
Annelida (segmented worms), *1:* 69
Anoxia, *2:* 355
Antarctic Circumpolar Current (ACC), *1:* 37
Antarctic ice sheet, *1:* 160, 169
Antarctic melting, *3:* 406
Antarctica, *1:* 159, 168, 169–70
Anticyclones, *1:* 196
Antikythera Mechanism, *2:* 364
Appalachian Mountains, acid deposition in, *3:* 380
**Aquaculture**, *2:* **279–83**
  drawbacks to, *2:* 280, 282–83
  economics of, *2:* 282–83
Aquaculture center, *2:* 282 (ill.)
Aqualung, *2:* 357
Aquarists, *2:* 234
**Aquariums**, *2:* **233–37**
  development of modern, *2:* 234–36

in the home, *2:* 235, 235 (ill.)
Aquatic life, *1:* 100
**Aqueducts**, *1:* 98; *2:* **199–203**, 202 (ill.), 205, 299, 366–67
  ancient, *2:* 199–200
  innovations in technology, *2:* 200–202
  Roman, *2:* 201, 201 (ill.)
  today, *2:* 203
Aquifers, *2:* 243, 287–88, 289; *3:* 422
  confined, *1:* 112
  defined, *1:* 1, 109–12, 113
  fossil, *3:* 457
  as source of freshwater, *3:* 457
Arabian Desert, *1:* 175
Arabian Sea, *1:* 183
Aral Sea, *1:* 116, 117–18
Arbitration, *3:* 492
Arch dams, *2:* 204
Archaeology
  exploring underwater sites in, *2:* 251–54
  marine, *2:* 251–54
Archimedes, *1:* 18, 19; *2:* 342, 365
Arctic Circle, *1:* 155
Arctic ice, *1:* 155, 156
Arctic ice caps, *1:* 38, 155, 156
Arctic Islands, *1:* 156
Arctic melting, *3:* 406, 406 (ill.)
Arctic Ocean, *1:* 156
**Arctic region**, *1:* **155–58**
  geography of, *1:* 156
  humans in, *1:* 157–58
**Arid climates**, *2:* **351–54**
  animals in, *2:* 352–54
  defined, *2:* 351
  plants surviving in, *2:* 351–52
Arid deserts, *1:* 176
Aristotle, *1:* 87; *2:* 256
Arkansas River, *1:* 129, 132, 133
Arno River, flooding of, *3:* 398
Arsenic, *3:* 387, 460
Arsenic antimony, *3:* 459

Art, acid rain and, *3:* 378, 379 (ill.)
Artesian Basin, *3:* 457
Artesian flow, *1:* 112
Artesian wells, *2:* 288
Arthropods, *1:* 69, 72–73
Artificial reefs, *1:* 32, 32 (ill.)
Asia
  rivers in, *1:* 128–29
  steppe in, *1:* 175
Asian monsoon, *1:* 183, 185–86
Aswan High Dam, *2:* 208, 208 (ill.), 209
Atacama Desert, water shortage in, *3:* 484
Athens, Greece, *2:* 368
Atlantic bottlenose dolphins, *1:* 75
Atlantic City, New Jersey, *3:* 385
Atlantic salmon, survival of, *3:* 472
Atmosphere, *1:* 173
Atmospheric chemistry, *1:* 8
Atmospheric pressure, *1:* 193, 194, 196
Atoms, *1:* 2, 8, 9
Australia
  Outback in, *1:* 175
  rivers in, *1:* 129
Autecology, *2:* 239
Autonomous underwater vehicles (AUVs), *2:* 262, 263, 356
Autotrophs, *2:* 240, 241
Avalanche forecasting, *1:* 161
Aviation meteorologists, *1:* 180

# B

Backstroke, *2:* 342
Bacteria, *2:* 297
Bahamas, *1:* 58, 59
Bahamian platform, *1:* 59
Baikal epischura crustacean, *2:* 249
Bald maples, *1:* 148
Baleen, *1:* 76; *2:* 329
Baleen whales, *1:* 75, 76
Bali, *1:* 58
Ballast water, *3:* 443–44

Bangladesh, *1:* 184–85
Barium, *2:* 296
Barium sulfate, *2:* 296
Barnacles, *1:* 69, 72, 143
Barometers, *1:* 194, 195 (ill.)
Barometric pressure, *1:* 194, 195
Barracuda, *2:* 349
Barrage, *2:* 224
Barrier islands, *1:* 29–30, 56, 57, 60, 93
Barton, Otis, *2:* 358, 358 (ill.)
Basalt, *1:* 53
Basement, *1:* 52
Basin, *1:* 132
Basket star, *1:* 68
Basking sharks, *1:* 85
Bass, *1:* 107
Bathymetric profile, *1:* 51
Bathymetry, *1:* 49, 86; *2:* 263
Bathypelagic zone, *1:* 66, 68
Bathyscaphes, *2:* 356, 370
Bathysphere, *2:* 358, 358 (ill.)
Baum, L. Frank, *1:* 189
Bay of Bengal, *1:* 183, 184
Bay of Fundy, tides in, *1:* 89
Beach, *1:* 29; *3:* 384
**Beach erosion**, *3:* **383–87**, 384 (ill.)
Beavers, *1:* 107
Beebe, Charles William, *2:* 358, 358 (ill.)
The Bends, *2:* 273, 347
Bengal tiger, *1:* 98 (ill.)
Benguela Current, *1:* 37
Benthic, *2:* 257
Bermuda, *1:* 58
Bermuda Triangle, *1:* 188
Big islands, *1:* 58
**Bioaccumulation**, *3:* **389**, 439, 439 (ill.)
  effect of, on water organisms, *3:* 389–90
  **of heavy metals**, *3:* **387–90**
**Biochemistry**, *1:* **1–7**, 8; *2:* 257
Biodiversity, *1:* 149; *2:* 255; *3:* 442
Biological limits, *2:* 354
Biological limnology, *2:* 249–50

Biological oceanography, *2:* 265, 266
Biological sciences, ecology as part of, *2:* 237–38
**Biology**
  lake, *1:* 116, 118–19
  marine, *2:* 359–60
  **oceans,** *1:* **23–28**
Bioluminescence, *1:* 43, 68, 83
Bioremediation, *1:* 123; *3:* 509
Biosphere, *2:* 238
Biotechnology, *2:* 257, 258
Biotic part of environment, *2:* 237
Birds, polychlorinated biphenyls effects on, *3:* 440, 440 (ill.)
Bitumen, *2:* 303
Bivalves, *1:* 71–72
Bjerknes, Jacob, *1:* 41
Black Forest, Germany, *3:* 381, 382
Black mangroves, *1:* 150
Black Sea, *1:* 119
Black smokers, *2:* 294
Black willows, *1:* 148
Blackbar sunfish, *1:* 44 (ill.)
Blackfly larvae, *1:* 103
Bladderworts, *1:* 106, 151
Blizzards, *1:* 186, 187, 197
Blowhole, *1:* 75
Bluegills, *1:* 107
Blue-green algae, *3:* 395
Blue Nile, *1:* 128
Blue whale, *1:* 76, 78; *2:* 329
Boardwalks, *1:* 152 (ill.)
Boat people, *3:* 490 (ill.)
Boating, *2:* 342–43
Bogs, *1:* 147, 150–51
Boiling, *1:* 21
Bonds
  covalent, *1:* 2, 8
  hydrogen, *1:* 4, 5, 9, 10, 20
  ionic, *1:* 4
Bony fish, *1:* 46–47
Bonytail, *3:* 417
Boreal forests, *1:* 156, 175
Borneo, *1:* 55, 175
Boundary layer, *1:* 102
Brackish water, *1:* 142; *2:* 210

*Braer* (ship) oil spill, *3:* 431
Brahmaputra Delta, *1:* 97
Brahmaputra River, *1:* 184
Braided streams, *1:* 134
Brazil Current, *1:* 36
Brazos River, *1:* 131
Breakwaters, *2:* 222
Breaststroke, *2:* 342
Brine, *2:* 309
Brine shrimp, *1:* 72
British Isles, *1:* 55
British Petroleum–Amoco (BP), *2:* 302, 304
Brittle stars, *1:* 73
Bromine as greenhouse gas, *3:* 407
Brown algae, *1:* 62; *2:* 280
Brown pelicans, *1:* 144
Bubonic plague, *3:* 448
Budapest River, *1:* 129
Bulk carriers, *2:* 317
Bulk container ships, *2:* 318
Bull sharks, *1:* 45
Buoyancy, *1:* 18, 19, 19 (ill.); *2:* 341, 342, 365
Bush, George W., *3:* 408, 504 (ill.)
Butterfly, *2:* 342
Button bush, *1:* 106
Buttonwood, *1:* 150
Buttress dams, *2:* 204
Byssal threads, *1:* 72

# C

Cacti, *2:* 352
Caddis fly, *1:* 103, 107; *2:* 239
Cadmium, *3:* 387, 459
  effects of, *3:* 389
  in sediment contamination, *3:* 441
Calcium, *1:* 24
Calcium carbonate, *1:* 58; *2:* 267, 296; *3:* 381, 382
Calcium sulfate, *2:* 296
California Coastal Act (1972), *3:* 386
California Current, *1:* 37, 38
California Gold Rush, *2:* 296
California gray whale, *2:* 330–31

California sea lions, *1:* 75
California sea otter, *3:* 475 (ill.)
*Calypso* (ship), *2:* 357
*Calyptogena, 1:* 26
Camels, *1:* 8; *2:* 353
Canadian Falls, *2:* 345
Canal lock, *2:* 373
Canals, *2:* 205, 312–13, 373. See also specific canals
Canary Current, *1:* 37, 38
*Cannery Row* (Steinbeck), *1:* 67
Canoeing, *2:* 343–44
Cap rock, *2:* 303
Cape Hatteras Lighthouse, *3:* 385
Cape Horn, *2:* 334, 336 (ill.)
Capillaries, *1:* 10
Capillary action, *1:* 10
Carbohydrates, *1:* 23
Carbon, *1:* 24
Carbon dioxide, *1:* 85; *2:* 267
    atmospheric levels of, *3:* 381
    as greenhouse gas, *3:* 407, 408–9
Carbonate Islands, *1:* 58–59
Carbonate shelves, *1:* 54
Carbonates, *1:* 58
Carbonic acid, *3:* 381
Cargo hold, *2:* 317
Caribou, *1:* 157
Carnivores, *1:* 76; *2:* 241
Carolina Outer Banks, *3:* 385, 385 (ill.)
Carson, Rachel, *3:* 450
Carter, Jimmy, Love Canal and, *3:* 420
Cartilaginous fish, *1:* 45
Caspian Sea, *1:* 116, 119; *2:* 250
Catadromous fish, *1:* 103
Catalina Island, *1:* 56
Catfish, *1:* 130; *2:* 279, 280
Catskill Mountains, acid deposition in, *3:* 380
Cattails, *1:* 106
Centre for Hydrology (Britain), *2:* 243
Centrifugal force, *1:* 87
CERCLA Superfund, *3:* 508
Cetaceans, *1:* 75

Ceylon, *1:* 184
Chalcopyrite, *2:* 294
Challenger Deep, *1:* 49
*Challenger* (ship), *1:* 49, 50; *2:* 265
Chang Jiang River, *1:* 128
Channel, *1:* 134, 136
Channel Tunnel, *2:* 374
Charge zones, *1:* 111
Charybdis, *2:* 333
Chemical limnology, *2:* 248–49
Chemical oceanography, *2:* 265, 266–67
Chemical spills, *2:* 318
Chemical tankers, *2:* 317
Chemical weathering, *1:* 137–38
Chemistry, *1:* 8
**Chemistry of water**, *1:* **8–12**, 115–16
Chemosynthesis, *2:* 360, 371
Chert, *1:* 138
Chesapeake Bay, *1:* 145, 146 (ill.); *3:* 397
Chesapeake Bay Program, *1:* 145
Chesapeake River, *1:* 144 (ill.)
Chevron–Texaco, *2:* 304
Chickasaw people, *1:* 133
*Chiku* (ship), *2:* 262
China, Three Gorges Dam in, *2:* 207, 207 (ill.)
Chinese junk, *2:* 363
Chinese water chestnuts, *2:* 280
Chlordane, *3:* 441
Chlorine, *2:* 298
    as greenhouse gas, *3:* 407
Chlorofluorocarbons (CFCs), *3:* 408
Chlorophyll, *1:* 62
Choctaw people, *1:* 133
Cholera, *2:* 372; *3:* 444, 448
*Chondrichthyes, 1:* 44
Chromium, *2:* 293; *3:* 387, 458
Churchill River, *1:* 129
Cichlids, *1:* 116
Cirrocumulus clouds, *1:* 178, 179, 180

Cirrostratus clouds, *1:* 178, 179, 180
Cirrus clouds, *1:* 178, 179, 180
Cisterns, *2:* 200, 201, 365
Cities, growth of, *3:* 416
Clams, *1:* 71, 143, 145; *2:* 257
Clark, William, *1:* 131
Clean Air Act (1990), *2:* 325; *3:* 382, 505
Clean Water Act (1972), *1:* 121; *2:* 325; *3:* 428–29
Clearcutting, *3:* 417, 468
**Climate**, *1:* **173–77**, 193. See also Global climate
    changes in, *1:* **176–77**
Climate zones, *1:* 173, 174–76
    cold, *1:* 175
    polar, *1:* 175
    semi-arid, *1:* 175
    subtropical arid, *1:* 175
    temperate, *1:* 175
    tropical, *1:* 175
Clocks, water, *2:* 365
**Clouds**, *1:* **177–83**
    altocumulus, *1:* 178–79, 180, 181
    altocumulus castellanus, *1:* 181
    altostratus, *1:* 178–79, 180, 181
    cirrocumulus, *1:* 178, 179, 180
    cirrostratus, *1:* 178, 179, 180
    cirrus, *1:* 178, 179, 180
    cumuliform, *1:* 178
    cumulonimbus, *1:* 79, 182, 188
    cumulus, *1:* 179, 182
    families and types of, *1:* 178–79
    formation of, *1:* 178, 178 (ill.)
    lenticular altocumulus, *1:* 181
    mammatus, *1:* 189
    names of, *1:* 179
    nimbostratus, *1:* 178–79, 180, 181
    nimbus, *1:* 179

shape and color of, *1:* 179
standing, *1:* 181
stratocumulus, *1:* 179, 181
stratoform, *1:* 178
stratus, *1:* 179
wall, *1:* 189
Cloud seeding, *1:* 181
Cnidarians, *1:* 69, 70
Coal, *2:* 304
Coastal development laws and acts, *3:* 386
Coastal ecosystems, *1:* 31, 31 (ill.)
Coastal erosion, *2:* 209
Coastal islands, *1:* 56–58
Coastal marshes, *3:* 415
Coastal plains, *1:* 29
Coastal zone, *1:* 29
  features of, *1:* 29–30
  life in, *1:* 33–34
Coastal Zone Act Reauthorization Amendments (1990), *3:* 428–29
Coastal Zone Management Act (1972), *3:* 386
**Coastlines,** *1:* 29–34; *3:* 384–85
  depositional, *1:* 30–32
  erosional, *1:* 32–33
  processes that shape, *1:* 30
  types of, *1:* 30–33
Cobalt, *2:* 292, 293
  effects of, *3:* 389
  in sediment contamination, *3:* 441
Coelacanth, *2:* 360
Cold front, *1:* 192, 197
Cold War, *2:* 208
Coliseum, *3:* 378
Colonies, *1:* 106
Colorado River, *1:* 131; *2:* 320; *3:* 452, 456, 504
Columbia River, *2:* 207
**Commercial fishing,** *2:* 285, 285 (ill.)
  regulation of, *3:* 479–83
Commercial oyster beds, *2:* 279 (ill.)
**Commercial waste,** *3:* 418–22

**Commercial water uses,** *2:* 283–87
Communities, *2:* 238
Community ecologist, *2:* 238
Community overuse, *3:* 437–38
Compound, *2:* 308
Comprehensive Environmental Response, Compensation, and Liability Act (CERCLA) (1980), *3:* 508
Computer models, *2:* 243–44
Condensation, *1:* 13, 14, 177
Confined aquifers, *1:* 112
Congo River, *1:* 128
Conoco-Phillips, *2:* 304
Conrad, Joseph, *1:* 128
Conservation, *3:* 494
  defined, *3:* 445
  marine archaeology and, *2:* 254
  water, *3:* 445–54
Container ships, *2:* 317
Contamination
  cleanup of, *3:* 508–9
  sediment, *3:* 438–42
Continental crust, *1:* 52–53, 58
Continental Divide, *1:* 132
Continental drift, theory of, *1:* 50
Continental fragments, *1:* 58
Continental glaciers, *1:* 159, 168–69
Continental margins, *1:* 16, 53–54
Continental rise, *1:* 52
Continental shelf, *1:* 30, 51–52; *3:* 477
Continental slope, *1:* 52
Convection, *1:* 13, 14
Convention on International Trade in Endangered Species of Wild Fauna and Flora, *3:* 475
Convention on the Prevention of Marine Pollution by Dumping of Wastes and Other Matters (London Dumping Convention), *3:* 492–93

Convention on the Transboundary Movement of Hazardous Wastes (Basel Convention), *3:* 492–93
Convention Relating to Conservation and Management of Straddling Fish Stocks and Highly Migratory Fish Stocks, *3:* 491
Convergent plates, *1:* 50
Cook, James, *2:* 256
Cool surface currents, *1:* 37
Copepods, *1:* 69, 72, 83–84
Copper, *1:* 24; *2:* 292
Coral, *1:* 32, 55, 58, 69, 70, 85
Coral reef fish, *1:* 84
Coral reefs, *1:* 47, 58, 74
  destruction of, *3:* 481
  exploration of, *2:* 356
Coring (drilling) devices, *2:* 261
Coriolis effect, *1:* 35, 36, 36 (ill.)
Coriolis force, *1:* 36
Corrosion, due to acid deposition, *3:* 379 (ill.), 382
Cotopaxi, *1:* 159
Cottonwoods, *1:* 148
Cousteau, Jacques-Yves, *2:* 235, 356, 357, 357 (ill.)
Covalent bonds, *1:* 2, 8
Crabs, *1:* 69, 82, 83, 143; *2:* 257
Crappies, *1:* 107
Crater Lake, *1:* 120
Craters, *1:* 120
Crawfish, *2:* 280
Crest, *1:* 90
Cretaceous period, *1:* 166
Crevasses, *1:* 161
Cripple Creek, *1:* 132
Crocodiles, *1:* 124–25
Crude oil, *2:* 300; *3:* 430
Cruise line, *2:* 322–23
Cruises, *2:* 321–23
Cruise ship, *2:* 327
Crustaceans, *1:* 24, 72, 83, 99
Crystal, *1:* 18
Cuba, *1:* 55
Cultural eutrophication, *3:* 395

Cumuliform clouds, 1: 178
Cumulonimbus clouds, 1: 179, 182, 188
Cumulus clouds, 1: 179, 182
Curation, 2: 254
Currents. *See* Air currents; Ocean currents
Cuttle fish, 1: 72
Cuyahoga River, 1: 121
Cyanide, 3: 417
Cyanobacteria, 1: 106
Cyclones, 1: 97, 189, 196; 2: 335
   mid-latitude, 1: 192
   tropical, 1: 189–92

# D

Daldsterben, 3: 382
**Dams and reservoirs**, 1: 13, 16, 113, 127; 2: **203–9**, 218, 243, 321, 374. *See also* specific dams and reservoirs
   arch, 2: 204
   buttress, 2: 204
   to control flood waters, 3: 403
   embankment, 2: 204
   gravity, 2: 204
   in history, 2: 204–5
   modern, 2: 206
   petroleum, 2: 301
**Dangerous waters**, 2: **333–40**
Danube River, 1: 129
Daphnia, 1: 84
Darling River, 1: 129
Darwin, Charles, 1: 57, 60; 2: 256
DDT, 3: 441
De Orellana, Francisco, 1: 130
De Soto, Hernando, 1: 133
Dead Sea, 1: 10, 116, 119
Decomposers, 2: 240
Decompression sickness, 2: 347
Deep ocean currents, 1: 38
Deep ocean drilling, 2: 262
Deep ocean sampling device, 2: 267 (ill.)
Deep Sea Drilling Project (DSDP), 2: 262

Deep-sea fishing, 2: 324, 349
Deep-sea submersibles, 2: 359
Deforestation, 1: 130; 3: 393, 468
Delaware River, 1: 131
**Deltas**, 1: 16, **95–100**, 96 (ill.)
   Brahmaputra, 1: 97
   defined, 1: 13, 29
   formation of, 1: 95–96
   Ganges, 1: 97, 185
   humans and, 1: 98–99
   life in, 1: 99–100
   Mississippi, 1: 56, 93, 96 (ill.), 97, 133
   Nile, 1: 98; 2: 271 (ill.)
   structure of, 1: 96
   types of, 1: 96–98
Density, 1: 2
Dentricles, 1: 45
Denver, Colorado, 2: 244
Deposition, 1: 136–38; 2: 363. *See also* Acid deposition
   dry, 3: 377
   wet, 3: 377
Depositional coastlines, 1: 30–32
**Desalination**, 2: **210–12**, 211 (ill.), 309 (ill.), 372; 3: 496, 504
   manipulated, 2: 210
   natural, 2: 210
Desert oases, 1: 116
Desert Paintbrush, 2: 352
Desert Sand Verbena, 2: 352
**Desertification**, 3: **390–94**
   causes of, 3: 393
   halting, 3: 393–94
   impact of, on environment, 3: 392 (ill.), 392–93
Deserts
   arid, 1: 176
   defined, 3: 390
   rainshadow, 3: 393
Developed nations, water use in, 3: 455
Dew, 2: 354
Diadromous fish, 1: 103
Diamonds, 2: 292
Diatoms, 1: 24, 102

Dichlorodiphenyl trichloroethane (DDT), 3: 441
Diesel-powered ships, 2: 311
Dikes, 2: 370, 371 (ill.)
Dimethyl mercury in water pollution, 3: 460
Dinoflagellates, 1: 83, 106; 2: 258
Dipolar molecule, 1: 8
Dipolarity, 1: 9
Discharge zones, 1: 109; 2: 245
Dissolution, 1: 137
Distillation
   multistage, 2: 212
   solar, 2: 211
Distributaries, 1: 96
Divergent plates, 1: 50
Diversion hydropower facilities, 2: 216
Diving, 2: 355–56
Diving bell, 2: 355
Diving suits, 2: 355
Doctors Without Borders, 3: 487
Doctrines, 3: 499
Dodo, 3: 472
Dolphins, 1: 75, 76 (ill.); 2: 257
   Atlantic bottlenose, 1: 75
   Pacific white-sided, 1: 75
Downdrafts, 1: 188
Downwellings, 1: 38–39
Dowsing, 2: 289
Drag, 1: 102
Dragonflies, 1: 107, 148
Drainage divides, 1: 132
Drainage patterns, 1: 133–34
Dredges, 2: 261
Dredging, 2: 221, 254, 314–15
Drilled wells, 2: 289
Drinking water, 2: 319–20
Drip irrigation, 2: 276–77
Driven wells, 2: 289
Drogues, 2: 268
Droughts, 1: 193; 3: 445
Dry deposition, 3: 377
Dry season, 1: 185
Ducks, 1: 148
Duckweed, 1: 106, 148

Dugongs, *1:* 78
Dustbowl, *3:* 391, 391 (ill.)
Dwarf seahorse, *3:* 418
Dwarf treefrog, *1:* 124 (ill.)
Dynamic equilibrium, *1:* 13, 15–16
Dynamite fishing, *3:* 481
Dysentery, *3:* 448

# E

Earth
   highest point on, *1:* 49
   lowest point on, *1:* 49
   water budget of, *1:* 12–13, 163–64
   water on, *1:* 1, 5, 8, 17; *3:* 446–47
Earthworm, *1:* 71
East Antarctica, *1:* 169
East Australian Current, *1:* 36, 64
Easterlies, *1:* 192
Easterly jet streams, *2:* 231
Ebro River, *1:* 129
Echinoderms, *1:* 68, 69–70, 73–74, 84; *2:* 256
Echolocation, *1:* 75, 76
Echosounders, *1:* 50, 51
Ecological damages of oil spills, *3:* 434
Ecological pyramid, *2:* 241
Ecological system, *2:* 238
Ecologist
   community, *2:* 238
   ecosystem, *2:* 238
   population, *2:* 238
**Ecology,** *1:* 80, 113, 149; *2:* **237–42,** 255; *3:* 449
   important concepts in, *2:* 239–40
   as part of biological sciences, *2:* 237–38
   subdivisions of, *2:* 239
**Economic uses of groundwater,** *2:* **287–91**
Ecosystem ecologist, *2:* 238
Ecosystems, *1:* 55; *2:* 238, 239–40
   coastal, *1:* 31, 31 (ill.)
   energy in, *2:* 241

Ecotourism on the ocean, *2:* 324
Ectotherms, *1:* 24, 25–26, 43
Eddies, *1:* 137
Ederle, Gertrude Caroline, *2:* 348, 348 (ill.)
Edwards Aquifer, *1:* 110
Eelgrass, *1:* 143, 144
Eels, *1:* 47
Effluent, *2:* 372
Egrets, *1:* 150
Egypt
   ancient, *2:* 363, 363 (ill.)
   Aswan High Dam in, *2:* 208, 208 (ill.), 209
   shipping in ancient, *2:* 310
Ekofisk blowout, *3:* 432
**El Niño,** *1:* **39–43,** 41 (ill.); *2:* 268
   discovery of, *1:* 40–41
   effects of, *1:* 41–42
El Niño Southern Oscillation (ENSO), *1:* 39, 42
Elbe River, *1:* 129
Electromagnetic spectrum, *1:* 18
Electron shells, *1:* 2
Electrons, *1:* 2, 8–9
Elements, *1:* 8
Elephant Island, *1:* 170
Embankment dams, *2:* 204
Emissions allowances, *3:* 382
**Endangered species**
   heightened need for protection of, *3:* 473–75
   **laws on,** *3:* **471–76**
   whales as, *2:* 331
Endangered Species Act (1973), *1:* 78; *3:* 474, 506
Endangered Species Conservation Act (1969), *3:* 472, 473
Endangered Species Protection Act (1966), *3:* 472–73
Endothermic process, *1:* 18
Endotherms, *1:* 25–26
*Endurance* (ship), *1:* 170, 171 (ill.)
Energy Policy Act (1992), *2:* 307

English Channel, *2:* 348, 348 (ill.), 374
Environment, protecting, *2:* 324
Environmental Protection Agency, U.S. (EPA), *3:* 439, 505, 505 (ill.)
   acid rain and, *3:* 379, 382
   landfills and, *3:* 422
   pesticide contamination and, *3:* 413
   survey of acid deposition, *3:* 380
   water pollution and, *3:* 462
   water quality monitoring, *3:* 418
Epilimnion, *1:* 104
Epipelagic zone, *1:* 66–67, 68
Equator, *1:* 20
Equatorial current, *1:* 40
Erie Canal, *1:* 121; *2:* 312
Erosion, *1:* 56, 136–38
   beach, *3:* 383–87, 384 (ill.)
   coastal, *2:* 209
   development and, *3:* 385–86
   problems caused by, *3:* 384–85
Erosional coastlines, *1:* 32–33
Erosional features, *1:* 161
*Escherichia coli,* *2:* 297; *3:* 464
Eskimo, *1:* 157–58
**Estuaries,** *1:* 29, 31, **141–47;** *2:* 229
   animal life in, *1:* 143–44
   danger to, *1:* 145–46
   general structure of, *1:* 141–42
   importance of, *1:* 145
   plant life in, *1:* 143, 143 (ill.)
Estuaries Environmental Studies Lab, *1:* 146 (ill.)
Euphausids, *1:* 69, 82, 84, 85
Euphotic zone, *1:* 118
Euphrates River, *1:* 127, 129; *2:* 205
Europe, rivers in, *1:* 129
European Union, Kyoto Treaty and, *3:* 408

Eutrophic "dead zone," *3:* 396
Eutrophic food webs, *1:* 25
Eutrophic lakes, *1:* 118–19
**Eutrophication**, *1:* 25, 151–52; *3:* **394–97**, 427
   consequences of, *3:* 395–96
   cultural, *3:* 395
   effects of, *3:* 396–97
   gulf, *3:* 396
   process of, *3:* 394–95
Evaporation, *1:* 13–14; *2:* 276
Evaporative cooling, *1:* 5
Evaporite deposits, *2:* 296
Evolution, *2:* 261
Excavation, *2:* 253, 254
**Exclusive economic zones**, *3:* 476–79, 489
   establishing territorial waters, *3:* 476–77
   United Nations and Law of the Sea, *3:* 477–78
Exothermic process, *1:* 18
Exports, *2:* 220
Exxon-Mobil, *2:* 304
*Exxon Valdez,* oil spill from (1989), *2:* 318, 339; *3:* 431, 431, 432 (ill.), 433
Eye of hurricane, *1:* 191; *2:* 335

# F

Fall turnover, *1:* 105
Faraday, Michael, *2:* 214
Feather stars, *1:* 73
Fens, *1:* 147
Ferries, *2:* 328
Fertile Crescent, *2:* 205
Fertilizer in water pollution, *3:* 427
Fetch, *1:* 90
Field flooding, *2:* 276
Fiji, *2:* 351
Filtration systems, *2:* 234
Fin whale, *1:* 76
Finback whale, *1:* 78
Fire, impact on watersheds, *3:* 467
First in time, first in right, *3:* 499

Fish, *1:* **43–48**
   *Agnatha, 1:* 44–45
   anadromous, *1:* 103
   catadromous, *1:* 103
   *Chondrichthyes, 1:* 45–46
   diadromous, *1:* 103
   diversity of, *1:* 43–44
   *Osteichthyes, 1:* 46–47
Fish keeping, history of, *2:* 233–34
Fishing, *2:* 341–42
   commercial, *2:* 285, 285 (ill.); *3:* 479–83
   deep-sea, *2:* 324, 349
   dynamite, *3:* 481
   effect of acid rain on, *3:* 380
   fly, *2:* 341
   habitat loss and, *3:* 416
   ice, *2:* 346
   on the ocean, *2:* 324
   recreational, *2:* 349
Fishing limits, *3:* 482–83
Fjord, *1:* 162
Flagella, *1:* 106
Flash floods, *1:* 139, 139 (ill.); *2:* 351, 352–53; *3:* 398–99, 400
   warnings, *3:* 400, 402
   watches, *3:* 400, 401
Flevoland, *2:* 370
Float research, *2:* 268
Floating devices, *2:* 231
Floating-leaf and emergent zone, *1:* 106
Flood control, *1:* 133; *3:* 402–3
Flood Waters Control Act (1928), *3:* 402
Floodplains, *1:* 13, 16, 99, 126, 134; *3:* 398
**Floods**, *1:* 15, 134; *3:* **397–403**
   damage from, *3:* 400
   describing, *3:* 398–400
   flash, *1:* 139, 139 (ill.); *2:* 351, 352–53; *3:* 398–99, 400
   height of, *3:* 398
   100-year, *3:* 400
   size and frequency of, *3:* 399–400
   speed of, *3:* 398–99

   warnings, *3:* 400–402
   watches, *3:* 400–402
Floodways, *3:* 403
Florida Keys, *1:* 58, 59
Florida Keys National Marine Sanctuary, *3:* 482
Florida manatee, *3:* 418
Flounder, *1:* 144, 145
Flow method, *2:* 268
Fluoride, *1:* 11
Fluorine, as greenhouse gas, *3:* 407
Fly fishing, *2:* 341
Flycatchers, *1:* 107
Fongafale Island, *3:* 405 (ill.)
Food and Drug Administration (FDA), recommendation on tuna in diet, *3:* 439
Food chain, *1:* 23; *2:* 371; *3:* 415, 439, 481
Food webs, *1:* 25, 25 (ill.); *3:* 415, 439
Fool's gold (iron sulfide), *2:* 294
Foraminifera, *1:* 84
Forbes, Edward, *2:* 256
Forbes, Stephen Alfred, *2:* 247
Forel, François-Alphonse, *2:* 246–47
Forests
   acid deposition in, *3:* 381, 382 (ill.)
   boreal, *1:* 156, 175
   kelp, *2:* 240
   mangrove, *1:* 97, 99, 150
Fossil aquifers, *3:* 457
Fossil fuels, *1:* 85; *3:* 380–81
Foxes, *1:* 157
Free-floating plant zone, *1:* 107
Freestyle swimming, *2:* 342
Freezing, *1:* 15
**Freshwater**, *2:* 310
   fishing regulations, *3:* 483
   household uses of, *2:* 372
   **life in**, *1:* **100–108**, 101 (ill.)
   recreation in and on, *2:* 341 (ill.), 341–46
   shipping on, *2:* 310–15
   sources of, *3:* 498

types of, *2:* 311–12
wasting of, in irrigation, *3:* 497
Freshwater lakes, *1:* 113
Freshwater marshes, *1:* 147–49
Freshwater swamps, *1:* 148–49
Friction, *1:* 35
Fronts, *1:* 197
Fur seals, *1:* 76

# G

Gagnan, Emile, *2:* 356, 357
Galapagos Islands, *1:* 26, 55, 60
Galena, *2:* 294
Gallium, *2:* 292
Galveston, Texas, *1:* 30, 191; *3:* 386
Gamma rays, *2:* 270
Ganges Delta, *1:* 97, 185
Ganges River, *1:* 126, 129, 184; *2:* 243, 362, 375
Ganges-Brahmaputra Delta, *1:* 98
Gases, *1:* 5, 18
  greenhouse, *1:* 21, 164, 174; *3:* 407–9
  natural, *2:* 301; *3:* 477
  in North Sea, *2:* 302, 302 (ill.)
Gastropods, *1:* 58, 71
Geochemistry, *1:* 8
Geologic time, *1:* 16
Geologic uplift, *1:* 139
Geological limnology, *2:* 247
Geologists, *1:* 114; *2:* 358
**Geology**
  marine, *2:* 265, 268–69, 360–61
  **of ocean floor, *1:* 48–54**
**Geophysics, marine geology and, *2:* 259–64**
Geothermal warming, *2:* 345
Geyser, *2:* 244 (ill.)
Ghost crabs, *3:* 415
Giant kelp, *1:* 64; *2:* 257
Giardia, *2:* 354
Glacial cycles, *3:* 404
Glacial erratic, *1:* 163
Glacial flour, *1:* 162

Glacial ice, *1:* 159, 162
Glacial lakes, *1:* 120–21
Glacial landscapes, *1:* 161–63
Glacial polish and striations, *1:* 162
Glacier Bay National Park, Alaska, *1:* 160 (ill.)
**Glaciers, *1:* 1, 13, 15, 58, 128, 158–63**
  alpine, *1:* 159
  continental, *1:* 159, 168–69
  formation of, *1:* 159–60
  mountain, *1:* 159, 161, 163, 164
  movement of, *1:* 160–61
  Pleistocene, *1:* 165
  tributary, *1:* 161
Glen Canyon Dam, *2:* 209, 320
**Global climate**
  changes in, *3:* **404–10**
  links between Asian monsoon and, *1:* 185–86
Global warming, *1:* 85, 164, 176; *3:* 404–7
Global Water Partnership, *3:* 485, 488
*Glomar Challenger* (ship), *2:* 262
Gobies, *1:* 144
Gold, *2:* 292
  fool's, *2:* 294
  panning for, *2:* 295 (ill.), 296
Gold rush
  Alaskan, *1:* 129–30
  California, *2:* 296
Golden apple snail, *3:* 442
Golden Gate Bridge, *1:* 181 (ill.)
Goldfish, *2:* 233
Golomyanka, *2:* 249
Grabens, *2:* 247
Graded profile, *1:* 114
Graded streams and base level, *1:* 138–40
Grand Banks, *2:* 285; *3:* 436
Grand Canyon, *2:* 320
Grand Coulee Dam, *2:* 207, 214; *3:* 450
Grand Dixence Dam, *2:* 204
Gravity, *1:* 87

Gravity dams, *2:* 204
Gray water, *3:* 494
Gray whale, *1:* 76, 78
Great Britain, *1:* 55
Great Depression, *3:* 391
Great Lakes, *1:* 113, 120–22, 129, 165; *2:* 250
  shipping on, *2:* 314
  zebra mussels in, *3:* 444
Great Lakes Water Quality Act, *1:* 121
Great Lakes-St. Lawrence River system, *2:* 311, 314
Great Midwest Flood of the Mississippi, *3:* 400
Great Plains, *1:* 175
Great Rift Valley, *1:* 116, 119
Great Salt Lake, *1:* 10, 116, 117–18; *2:* 246; *3:* 484
Great white sharks, *1:* 45, 46 (ill.)
Greece, *2:* 363–64
Greek mythology, *2:* 361
Green seaweed, *1:* 64
Greenhouse effect, *3:* 404–5, 407
Greenhouse gases, *1:* 21, 164, 174; *3:* 407–9
Greenhouse layer, *1:* 164
Greenhouse warming, *1:* 167
Greenland, *1:* 54, 58, 157, 159, 167, 168–69
Greenland ice sheet, *1:* 160, 167, 170–71
Greenpeace, *3:* 487–88
**Groundwater, *1:* 8, 10, 15; *2:* 298; *3:* 411–14, 422**
  contamination, *3:* 413 (ill.), 413–14, 424 (ill.), 507–8
  economic uses of, *2:* 287–91
  individual versus community use, *3:* 412
  pesticides in, *3:* 413
  protecting, *3:* 457
  as source of freshwater, *3:* 498
  sources of depletion, *3:* 412
  surface water, *3:* 452–53
  threats to, *3:* 411–12
  **uses of, *2:* 319–21; *3:* 457**

Groundwater discharge, *1:* 109
Groundwater discharge lakes, *1:* 122
Groundwater flow, *1:* 15
**Groundwater formation**, *1:* 108–12
**Groundwater rights**, *3:* 498–501
Grouper, *1:* 144
Groynes, *3:* 385, 386
Guam, *1:* 54, 60
Gulf eutrophication, *3:* 396
Gulf of Ababa, *1:* 119
Gulf of Mexico, *1:* 93; *3:* 396
Gulf Stream, *1:* 35–36, 38, 55, 191–92
Gulf War (1991), oil spill during, *3:* 432
Gullies, *1:* 132
Guyots, *1:* 57
*Gymnodinium breve*, *1:* 83
Gypsum, *1:* 138; *2:* 296; *3:* 484
Gyres, *1:* 37– 38

# H
**Habitat loss and species extinction**, *3:* 414–18
Hadley cells, *1:* 174
Haeckel, Ernst, *2:* 237
Hagfish, *1:* 44–45
The Hague, *2:* 370
Hail, *1:* 182
Halibut, *1:* 144
Halite, *2:* 308–9
Halocarbons as greenhouse gas, *3:* 407
Halocline, *1:* 142
Halogens as greenhouse gas, *3:* 407
Hand-dug wells, *2:* 288, 290
Hanging valley, *1:* 161
Harbors. *See* Ports and harbors
Hares, *1:* 157
Harrison, John, *2:* 338
Hawaiian Islands, *1:* 56, 57, 59, 60
Hawaiian monk seal, *1:* 78
Hawaiian-Emperor seamount chain, *1:* 57

Hawaiian-Emperor volcanoes, *1:* 57
Headwater streams, *1:* 126
*Heart of Darkness* (Conrad), *1:* 128
Heavy metals, *3:* 421
    bioaccumulation of, *3:* 387–90
    as non-source pollutants, *3:* 426
    in sediment contamination, *3:* 441
Heezen, Bruce, *1:* 51
Henley, Don, *1:* 125
Herbivores, *2:* 241
Herodotus, *1:* 95; *2:* 208, 265
Herons, *1:* 107, 144, 148, 150
Hetch-Hetchy reservoir, debate over, *3:* 451, 451 (ill.)
Heterotrophs, *2:* 240
Heyerdahl, Thor, *2:* 364
High seas, *3:* 476
High-pressure systems, *1:* 196
Himalayan Mountains, *1:* 50, 97, 126, 129, 183, 185
Hindus, *1:* 129; *2:* 375
Hispanola, *1:* 55
Historical groundwater use, *2:* 289–90
Hohokam, *2:* 366
Holdfasts, *1:* 62, 64, 102
Holoplankton, *1:* 84
Homeostasis, *2:* 240
Homer, *2:* 333, 361–62
Hong Kong, ports of, *2:* 221, 221 (ill.)
Honolulu, Hawaii, *3:* 385
Hooker Chemical Company, *3:* 420
Hoover Dam, *2:* 209, 214, 217, 217 (ill.), 218, 353 (ill.); *3:* 450
Horseshoe Falls, *2:* 345
Hot spot, *1:* 56, 57
Hot springs, *2:* 344, 368
Hot Springs, Arkansas, *2:* 345
Houseboats, *2:* 343
Hovercraft, *2:* 328
Hualalai, *1:* 57
Huang He River, *1:* 128

Hudson River, *1:* 130
Human body, water in, *1:* 1, 16
Humans, in Arctic, *1:* 157–58
Humboldt, Alexander von, *2:* 256
Hurricanes, *1:* 38, 89, 186, 189; *2:* 335–37
    Andrew, *1:* 191
    categories, *2:* 336
    eye of, *1:* 191; *2:* 335
    Isabel, *1:* 36, 36 (ill.)
    Mitch, *1:* 190 (ill.)
    names of, *1:* 192
    storm surge from, *3:* 398
    strength of, *1:* 191
Hutchinson, George Evelyn, *2:* 247
Hydrocarbons, *2:* 261, 300–301, 305; *3:* 430
Hydroelectric technology, *2:* 214–15, 374
Hydroelectricity, *1:* 113
Hydrofoil, *2:* 328
Hydrogen atoms, *1:* 2
Hydrogen bonds, *1:* 4, 5, 9, 10, 20
Hydrogeologic maps, *2:* 245
Hydrogeologists, *1:* 113; *2:* 242
**Hydrogeology**, *2:* **242–46**
**Hydrologic cycle**, *1:* **12–17**, 14 (ill.), 126, 136, 173; *2:* 210; *3:* 446
Hydrologic potential, *2:* 205
Hydrologists, *1:* 113, 136; *2:* 242
**Hydrology**, *2:* **242–46**
Hydrophilic molecules, *1:* 2, 4
Hydrophobic molecules, *1:* 2, 4
**Hydropower**, *2:* 205, 206, **212–19**
    benefits and drawbacks of, *2:* 218
    future of, *2:* 218
    in history, *2:* 213–14
    sizes of facilities, *2:* 217–18
    types of facilities, *2:* 215
Hydrosphere, *1:* 8; *2:* 238
Hydrothermal deposits, *2:* 293–94

Hydrothermal vents, *1:* 24–26, 27 (ill.); *2:* 263, 360, 371
Hypolimnion, *1:* 104, 105
Hypopycnal flow, *1:* 96
Hypothermia, *2:* 333, 335
Hypoxia, *2:* 355

# I

Ibis, *1:* 150
Ice, *1:* 5–6, 21
Ice age, *1:* 163; *3:* 404
Ice caps, *1:* 163, 168
    Arctic, *1:* 38
    polar, *1:* 164, 168–72, 175
Ice cave, *1:* 166 (ill.)
Ice fishing, *2:* 346
Ice hockey, *2:* 346
**Ice, sea-level, and global climate, *1:* 163–68**
Ice sheets, *1:* 159, 168–71
    Antarctic, *1:* 160, 169
    Greenland, *1:* 160, 167, 170–71
    West Antarctic, *1:* 167, 169–70
Ice shelves, *1:* 165, 170
Ice skating, *2:* 346
Ice streams, *1:* 165
Iceberg alley, *1:* 156
Icebergs, *1:* 20 (ill.), 21, 156; *2:* 323, 337–38
Iceland, *1:* 56, 156; *2:* 215
Ikysh River, *1:* 129
Immigration to New World, *2:* 326, 327 (ill.)
Imports, *2:* 220
Impoundment facilities, *2:* 215
Inactive volcanoes, *1:* 55
*In situ* cleanup of soil, *3:* 509
Indian Ocean, *1:* 184
Indian Ocean Sanctuary, *2:* 330
Indian peninsula, *1:* 183–84
Indonesia, *1:* 55
Indoor water usage, *2:* 306
Industrial areas as source of non-source pollution, *3:* 427–28
**Industrial waste, *3:* 418–22**
**Industrial water use, *2:* 283–8, 320–21**

Indus Water Treaty (1960), *3:* 493
Inland waterways, *2:* 311
Integrated Ocean Drilling Project (IODP), *2:* 262
Interdistributary areas, *1:* 96, 99
Interior, U.S. Department of, *3:* 504, 505, 506
Internal deformation, *1:* 160, 161
International Association for Environmental Hydrology, *3:* 487
International Commission on Irrigation and Drainage, *3:* 486
International Commission on Water Quality, *3:* 487
International Convention for the Prevention of Pollution from Ships at Sea (MARPOL), *2:* 325
International Convention for the Regulation of Whaling, *3:* 492
International Council of Cruise Lines (ICCL), *2:* 324
International Hydrological Program, *3:* 486
International Ice Patrol, *2:* 337
International Institute for Land Reclamation and Improvement, *3:* 485
International Maritime Organization (IMO), *2:* 323–24; *3:* 483
International Seabed Authority, *2:* 293
International Union for the Conservation of Nature and Natural Resources (IUCN), *3:* 453
International Water and Sanitation Center, *3:* 485
International Water Association, *3:* 487
**International water laws and enforcement, *3:* 488–93**

International Water Management Institute, *3:* 485
International Water Resources Association, *3:* 488
International Whaling Commission (IWC), *2:* 329–30
Intertidal zones, *1:* 70
Inuits, *1:* 157–58
Invertebrates, *1:* 24, 69–74, 144
Ionic bonds, *1:* 4
Ions, *1:* 2, 8, 137–38
Ireland, *1:* 55
Iron, *1:* 24
Irrigation, *2:* 276–77, 352 (ill.), 371–72
    agricultural overuse and, *3:* 435
    drip, *2:* 276–77
    spray, *2:* 277
    sprinkler, *2:* 277 (ill.)
    use of groundwater for, *2:* 290–91
    wasting of freshwater in, *3:* 497
**Islands, *1:* 54–61**
    barrier, *1:* 29–30, 56, 57, 60, 93
    big, *1:* 58
    carbonate, *1:* 58–59
    coastal, *1:* 56–58
    life on, *1:* 60–61
    volcanic, *1:* 55–56, 56 (ill.), 59, 60
Islets, *1:* 54
Isolation, ground- and surface-water treatment by, *3:* 509–10
Itaipu Dam, *2:* 204, 207

# J

Jack, *1:* 144
Japan, *1:* 55
Japanese shore crab, species introduction and, *3:* 444–45
*Jason Junior* (submersible), *2:* 359 (ill.)
Jawless fish, *1:* 44
Jellyfish, *1:* 68, 69, 70, 82, 84
    dangers from, *2:* 339

moon, *1:* 71 (ill.)
water in, *1:* 1, 16
Jet skis, *2:* 342, 343
Jet stream, *1:* 196
Jetties, *1:* 30; *2:* 222
John, Abbot of Wallingford, *1:* 86
Johnstown (PA), flood damage in, *3:* 400
Joint Oceanographic Institution for Deep Earth Sampling (JOIDES), *2:* 262
*Joola* (ferry), *2:* 328
Jurassic Period, *1:* 12

## K
Kahoolawe, *1:* 57
Kalahari Desert, *1:* 175; *3:* 457
Karst, *1:* 110, 122; *3:* 484
Kauai, *1:* 15, 57
Kayaking, *2:* 343–44
Kazakhstan, *1:* 117
Keel, *2:* 342
Keiko, the killer whale, *1:* 77, 78 (ill.)
**Kelp,** *1:* **61–65,** 65 (ill.); *2:* 257, 280
Kelp forests, *2:* 240
Kelvin, Lord, *1:* 87
Kerguelan Islands, *1:* 56
Kesterson National Wildlife Refuge, *3:* 417, 418
Kettle pond, *1:* 163
Khartoum, *1:* 128
Kilauea, *1:* 57, 58 (ill.)
Kilimanjaro, *1:* 159
Kitty Hawk, North Carolina, *3:* 385
Klettvik Bay, *1:* 77
Koi, *2:* 233
*Kon-Tiki* (raft), *2:* 364
Krill, *1:* 25 (ill.), 84
Kudzu plant, *3:* 467
Kuroshio, *1:* 36, 38
Kyoto Treaty, *3:* 408

## L
La Grande Dams, *2:* 207
La Rance (Brittany, France), *2:* 223

**La Niña,** *1:* **39–43;** *2:* 268
discovery of, *1:* 40–41
effects of, *1:* 41–42
Lagoons, *1:* 29, 56–57, 93, 141; *2:* 228
Lake Baikal, *1:* 119, 174 (ill.); *2:* 247, 249
Lake basins, *1:* 119–20, 122
Lake Erie, eutrophication of, *3:* 396
Lake Nasser, *2:* 208
Lake Okeechobee, *1:* 122
Lake Powell, *1:* 120 (ill.)
Lake St. Clair, *3:* 444
Lake systems, *2:* 311
Lake Tahoe, *1:* 120
**Lakes,** *1:* **113–23**
acid deposition and, *3:* 379–80
biology of, *1:* 116, 118–19
chemistry of, *1:* 115–16
difference between pond and, *1:* 123
dying, *1:* 117–18
eutrophic, *1:* 118–19
freshwater, *1:* 113
glacial, *1:* 120–21
groundwater discharge, *1:* 122
life cycle of, *1:* 113–14
life in, *1:* 104–8
monomictic/dimictic/polymictic, *1:* 115
saline, *1:* 115–16
volcanic, *1:* 120
Lampreys, *1:* 44–45, 45
Lanai, *1:* 57
Land bridges, *1:* 166
Land crabs, *1:* 149
Land reclamation, *1:* 99
Land snails, *1:* 149
**Landfills,** *3:* **422–25**
construction of, *3:* 423–24
defined, *3:* 423
monitoring of, *3:* 424–25
Laplace, Pierre Simon, *1:* 87
Larsen B ice shelf, *1:* 165, 166 (ill.)
Larval fish, *1:* 82

Las Vegas, Nevada
demand for water in, *3:* 412
water use in, *2:* 353; *3:* 437–38, 452
**Layers of the ocean,** *1:* **66–69**
Le Maire, Isaac, *2:* 334
Leachate, *3:* 422, 423
Lead, *2:* 292; *3:* 387, 459
effects of, *3:* 389
in sediment contamination, *3:* 441
Leatherneck turtles, *3:* 416 (ill.)
Lemmings, *1:* 157
Lena River, *1:* 129
Lentic waters, *1:* 101
Lenticels, *1:* 150
Lenticular altocumulus cloud, *1:* 181
Leopold, Aldo, *3:* 450
Lesser Antilles, *1:* 55
Levees, *1:* 96, 127, 133; *2:* 243, 370; *403*
Lewis, Meriwether, *1:* 131
Light, *1:* 23–24
regulating sun, *1:* 173–74
ultraviolet, *1:* 8–9
Lighthouses, *3:* 385
Lightning, *1:* 186
Limestone, *1:* 58, 138; *2:* 296, 303; *3:* 484
Limnetic zone, *1:* 104, 118
Limnologists, *1:* 115, 118
**Limnology,** *1:* 113; *2:* **246–51**
biological, *2:* 249–50
chemical, *2:* 248–49
geological, *2:* 247
history of, *2:* 246–47
physical, *2:* 247–48
Limpets, *1:* 71, 103
Limpopo River, *1:* 128
Lindisfarne (Holy Island), *2:* 223
Liquids, *1:* 5, 18
Lithosphere, *1:* 119; *2:* 238
Lithospheric plates, *1:* 50
Littoral zone, *1:* 104
Liverworts, *1:* 102
Livestock industry, use of groundwater by, *2:* 291

Livingstone, David, *1:* 138
Lizards, *2:* 354
Lobsters, *1:* 83, 84
Lock, *2:* 313
Logging, *3:* 416–17
    clearcutting in, *3:* 417, 468
    impact on watersheds, *3:* 467
Loihi, *1:* 57
Long Island, New York, *1:* 58
Longshore currents, *1:* 93
Loons, *1:* 107
Los Angeles, California, water needs of, *3:* 452
Lost at sea, *2:* 338
Lotic waters, *1:* 101
Louisiana Purchase (1803), *2:* 312
Love Canal, *3:* 420, 420 (ill.)
Love, William, *3:* 420
Low-pressure centers, *1:* 196
Low-pressure systems, *1:* 196

# M

Mackenzie River, *1:* 129
Macroalgae, *1:* 62
Macrocystis, *1:* 64
Macroplankton, *1:* 81–82
Madagascar, *1:* 58
Maelstrom, *2:* 333
Magellan, Ferdinand, *2:* 334
Magnesium, *1:* 24
Magnetometers, *2:* 253
Malacostracans, *1:* 72–73
Mammals, marine, *1:* 74–79
Mammatus clouds, *1:* 189
Manatees, *1:* 78, 150; *3:* 418, 473 (ill.)
Manganese, *2:* 261, 293
Manganese nodules, *2:* 293
Mangrove forests, *1:* 97, 99, 150
Mangrove swamps, *1:* 149–50
Mangroves, *2:* 280
Mantle, *1:* 71
Mapping the oceans, *2:* 357–59
Mariana Trench, *1:* 49; *2:* 356, 360, 370
Mariculture, *2:* 258, 279–80, 282–83

Marine animals, impact of sound on, *2:* 273
**Marine archaeology**, *2:* **251–55**
Marine Biological Laboratory, *2:* 266
**Marine biology**, *2:* **255–59**, 359–60
    history of, *2:* 256–57
    research areas in, *2:* 258
    types of organisms studied, *2:* 257
**Marine geology**, *1:* 48–49; *2:* 265, 268–69, 360–61
    **geophysics and**, *2:* **259–64**
Marine geoscientists, *2:* 260
**Marine invertebrates**, *1:* **69–74**
    Annelida, *1:* 70–71
    Arthropoda, *1:* 72–73
    Cnidaria, *1:* 70
    Echinodermata, *1:* 73–74
    Molluska, *1:* 71–72
    Porifera, *1:* 70
Marine Mammal Protection Act (1972), *3:* 473
**Marine mammals**, *1:* **74–79**
    Carnivora, *1:* 76–77
    Cetacea, *1:* 75
    endangered, *1:* 78–79
    in military, *1:* 75
    Odontoceti, *1:* 75–76
Marine protection areas, *3:* 482
Marine science, *2:* 264
Marine sea otter, *1:* 78
Marine snails, *1:* 149
Marlin, *2:* 349
MARPOL 73/78, *3:* 483
Mars, water on, *1:* 3, 3 (ill.)
Marsh, *1:* 141
    freshwater, *1:* 147–49
    salt, *1:* 149
Marsh, George Perkins, *3:* 449
Marsh grasses, *1:* 149
Maryland crabs, effect of eutrophication on, *3:* 397
Maui, Hawaii, *1:* 57; *2:* 334 (ill.)
Mauna Loa, *1:* 57
Mayflies, *1:* 103, 107
Meandering streams, *1:* 134
Meanders, *1:* 134, 135

Meat processing industry, water uses by, *2:* 285–86
Mediterranean Sea, *1:* 119; *2:* 362
Medusa, *1:* 70
Mekong River, *1:* 129
Melting, *1:* 15, 18
Meniscus, *1:* 10
Merchant ships, types of, *2:* 316–17
Mercury, *2:* 249; *3:* 387
    effects of, *3:* 389
    in sediment contamination, *3:* 441
    in water pollution, *3:* 458, 459–60, 502
Meromictic lake, *1:* 115
Meroplankton, *1:* 84
Mesopelagic zone, *1:* 67–68
Mesoplankton, *1:* 82
Mesopotamia, *1:* 129
Mesotrophic lakes, *1:* 119
Metabolic rate, *1:* 24–25
Metabolism, *1:* 47
Metals, bioaccumulation of heavy, *3:* 387–90
Meteorologists, *1:* 180, 189, 193
Methane, *3:* 409
    as greenhouse gas, *3:* 407, 422
    landfills and, *3:* 424
Methylmercury, *3:* 388–89
*Metula* (ship), oil spills from, *3:* 431
Mexican monsoon, *1:* 183
Miami Beach, Florida, *3:* 385
Micro-hydropower plants, *2:* 217
Microplankton, *1:* 82
Microwaves, *2:* 270, 271–72
Mid-Atlantic Ridge, *1:* 50, 52; *2:* 360, 370
Middle East, rivers in, *1:* 129
Mid-latitude cyclones, *1:* 192
Mid-oceanic ridge, *1:* 52; *2:* 260
Mid-oceanic ridge volcanoes, *1:* 53
Milankovitch cycles, *1:* 164

Mile
  nautical, 2: 349
  statutory, 2: 349
Milfoil, 1: 106
Military, marine mammals in, 1: 75
Miller, Stanley, 1: 2 (ill.)
**Minerals**
  importance of, 2: 292–93
  **mining and,** 2: **292–97**
  water-laid, 2: 293
Mining, 3: 416–17
  minerals and, 2: 292–97
  Ogallala water, 3: 457
  open-pit, 2: 294–95
  sea, 2: 339
  solution, 2: 309
  strip, 2: 295
  water uses in, 2: 285
Mississippi levees, 1: 133
Mississippi River, 1: 126, 127, 127 (ill.), 129, 131, 132, 134; 2: 243, 313 (ill.)
  control of nature on, 1: 133
  drainage basin for, 3: 402
  flood control measures along, 3: 449
  flooding of, 3: 402
Mississippi River and Tributaries Project, 3: 402
Mississippi River Delta, 1: 56, 93, 96 (ill.), 97, 133
Mississippi-Missouri river system, 2: 311, 312
Missouri River, 1: 129, 131, 133
Mistral, 1: 176
Molecular biology, 2: 257, 258
Molecular probes, 2: 258
Molecule, 1: 8, 18
Mollusks, 1: 24, 58, 69, 71, 82, 84, 85, 99; 2: 256, 279
Molokai, 1: 57
Mongooses, 1: 60
Monomictic/dimictic/polymictic lake, 1: 115
**Monsoons,** 1: 42, 97, 175, 175 (ill.), **183–86**
  Asian, 1: 183, 185–86
  Mexican, 1: 183

Mont-St.-Michel, 2: 223
Moon, gravitational pull of, 1: 87–88
Moon jellyfish, 1: 71 (ill.)
Moraines, 1: 122, 163
Mosquitoes, 1: 107
Mosses, 1: 102, 106, 143
Motorboats, 2: 342–43
Mt. Everest, 1: 49, 194
Mt. Waialeale, 1: 15, 57
Mt. Waialeale Crater, 1: 59 (ill.)
Mountain glaciers, 1: 159, 161, 163, 164
Mousse, 3: 434
Mudflats, 1: 142
Muir, John, 3: 450, 451
Mullet, 1: 144
Multistage distillation, 2: 212
Municipal solid waste landfills, 3: 423
**Municipal water**
  protecting, 2: 298–99, 300
  **uses of,** 2: **297–300,** 300 (ill.)
Murray River, 1: 129
Muskoxen, 1: 157
Muskrats, 1: 107
Mussels, 1: 69, 71, 72
Mustang Island, 1: 30

# N

Nannoplankton, 1: 82
Nantucket, 1: 58
Nasser, Gamal Abdel, 2: 208
National Aeronautics and Space Administration, U.S. (NASA), measurement of ice cover by, 3: 406
National Coalition for Marine Conservation (NCMC), 3: 436
National Forest Service, 3: 449
National Geographic Society, 1: 51
National Marine Fisheries Service, 3: 474
National parks, 3: 505
National Weather Service, 1: 195; 3: 400–402

National wildlife refuges, 3: 505
Native Americans, Southwestern, 2: 366
Natural gas, 2: 301; 3: 477
Natural rainwater, pH of, 3: 378
Nature Conservancy, 3: 418, 486
Nautical mile, 2: 349
Nautiluses, 1: 72
Naval Depot of Charts and Instruments, 2: 266
Navigation, 2: 338
Navigation channels, 2: 220
Neap tides, 1: 88
Neckton, 2: 257
Neptune, 2: 361
Nerpa, 2: 249
Net bucket, 1: 80
Net plankton, 1: 81
Net ring, 1: 80
Netherlands, life below sea level in, 2: 370
Neurobiology, 2: 257
Neutralization, 3: 378
Neutron, 1: 2
New Guinea, 1: 58; 2: 364
New Orleans, Louisiana, 1: 127, 132
New South Wales, Australia, 1: 129
New York City, municipal water in, 2: 299, 299 (ill.)
Newton, Isaac, 1: 87
Niagara Falls, 1: 121; 2: 345–46; 3: 448
Nickel, 2: 261
  effects of, 3: 389
  in sediment contamination, 3: 441
Niger River, 1: 128 (ill.)
Nihau, 1: 57
Nile River, 1: 126, 126 (ill.), 127, 128; 2: 209, 220, 243, 271 (ill.), 310, 362, 363, 363 (ill.)
Nile River Delta, 1: 98; 2: 271 (ill.)

Nimbostratus clouds, *1:* 178–79, 180, 181
Nimbus clouds, *1:* 179
Nitrate, *1:* 24; *3:* 464
Nitric acid (HNO₃), acid rain and, *3:* 377
Nitrogen, *1:* 64
Nitrogen dioxide (NO₂), acid rain and, *3:* 377
Nitrogen oxides
  acid rain and, *3:* 377
  source of, *3:* 378
Nitrous oxides
  acid rain and, *3:* 503
  as greenhouse gas, *3:* 407
Nixon, Richard, *3:* 473
Non-point source wastewater, *2:* 225
**Non-point sources of pollution,** *3:* 425–30, 459
  control of, *3:* 428–29
  defined, *3:* 425
**Nonprofit international organizations,** *3:* 483–88
  education and, *3:* 488
  pollution prevention and conservation, *3:* 487–88
  sustainable water supplies and, *3:* 485
  water shortages and, *3:* 484–85
  water supply management and, *3:* 485–86
Non-source pollutants, types of, *3:* 426
Non-source pollution, origins of, *3:* 426–28
Nor'easters, *1:* 192; *2:* 337
Norias, *2:* 205
Norsk Hydro, *2:* 302
North America, rivers in, *1:* 129–31
North American Plate, *1:* 50
North Atlantic Gyre, *1:* 38
North Equatorial Current, *1:* 37, 38
North Pole, *1:* 155
North Sea, oil and gas in, *2:* 302, 302 (ill.)
Northeasterly winds, *1:* 183

Northwest Territories, *2:* 312
No-take zones, *3:* 481–82
Nova Zemlya, *1:* 156
Nucleus, *1:* 2
Nurse sharks, *1:* 85
Nutrient recharge zones, *1:* 99–100
Nutrients as non-source pollutants, *3:* 426

## O

Oahu, *1:* 57
Ob River, *1:* 129
Ocean basins, *1:* 54, 119
Ocean currents, *1:* 20, 34, 37 (ill.); *2:* 224
Ocean dumping, *3:* 462, 462 (ill.)
Ocean floor, geology of, *1:* 48–54
Ocean trenches, *1:* 52
Oceanic crust, *1:* 53
Oceanographers, *1:* 66; *2:* 242, 260
**Oceanography,** *1:* 49; *2:* 246, **264–69**
  biological, *2:* 265, 266
  chemical, *2:* 265, 266–67
  history of, *2:* 265–66
  physical, *2:* 265, 267–68
Ocean rocks and sediments, *1:* 52–54
**Oceans,** *1:* 20
  acid deposition in, *3:* 380–81
  biology of, *1:* 23–27
  currents and circulation patterns in, *1:* **34–39**
  exploration of, *2:* **354–61,** 369–71
  layers of, *1:* 66–69
  mapping of, *2:* 357–59
  recreation in and on, *2:* 347–50
  resource management in, *3:* 477
  salts in, *1:* 10
  shipping on, *2:* 315–18
  tourism on, *2:* 321–25
  transportation on, *2:* 325–28

Octopuses, *1:* 69, 71, 72
Oder River, *1:* 129
*The Odyssey* (Homer), *2:* 361–62
Offshore turbines, *2:* 224
Off-site cleanup of soil, *3:* 509
Ogallala aquifer, *3:* 457
Ogallala groundwater reservoir, *1:* 16
Ogallala water mining, *3:* 457
Ohio River, *1:* 129, 133; *2:* 312
Oil in North Sea, *2:* 302, 302 (ill.). *See also* Petroleum
Oil exploration on seabed, *3:* 477
Oil fish, *2:* 249
Oil Pollution Control Act, *2:* 325
Oil pollution of waters, *3:* 430–31
**Oil spills,** *2:* 318; *3:* **430–35,** 459
  ecological damages of, *3:* 434
  post, *3:* 433–34
  wartime, *3:* 432–33
Oil storage tanks, *2:* 303 (ill.)
Oil tankers, *2:* 317
Ojibwe people, *1:* 133
Okavango River, *1:* 128
Oligomictic lake, *1:* 115
Oligotrophic lakes, *1:* 118
Oligotrophic waters, *1:* 25
100-year flood, *3:* 400
Open ocean, *3:* 476
Open-pit mines, *2:* 294–95
Ophiuroids, *1:* 73
*Opportunity* (spacecraft), *1:* 3
Orbitals, *1:* 2
Ores, *2:* 292, 293
Organ systems, *2:* 238
Organs, *2:* 238
Orinoco River, *1:* 131
Oscillating water channels (OWCs), *2:* 231
Oscillation, *1:* 39
Osmosis, *1:* 26, 47–48, 142; *2:* 212
Osprey, *1:* 107
Osteichthyes, *1:* 44, 46–48

Index | lxxi

Out banks, *1:* 29–30
Outdoor water usage, *2:* 306
Outer Banks, *1:* 57, 93
Outwash, *1:* 162
Overfishing, *2:* 369; *3:* 436, 437 (ill.), 477
Overseas trade, *2:* 220
**Overuse,** *3:* **435–38**
  agricultural, *3:* 435
  community, *3:* 437–38
  residential, *3:* 435–37
Overwhaling, *3:* 477, 492
Owls, *1:* 149
Oxbows, *1:* 135
Oxygen, *1:* 24; *3:* 464
Oysters, *1:* 71, 72, 143, 145
Ozone, *3:* 407–8
Ozone layer, *1:* 173–74

## P

Pacific Plate, *1:* 57; *2:* 361
Pacific white-sided dolphins, *1:* 75
Pack ice, *1:* 156
Palladium, *2:* 293
Panama Canal, *2:* 334, 373
Panning for gold, *2:* 295 (ill.), 296
Papagayo, *1:* 176
Paraná River, *1:* 131; *2:* 207
Paranhas, *1:* 130
Parthenogenesis, *1:* 84
Parthenon, *3:* 378
Passenger ships, *2:* 374
Passive margins, *1:* 50
Pathogens as non-source pollutants, *3:* 426
Peacocks, *1:* 184
Pearl River, *1:* 128
Pedicellariae, *1:* 73
Pelagic ooze, *1:* 53
Pelicans, *1:* 150
*The Perfect Storm, 1:* 187 (ill.)
Permafrost, *1:* 156, 157, 158 (ill.)
Permanent ice, *1:* 159
Permeability, *1:* 110–11
Personal watercraft, *2:* 342, 343
Peru Current, *1:* 37
Peru-Chile Trench, *1:* 53

Pesticides, *1:* 11; *2:* 371–72; *3:* 413
**Petroleum,** *2:* 261. *See also* Oil
  **exploration and recovery,** *2:* 300–306
  formation of deposits, *2:* 301–3
  history of modern industry, *2:* 303–4
  in North Sea, *2:* 302, 302 (ill.)
  problems of use, *2:* 304–5
  reservoirs of, *2:* 301
*Pfisteria*, growth of, *2:* 228
pH scale, acid rain and, *3:* 377–78
Phase change, *1:* 18–19
Phelan, James, *3:* 451
Philippines, *1:* 55
Phoenicians, *2:* 362
Phoenix, Arizona, water needs of, *3:* 452
Phosphate, *1:* 24
Phosphorus, *1:* 64; *3:* 465
Photic zone, *1:* 66
Photosynthesis, *1:* 1, 2, 9, 23, 85, 100–101, 124; *2:* 240, 241, 257, 359, 371
Physical limnology, *2:* 247–48
Physical oceanography, *2:* 265, 267–68
**Physics of water,** *1:* **17–22**
Phytoplankton, *1:* 23, 24, 35, 40, 66, 82–83, 85, 104, 105, 143; *2:* 257, 258
Picoplankton, *1:* 82
Pike's Peak, *1:* 132
Pinchot, Gifford, *3:* 448–49, 450, 453
Pinnipeds, *1:* 76
Pinzon, Vicente Yañez, *1:* 130
Pipefish, *1:* 144
Pitcher plants, *1:* 151
Placer deposits, *2:* 295, 296
**Plankton,** *1:* **79–86,** 81 (ill.), 104, 143; *2:* 257
  cell structure of, *1:* 82–84
  importance of, *1:* 85
  life history of, *1:* 84–85
  size of, *1:* 81–82

  studying and classifying, *1:* 80–85
Plankton nets, *1:* 80
Plants
  in arid climate, *2:* 351–52
  in estuaries, *1:* 143, 143 (ill.)
  in lakes and ponds, *1:* 106–7
  in rivers and streams, *1:* 102
  on the tundra, *1:* 156–57
Plate, *1:* 48–49
Plate tectonics, *1:* 48–49, 50, 119, 126; *2:* 260–61
Platinum, *2:* 292, 293
Playa lakes, *1:* 116
Pleistocene, *1:* 12, 156, 164, 167, 171
Pleistocene glaciers, *1:* 165
Po River, *1:* 129
Poachers, *3:* 472
Point bars, *1:* 135, 137
Point source wastewater, *2:* 225
Point sources of water pollution, *3:* 459
Polar bears, *1:* 77, 157
**Polar ice caps,** *1:* 164, **168–72,** 175
Polar molecules, *1:* 2, 4
Polar substances, *1:* 4
Polders, *2:* 370
Pollutants, *1:* 121; *3:* 426
Pollution. *See* Air pollution; Water pollution
Pollution stress, *2:* 369
Polychaete worms, *1:* 143
Polychlorinated biphenyls (PCBs), *2:* 226; *3:* 440, 440 (ill.)
Polycyclic aromatic hydrocarbons (PAHs), *3:* 440–41
Polynesians, ancient, *2:* 364
Polyps, *1:* 70
**Ponds,** *1:* **123–25**
  differences between lake and, *1:* 123
  famous and infamous, *1:* 125
  fate of, *1:* 124–25
  formation of, *1:* 123

life in and around, *1:* 104–8, 124
Pontoon boats, *2:* 343
Population ecologist, *2:* 238
Populations, *2:* 238
Porifera, *1:* 69
Porosity, *1:* 110
Porphyry, *2:* 294
Porpoises, *1:* 75
Port state, *2:* 324
**Ports and harbors, *2:* 219–22**
   building and maintaining successful, *2:* 220–21
   modern, *2:* 220
   problems, concerns, and future of, *2:* 221–22
Potability, *3:* 463
Potable water, *2:* 210, 297
Potassium chloride, *2:* 296
Potassium nitrate, *2:* 296
Potomac River, *1:* 131
Powell, John Wesley, *1:* 131; *3:* 449
Powerboats, *2:* 342–43
Precipitation, *1:* 8, 13, 14–15, 136, 138
Preservationist movement, *3:* 450
Pressure, *1:* 27
Pressure changes, *1:* 18
Pressurized water, *2:* 202
*Prestige* (ship), oil spills from, *3:* 431
Primary consumers, *1:* 25
Primary water treatment, *2:* 226
Prince William Sound, *2:* 318, 339
Prior appropriation doctrine, *3:* 499–500, 501
Profundal zone, *1:* 104
Prop roots, *1:* 150
Propane, *2:* 301
Propulsion systems, *2:* 310–11
Prospectors, *2:* 296
Protons, *1:* 2, 9
Protozoans, *1:* 82, 84
Ptarmigan, *1:* 157
Public supply water system, *2:* 306

Puerto Rico, *1:* 55
Pulp and paper industry, water use in, *2:* 286
Pulse transmission, *2:* 273
Pumped storage hydropower facilities, *2:* 215–16
Purification, *2:* 306
Pyrite, *2:* 228

## Q

Quartz, *2:* 292
Queen Elizabeth Islands, *1:* 156
*Queen Mary 2*, *2:* 322, 327
Queensland, Australia, *1:* 129

## R

Raccoon River, flooding of, *3:* 399 (ill.)
Radio waves, *2:* 270
Rafting, *2:* 343–44, 344 (ill.)
Rainbow trout, *1:* 102 (ill.)
Rainforest, *1:* 130
Rainshadow deserts, *3:* 393
Rainy season, *1:* 184–85
Rapid City, South Dakota, flood damage in, *3:* 400
Rays, *1:* 45, 46
Razorback sucker, *3:* 417
Reasonable use doctrine, *3:* 499
Recharge zones, *1:* 109, 111, 112; *2:* 245, 287
Reclamation, Bureau of, *2:* 243; *3:* 449–50
**Recreation**
   **in and on freshwaters**, *2:* 341 (ill.), **341–46**
   **in and on oceans**, *2:* **347–50**
   water use for, *2:* 320
Recreational fishing, *2:* 349
Red algae, *1:* 63–64
Red mangroves, *1:* 150
Red maple, *1:* 148
Red Sea, *1:* 26, 119
Red tides, *1:* 83
Redfish, *1:* 144; *2:* 349
Redirecting excess water, *3:* 495
Reeds, *1:* 106

Reefs
   artificial, *1:* 32, 32 (ill.)
   coral, *1:* 47, 58, 74; *2:* 356; *3:* 481
   near the shore, *2:* 338–39
Reestablishment, *3:* 465–66
Regional Seas Conventions, *3:* 492
Religion and popular culture, *2:* 375
**Remote sensing, *2:* 253, 261, 270–73**
   energy of, *2:* 270–72
   history of, *2:* 272
Remote-operated vehicles (ROVs), *2:* 263, 356
Reservoirs. *See* Dams and reservoirs
Residence time, *1:* 13, 16, 111, 114
Residential overuse, *3:* 435–37
**Residential water use, *2:* 306–8**
*Resolution* (ship), *2:* 262
Restoration of watersheds, *3:* 465–67
Reverse osmosis, *2:* 212
Rhine River, *1:* 129
Rhone River, *1:* 129
Ridge, Tom, *3:* 504 (ill.)
Rift zones, *1:* 119
*Riftia*, *1:* 26
Right whale, *2:* 329
Ring of Fire, *1:* 52, 53, 55; *2:* 361
Rio Grande River, *1:* 131
Riparian doctrine, *3:* 499
Riparian zone, *3:* 467–68
Rip current, *1:* 93
**Rivers, *1:* 125–31**
   acid deposition and, *3:* 379–80
   lengths of, *1:* 128
   life in, *1:* 102 (ill.), 102–4
   major, *1:* 127–31
Rock salt, *2:* 308–9
Rock weir, *2:* 205
Rockefeller, John D., *2:* 304
Rocks, near the shore, *2:* 338–39

Roman aqueducts, 2: 201, 201 (ill.)
Roman Empire, power of, 2: 315–16
Romans, 2: 362
Rome, Italy, 2: 368
Roosevelt, Franklin Delano, 2: 213, 216; 3: 449
Roosevelt, Theodore, 3: 449
Roseate spoonbills, 1: 150
Ross Ice Shelf, 1: 165
Ross Sea, 1: 165, 171
Rotifer, 1: 107
Rotterdam, 2: 370
Rowing, 2: 343–44
Royal Bengal tigers, 1: 97
Royal shroud bird, 3: 461 (ill.)
Runoff, 1: 15; 3: 397–98
 agricultural, 2: 228; 3: 429
 urban, 2: 229
Run-of-river systems, 2: 216
Rural areas
 as source of non-source pollution, 3: 427–28
 watersheds in, 3: 465
Rushes, 1: 106

# S

Safety, ships and, 2: 328
Sahara Desert, 1: 175; 3: 391, 457
Sailboats, 2: 342, 348, 374
Sailing, 2: 348
St. Lawrence River, 1: 129
St. Lawrence Seaway, 2: 314
St. Mary's River, 2: 314
St. Paul's Cathedral, 3: 378
Saline lakes, 1: 115–16; 2: 246
Saline water, 3: 456
Salinity, 1: 26–27, 33, 34, 38, 142; 3: 464–65
Salinization, 3: 392
Salmon, 1: 107, 144; 2: 280
 farming in raising, 2: 281, 281 (ill.)
 survival of Atlantic, 3: 472
**Salt,** 1: 138; 2: **308–10**
 getting, 2: 308–9
 making, 1: 11 (ill.)
 need for, 2: 308

 table, 2: 308
Salt marsh, 1: 141, 149
Salt marshgrass, 1: 143
Salt wedge, 1: 96
Salter Duck, 2: 231–32
Salter, Steven, 2: 231–32
Saltpeter, 2: 296
*Samuel B. Roberts* (ship), 2: 339
San Joaquin Valley, California, agriculture in, 2: 276
Sand bars, 1: 30, 93, 97, 141, 142
Sand dunes, 3: 385–86, 392, 415
Sandstone, 2: 303
Sanitary sewers, 2: 225
Santa Ana fires, 1: 176
Santa Ana winds, 1: 176
Sao Francisco River, 1: 131
Saprotrophs, 2: 240
*Sargassum,* 1: 82
Scaling, 2: 212
Scallops, 1: 69, 71, 72
Scuba diving, 2: 234, 257, 324, 347, 349 (ill.), 355–56
Scurvy grass, 1: 143
Sea anemones, 1: 69, 70, 143; 2: 257
Sea cows, 1: 78
Sea cucumbers, 1: 68–70, 73, 74, 143; 2: 257
Sea grasses, 2: 257
Sea gulls, 3: 415
Sea ice, 1: 156, 168, 171
*Sea Island Terminal,* 3: 432
Sea lamprey infestation, 3: 443 (ill.)
Sea lions, 1: 75, 76, 157
Sea mines, 2: 339
Sea of Cortez, 3: 504
Sea of Galilee, 1: 119
Sea otters, 1: 77; 2: 240; 3: 475 (ill.)
Sea pigs, 1: 68
Sea salt, 2: 309
Sea slugs, 1: 84
Sea stars, 1: 69–70, 73; 2: 257
Sea urchins, 1: 64, 68, 69–70, 73, 77, 82, 84; 2: 240
Sea-aster, 1: 143

Seabed, oil and natural gas exploration on, 3: 477
Seafaring in ancient world, 2: 362–64
Seafloor
 depth and shape of, 1: 49–51
 features of, 1: 51–52
 reasons for studying, 2: 260–61
 studying, 2: 261–64
Sea-lavender, 1: 143
Seal furs, 3: 473
Seals, 1: 76, 157
 fur, 1: 76
 Hawaiian monk, 1: 78
Seamount, 1: 56
Seatrout, 2: 349
Seawalls, 3: 386
Seawater, 1: 11
**Seaweed,** 1: **61–65,** 63 (ill.), 82
 categories of, 1: 62–64
 characteristics of, 1: 62
Secondary consumers, 1: 25
Secondary water treatment, 2: 226
Sedges, 1: 106, 145
Sediment, 2: 301; 3: 426
**Sediment contamination,** 3: **438–42**
 consequences of, 3: 439, 439 (ill.)
 examples of, 3: 440–41
 historical, 3: 441
Sedimentary rock, 2: 301
Sedimentation, 1: 146; 2: 367; 3: 438
Seeps, 2: 287
Segmented worms, 1: 69
Seine River, 1: 129
Seismologists, 2: 358
Seismology, 2: 264
Selenium, 3: 417, 418
Self-Contained Underwater Breathing Apparatus (SCUBA), 2: 356
Self-supplied water system, 2: 306
Semiarid grasslands, 1: 176

Semipermeable barrier, *1*: 26
Sewage, *3*: 459 (ill.), 460, 460 (ill.)
Sewage treatment, *2*: 226, 227 (ill.), 228
Sewage treatment pond, *1*: 123
Sewer systems, *2*: 306
Sewers, *2*: 367–68
    sanitary, *2*: 225
    storm, *2*: 228
Shackleton, Ernest, *1*: 170
Shaker tables, *2*: 296
Sharks, *1*: 45–46, 85
    basking, *1*: 85
    bull, *1*: 45
    dangers from, *2*: 339
    great white, *1*: 45, 46 (ill.)
    nurse, *1*: 85
    tiger, *1*: 45
Shellfish, *2*: 280; *3*: 389–90
Shinto shrines, *2*: 375
**Shipping**
    **on freshwater waterways, *2*: 310–15**
    on Great Lakes, *2*: 314
    **on oceans, *2*: 315–18**
    problems with, *2*: 317–18
Shipyard, *2*: 362
Shoreline, *1*: 29
Shortage sharing, *3*: 501
Shredders, *1*: 107
Shrimp, *1*: 69, 72, 82, 83, 144; *2*: 280
Sicily, *1*: 56
Sidescan sonar, *2*: 253, 273, 359
Sierra Mountains, *1*: 120
*The Silent World* (World), *2*: 357
Silica, *1*: 24, 106
Silver, *2*: 292
Sinagua, *2*: 366
Sinkers, *2*: 341
Sinkhole, groundwater contamination and, *3*: 413–14
Skin diving, *2*: 347
Slave ships, *2*: 326
Slugs, *1*: 71
Snails, *1*: 69, 71, 84, 103; *2*: 257

Snake River, *3*: 504
Snook, *1*: 144; *2*: 349
Snorkeling, *2*: 347
Sockeye salmon, *1*: 104 (ill.)
Sodium chloride, *2*: 296
Soil
    off-site cleanup of, *3*: 509
    *in situ* cleanup of, *3*: 509
Soil compaction, *3*: 401
Soil Conservation Service, *3*: 450
Soil venting, *3*: 509
*Sojourner*, *1*: 3 (ill.)
Solar distillation, *2*: 211
Solar salt production, *2*: 309
Solids, *1*: 5, 18
Solomon Islands, *1*: 55
Solution, *1*: 8, 11
Solution mining, *2*: 309
Solvents, *3*: 411
    universal, *1*: 10–11; *3*: 411
    water as a, *1*: 1–2
Sonar, *1*: 18; *2*: 253, 262–63, 272, 359
Sonar echosounding, *1*: 50–51
Sonoran Desert, *2*: 352
Soo Locks, *1*: 121; *2*: 314
Sound, impact of, on marine animals, *2*: 273
Soundings, *1*: 49; *2*: 358
South America, rivers in, *1*: 131
South Fork Salmon River, *3*: 417
South Padre Island, *1*: 30, 57
South Pole, *1*: 169, 169 (ill.)
Southwestern Native Americans, *2*: 366
Species
    causes of extinction, *3*: 471–72
    preventing loss of, *3*: 418
**Species introduction, *3*: 442–45**
    ballast water in, *3*: 443–44
    examples of, *3*: 444–45
    problem of, *3*: 442–43
Specific heat, *1*: 18
Speedboats, *2*: 342–43

Sperm whales, *1*: 27, 28 (ill.); *2*: 329
Sphagnum moss, *1*: 151
Sphalerite, *2*: 294
Spin fishing, *2*: 341
Spindletop well, *2*: 304
*Spirit* (spacecraft), *1*: 3
Spits, *1*: 30
Spitsbergen, *1*: 156
Sponsons, *2*: 343
Sports
    swimming as, *2*: 341–42, 347, 348, 348 (ill.)
    winter, *2*: 346
Spray irrigation, *2*: 277
Spring tides, *1*: 88
Spring turnover, *1*: 105
Springs, *2*: 287, 288
Sprinkler irrigation, *2*: 277 (ill.)
Squid, *1*: 68, 71, 72, 84; *2*: 257
Sri Lanka, *1*: 184
Stacks, *1*: 33
Standard Oil Company, *2*: 304
Standing cloud, *1*: 181
Starfish, *1*: 68, 73
Stationary fronts, *1*: 197
Statue of Liberty, *3*: 378
Statutory mile, *2*: 349
Steam propulsion, *2*: 311
Steamship, *2*: 374
Steinbeck, John, *1*: 67
Stellar sea lion, *1*: 78
Stingray, *1*: 46
Stope and adit mines, *2*: 295
Storm drains, *1*: 137 (ill.); *2*: 225
Storm sewers, *2*: 228
Storm surge, *2*: 335–36; *3*: 398
**Storms, *1*: 186–93; *2*: 336–37**
Storrie Lake, water levels in, *2*: 353
Strait, *3*: 490
Strait of Gibraltar, *3*: 490
Straits of Magellan, *2*: 334
Stratification, *1*: 114
Stratocumulus clouds, *1*: 179, 181
Stratoform clouds, *1*: 178
Stratus clouds, *1*: 179

Index    lxxv

Stream channels, *1*: 134–35
Stream piracy, *1*: 135 (ill.)
**Stream systems**, *1*: **131–36**
Stream valley, *1*: 134
Streambed, *2*: 352
**Stream water flow, 136–40**
Streams, *1*: 102 (ill.), 102–4
Streeter, Allison, *2*: 348
Striations, *1*: 162
Strip mines, *2*: 295
Striped bass, *1*: 144, 145
**Subarctic regions**, *1*: **155–58**
Subatomic particles, *1*: 8
Subclimates, *1*: 173
Subduction, *1*: 52, 55; *2*: 261
Subduction zone, *1*: 55
Submerged plant zone, *1*: 107
Submersible vehicles, *2*: 248 (ill.), 263, 356–57, 359
Sub-Saharan Africa, UN role in, *3*: 496
Subsidence, *3*: 401
Subtropical trade winds, *1*: 35
Sulfur, *1*: 24
Sulfur dioxide, acid rain and, *3*: 377, 503
Sulfuric acid, acid rain and, *3*: 377
Sumeria, *1*: 129
Sun, gravitational pull of, *1*: 88
Sun Yat Sen, *2*: 207
Sunderbans, *1*: 97
Sunlight, regulating, *1*: 173–74
Superdams, environmental and social implications of, *2*: 206–7, 209
Superfund, *3*: 420
Surf zone, *1*: 92
Surface currents, *1*: 35–38
Surface survey, *2*: 252–53
Surface tension, *1*: 5, 9–10
**Surface water**, *1*: 15, 34–35; *2*: 298
 commercial uses of, *2*: 284–85
 as source of freshwater, *3*: 498
 use of, *2*: **319–21**
 using and protecting, *3*: 456

Surface water groundwater, *3*: 452–53
**Surface water rights**, *3*: **498–501**
Surfers, *1*: 91, 92 (ill.)
Surfing, *2*: 349
Susquahana River, *1*: 131
**Sustainable development**, *3*: 453
 strategies for, *3*: **493–98**
Sustainable water supplies, working for, *3*: 485
Swamps
 freshwater, *1*: 148–49
 mangrove, *1*: 149–50
 plants in, *1*: 106
Swash, *1*: 92
Sweetgum trees, *1*: 148
Swimming, *2*: 341–42, 347, 348, 348 (ill.)
Sydney tar ponds, *1*: 125
Synecology, *2*: 239

# T

Table salt, *2*: 308
Tahiti, *1*: 59
Taj Mahal, *3*: 378
Tankers, *2*: 316–17
Tapered channels, *2*: 231–32
Tarpon, *2*: 349
Tasmania, *1*: 58
Taxonomical grouping, *2*: 239
Technology, hydroelectric, *2*: 214–15
Tectonic basins, *1*: 119
Tectonic plates, *1*: 32, 51 (ill.); *2*: 360–61
Teleost fish, *1*: 47–48
Temperature, *1*: 5, 24–26
Tennessee Valley Authority (TVA), *2*: 216; *3*: 403, 449
Tennessee Valley Authority (TVA) Act (1933), *2*: 213, 216
Tentacles, *1*: 70
Terns, *3*: 415
Terra cotta, *2*: 200, 202
Territorial water zone, *3*: 489
Territorial waters, establishing, *3*: 476–77

Tertiary water treatment, *2*: 228
Thallium, *3*: 387
Thames River, *1*: 129
Tharp, Marie, *1*: 51
Thebes, *1*: 128
Thermal springs and spas, *2*: 344–45
Thermoclines, *1*: 35, 66, 67, 105, 114
Third United Nations Conference on the Law of the Sea (1973), *3*: 478, 489
Thomson, William, *1*: 87
Thoreau, David, *1*: 125
Three Gorges Dam, *2*: 207, 207 (ill.)
Thunder, *1*: 186, 188
Thunderheads, *1*: 188
Thunderstorms, *1*: 186, 187–88, 197
Tiber River, *1*: 129
Tibetan Plateau, *1*: 97
Tidal creeks, *1*: 141
Tidal fences, *2*: 224
Tidal flats, *1*: 99
Tidal inlets, *1*: 29, 30, 93
Tidal turbines, *2*: 224
Tidal wetlands, *1*: 29
**Tide energy**, *2*: **223–25**
Tidepools, *1*: 47
**Tides**, *1*: **86–90**, 88 (ill.)
 neap, *1*: 88
 red, *1*: 83
 spring, *1*: 88
Tierra del Fuego, *2*: 334
Tiger sharks, *1*: 45
Tigris River, *1*: 126, 129; *2*: 205
Tilapia, *2*: 280
Till, *1*: 162
Tissues, *2*: 238
*Titanic* (ship), *1*: 156; *2*: 254, 323, 323 (ill.), 337
Titanium, *2*: 292
Titmice, *1*: 149
Todadzischini Navajo Medicine Man, *2*: 367 (ill.)
Toothed whales, *1*: 75–76
Topographic features, *1*: 48
Topography, *2*: 247
"Tornado Alley," *1*: 189

Tornadoes, *1:* 186, 188–89
Toronto, Ontario, Canada, landfills in, *3:* 424
*Torrey Canyon* (ship) spill, *3:* 434
Torricelli, Evangelista, *1:* 194
**Tourism**
　at Niagara Falls, *2:* 345–46
　**on oceans, *2:* 321–25**
Tow surfers, *2:* 349
Toxic chemicals as nonsource pollutants, *3:* 426
Toxins, *3:* 411
Trade, *2:* 220, 373–74
Trade winds, *1:* 40, 174, 196
Trans-Antarctic mountains, *1:* 169
Transatlantic journeys, *2:* 326–27
Transform plates, *1:* 50
Transformers, *2:* 215
Transit zone, *3:* 491
Transpiration, *1:* 13–14; *2:* 276
**Transportation on oceans, *2:* 325–28**
Travel, *2:* 374
Treaties, *3:* 488
Tree death, *3:* 382
Triangle trade, *1:* 38
Tributary glaciers, *1:* 161
Trickling filter, *2:* 226
Trocadero Fountains in Paris, *2:* 284 (ill.)
Tropical cyclones, *1:* 189–92
Tropical depression, *1:* 190; *2:* 337
Tropical storm, *2:* 336–37
Trough, *1:* 90
Trout, *1:* 103
Truman, Harry S., *3:* 477
Tsukubai, *2:* 375
Tsunamis, *1:* 53, 53 (ill.)
Tube feet, *1:* 73
Tuna, *2:* 349
　hazards of eating, *3:* 389
　safety of, in diet, *3:* 439
Tundra, *1:* 156–57
Tuolumne River, damming of, *3:* 451
Tupelos, *1:* 148

Turbidite flows, *1:* 52
Turbine, *2:* 214, 374
Twilight zone, *1:* 67–68
Typhoid, *3:* 448
Typhoons, *1:* 189; *2:* 335
Typhus, *3:* 448

**U**
Ubangi River, *1:* 128
Ultraviolet light, *1:* 8–9
Ultraviolet rays, *2:* 270–71
UN Educational Scientific and Cultural Organization (UNESCO), *3:* 496
Underground storage tanks, groundwater contamination and, *3:* 414
*Undersea World of Jacques Cousteau, 2:* 357
Undertow, *1:* 92
UNESCO-IHE Institute for Water Education, *3:* 488
United Nations, *2:* 323
　Agreement on Straddling Fish Stocks and Highly Migratory Fish Stocks, *3:* 482–83
　Children's Fund (UNICEF), *3:* 495 (ill.)
　Convention on the Law of the Sea, *2:* 293
　Development Program, *3:* 485
　Environment Program (UNEP), *3:* 453, 492
　Environment Program—Fresh Water Branch, *3:* 487
　Environment Program—Fresh Water Unit, *3:* 485
　environmental policies of, *1:* 118
　Food and Agricultural Organization, *2:* 279
　Framework Convention on Climate Change, *3:* 408, 496
　Intergovernmental Panel on Climate Change (IPCC), *3:* 409

　International Children's Fund, *3:* 485
　Law of the Seas, *3:* 477–78, 489–92
　Marine Protection Area, *3:* 482
　role in Sub-Saharan Africa, *3:* 496
　spread of species in ballast water and, *3:* 444
　UNESCO, *3:* 496
Universal solvents, *1:* 10–11; *3:* 411
Updrafts, *1:* 188
Upwellings, *1:* 38–39, 40, 67
Urban areas as source of non-source pollution, *3:* 426–27
Urban runoff, *2:* 229
Uruguay River, *1:* 131
**U.S. agencies and water issues, *3:* 502–6**
U.S. Army Corps of Engineers, *3:* 450
U.S. Centers for Disease Control, *3:* 487
U.S. Coast Guard, *2:* 324; *3:* 491, 491 (ill.)
U.S. Fish and Wildlife Service, *3:* 474, 506
U.S. Geological Survey, *3:* 503
U-shaped valley, *1:* 161
Uzbekistan, *1:* 117

**V**
Vanadium, *2:* 293
Vegetation, riparian, *3:* 468
Venice, Italy, *2:* 374; *3:* 401
Vent clams, *1:* 26
Venus flytraps, *1:* 151
Vertebrates, *1:* 43
*Vibrio cholera, 3:* 444
Victoria, Australia, *1:* 129
Victoria Falls, *1:* 138, 138 (ill.)
Viruses, *2:* 297
Viscosity of water, *1:* 5
Volcanic arcs, *1:* 55
Volcanic islands, *1:* 55–56, 56 (ill.), 59, 60
Volcanic lakes, *1:* 120

Volcanoes, *1:* 52, 55
  active, *1:* 55
  Hawaiian-Emperor, *1:* 57
  inactive, *1:* 55
  mid-oceanic ridge, *1:* 53
Volcanogenic deposits, 2: 294
Volga River, *1:* 129
Volvo Ocean Race Round the World, 2: 348–49

# W

Wakame, 2: 280
Wakeboarding, 2: 343
Walden Pond, *1:* 125
*Walden* (Thoreau), *1:* 125
Walden Woods Project, *1:* 125
Walker, Gilbert, *1:* 41
Wall clouds, *1:* 189
Walrus tusks, 3: 473
Walruses, *1:* 76, 77
Warblers, *1:* 107
Warm front, *1:* 197
Waste
  commercial, 3: 419–21
  industrial, 3: 421–22
**Wastewater**
  **management of**, 2: 225–30, 372
  purifying, 3: 485
Water
  agricultural uses of, 2: 275–78, 320
  ancient supply ystems, 2: 365–68
  characteristics of, *1:* 1–5
  chemistry of, *1:* 8–11
  commercial and industrial uses of, 2: 283–86
  conservation of, 2: 307
  contamination of, 3: 507–10
  on Mars, *1:* 3, 3 (ill.)
  oil pollution of, 3: 430–31
  phase changes of, *1:* 18–19
  physics of, *1:* 17–21
  potable, 2: 210
  redirecting excess, 3: 495
  shortages of, 3: 484–85
  states of, *1:* 5–6, 8, 17
  temperature of, *1:* 5
  transmission and absorption of light, *1:* 8–9
Water agencies, 3: 504–5
Water allotment, 3: 498
**Water and cultures**
  **in ancient world**, 2: 361–68
  **in modern world**, 2: 369–76
Water and Sanitation Program, 3: 485
Water budget, *1:* 12–13, 163–64
Water buoyancy, 2: 365
Water clocks, 2: 365
**Water conservation**, 3: 445–54, 494
  desertification and, 3: 393
  in history, 3: 447–48
  international, 3: 453
  need for, 3: 446–47
  in United States, 3: 448–50, 452–53
Water Environment Federation, 3: 488
Water flea, *1:* 107
Water footprints, 3: 455
Water hyacinth, *1:* 106; 2: 280; 3: 442–43
Water lentil, *1:* 106
Water lettuce, 3: 442–43
Water lilies, *1:* 106–7, 148
Water molecules, *1:* 1, 4, 8–9, 10, 13, 18
Water organisms, effect of bioaccumulation on, 3: 389–90
**Water politics, issues of use and abuse**, 3: 454–58, 455 (ill.)
**Water pollution**, 3: 458–63, 502 (ill.), 502–3
  estuaries and, *1:* 145–46
  fishing and, 3: 480–81
  laws to control, 2: 325
  levels of, 3: 458–60
  non-point sources of, 3: 425–30, 459
  as problem in aquaculture and mariculture, 2: 282
  sources and types of pollutants, 3: 460–62
Water processes, *1:* 13–15
**Water quality**
  **contamination cleanup and**, 3: 506–10, 507 (ill.)
  in watersheds, 3: 463–65
Water Resources Program of the World Meteorological Organization, 3: 486
Water rights, 3: 498
  combination of, 3: 500–501
  types of, 3: 499–501
Water screw, 2: 365
Water skiing, 2: 343
Water soldier, *1:* 106
Water standards, *1:* 11
Water supply
  ensuring, 3: 501
  managing, 3: 485–86
  shortages in, 3: 504
  sustainability of, 3: 497
Water Supply and Sanitation Collaborative Council, 3: 485
Water table, *1:* 15, 111–12, 122; 3: 503
Water vapor, *1:* 5, 7, 8, 12, 14, 21
Water witches, 2: 289
Waterborne diseases, 3: 448
Watercress, 2: 280
Watermeal, *1:* 106
WaterPartners International, 3: 485
Waters, dangerous, 2: 333–430
**Watersheds**, 2: 243, 247; 3: **463–69**, 500
  contaminated, 3: 465
  defined, 3: 463
  deforestation and, 3: 468
  impact of fire and logging on, 3: 467
  restoring, 3: 465–67, 466 (ill.)
  riparian zone, 3: 467–68
  risks in restoration, 3: 467
  in rural areas, 3: 465
  water quality in, 3: 463–65
Watersheds and drainage patterns, *1:* 27, 132–34

Waterspouts, *1:* 188, 189, 189 (ill.)
Waterways, changing, *3:* 417–18
WaterWeb, *3:* 488
Wave action, *3:* 383
Wave base, *1:* 90
**Wave energy,** *2:* **230–32**
Wave refraction, *1:* 92–93
Wavelength, *1:* 2, 7, 23
**Waves,** *1:* **90–94**
  breaking, *1:* 90–92
  radio, *2:* 270
  surfing perfect, *1:* 91
**Weather,** *1:* 173, **193–98;** *2:* 318
Weathering, *1:* 137–38
Webb, Matthew, *2:* 348
Weddell Sea, *1:* 165, 170, 171
Wegener, Alfred, *1:* 50
Wells, *2:* 288–89
  drilled, *2:* 289
  driven, *2:* 289
  hand-dug, *2:* 288, 290
West Antarctic, *1:* 169–70
West Antarctic Current, *1:* 37
West Antarctic ice sheet, *1:* 167, 169–70
West Bengal, *1:* 184
Westerly trade winds, *2:* 231
Western boundary currents, *1:* 35, 36
Westminster Abbey Cathedral, *3:* 378
Wet deposition, *3:* 377
**Wetlands,** *1:* **147–53;** *2:* 228; *3:* 415
  importance of, *1:* 151–53
  natural cycle of, *1:* 152–53
Whale oil, *2:* 329
Whales, *1:* 27, 157; *2:* 257, 330
  baleen, *1:* 75, 76
  blue, *1:* 76, 78; *2:* 329
  California gray, *2:* 330–31
  decline of, *2:* 329–31
  on endangered species list, *2:* 331
  fin, *1:* 76
  finback, *1:* 78
  gray, *1:* 76
  right, *2:* 329
  sanctuaries for, *2:* 330
  sperm, *1:* 27, 28 (ill.); *2:* 329
  toothed, *1:* 75–76
**Whaling,** *2:* **329–31**
Whirlpools, *2:* 333–34
Whitbread Round the World Race, *2:* 348–49, 350 (ill.)
White mangroves, *1:* 150
White Nile, *1:* 128
Whitewater rafting, *2:* 345
Whitewater rapids, *2:* 344
Whitman, Christie, *3:* 504 (ill.)
Wilderness, use of, *3:* 451
Willamette National Forest, *1:* 101 (ill.)
William of Orange, *2:* 370
Willows, *1:* 106
Wilson, Edward, *3:* 415
Windmills, *2:* 370
Winnebago people, *1:* 133
Winter sports, *2:* 346
*The Wizard of Oz* (Baum), *1:* 189
Wolves, *1:* 157
Woodpeckers, *1:* 149
Woods Hole Oceanographic Institute, *1:* 26; *2:* 266
World Bank, environmental policies of, *1:* 118
World Commission on Dams (WCD), *2:* 209
World Conservation Union, *3:* 475, 487
World Health Organization, *3:* 487
World Water Council, *3:* 487
World Wildlife Fund (WWF), *3:* 453
Worldwatch Institute, *3:* 487
Worms, *1:* 69, 84, 99, 143
Wrens, *1:* 149
Wright, Orville, *3:* 385
Wright, Wilbur, *3:* 385

# X

X rays, *2:* 270

# Y

Yachts, *2:* 350 (ill.)
Yangtze River, *1:* 126, 128; *2:* 207, 243
Yellow River, *1:* 126, 128
Yellowstone Lake, *1:* 120
Yellowstone National Park, *1:* 97
York Minster Cathedral, *3:* 378
Yukon River, *1:* 129

# Z

Zaire River, *1:* 128
Zambezi River, *1:* 128, 138
Zambia, *1:* 138
Zambizi River, *1:* 138
Zebra mussels, *2:* 250; *3:* 444
Zimbabwe, *1:* 138
Zinc, *1:* 24
Zones
  of infiltration, *3:* 411
  of saturation, *3:* 411
Zooplankton, *1:* 40, 66, 83–84, 85, 105, 143; *2:* 257